THE SLAIDBURN ANGEL

THE

SLAIDBURN

ANGEL

To Silvia

M. SHEELAGH

WHITTAKER

DUNDURN
TORONTO

Editor: Cheryl Hawley
Design: Courtney Horner
Printer: Webcom

Library and Archives Canada Cataloguing in Publication

Whittaker, M. Sheelagh
    The Slaidburn Angel / M. Sheelagh Whittaker.

Also issued in electronic format.
ISBN 978-1-4597-0363-6

    1. Gardner, Thomas, 1882-1885. 2. Isherwood, Grace.
3. Gardner, Isabella. 4. Murder--England--Slaidburn
(Lancashire). 5. Trials (Murder)--England--Leeds. I. Title.

HV6535.G6S53 2012   364.152'309427685   C2012-900126-0

1   2   3   4   5   16   15   14   13   12

We acknowledge the support of the **Canada Council for the Arts** and the **Ontario Arts Council** for our publishing program. We also acknowledge the financial support of the **Government of Canada** through the **Canada Book Fund** and **Livres Canada Books**, and the **Government of Ontario** through the **Ontario Book Publishing Tax Credit** and the **Ontario Media Development Corporation.**

Care has been taken to trace the ownership of copyright material used in this book. The author and the publisher welcome any information enabling them to rectify any references or credits in subsequent editions.

J. Kirk Howard, President

Printed and bound in Canada.
www.dundurn.com

Dundurn   Gazelle Book Services Limited   Dundurn
3 Church Street, Suite 500   White Cross Mills   2250 Military Road
Toronto, Ontario, Canada   High Town, Lancaster, England   Tonawanda, NY
M5E 1M2   LA1 4XS   U.S.A. 14150

Dedicated to three decent, loving, and self-sacrificing men:
John Green Isherwood, John Dean Whittaker, and
William John Morgan

Angel Stone from the tenth century found in Slaidburn.

PROLOGUE

The stone rested for centuries at what became the foot of the garden. It was covered by earth and then it wasn't. The residue of soil and the porous texture of the stone proved a fine surface for a luxuriant blanket of moss.

After what seemed like an eternity, but was in fact more like a thousand years, the white-haired lady came to sit by the stone to look out over the fells. For some reason she liked to sit there, gazing dreamily at the hills while running her hand gently over the stone's mossy surface. Slowly, over months blending into years, she decided that the stone's surface was too smooth, the edges too precise for nature to have been its only mason.

The gentle cleaning away of the moss was a labour of love, but as she worked she began to feel that there was something important here, some message from the past.

The early hints of a Celtic pattern of curves were encouraging, even exciting. The little pointed bits were harder to classify. They had none of the Celtic rhythms or symmetry. All the same, they were charming in their uniqueness and there seemed to be two of them. But two of what?

The revelation of the wings made her heart soar. Could it be an angel, resting here at the foot of the garden near the stream? Where could it have come from? What complex set of events had left it lying on a white stone bed here in Slaidburn?

Still, that is what it was. Carved on white stone. An angel wearing quaint pointed boots and what seemed to be a little petticoat.

A relic from long ago? Or a memorial?

INTRODUCTION

This book is about mothers and stepmothers, doomed children and children who feel lost.

It is about the power of love, and the fear of the loss of love, and the crazy things that love and fear can make people do.

This book is about untimely death and the possibility of murder.

And it is about devotion between sisters.

Mothers are the eternally missing part of our being. From our infinitesimal beginnings they surround us with warmth and sustenance. I read once that a woman is born with all the eggs she will ever ovulate. That being the case, then the original mother must have been born with all the other mothers-ever-to-be within her: a Russian doll opening inward to the tiniest of mothers, or outward to forever.

Stepmothers, by contrast, are natural villains. In becoming a stepmother, one develops sharp features overnight, accompanied by an obsession for having conversations with untrustworthy mirrors. The adjective "evil" seems to sit easily with "stepmother," in the same way as "loving" so naturally accompanies "mother."

My husband once said to me that at some level of consciousness we are all prepared to believe that stepmothers are murderers. I wrote down what he said because it rang so true.

Children are so precious and vulnerable; it physically hurts me even to think of a child being unloved, let alone deliberately harmed. But in the recent past, children were routinely unwanted or were viewed as a low-cost source of labour or a pension. Life could be short and was often cheap. Better medical care, easy divorce, and birth control changed all that. Now we are free to expose our children to the nuclear winter of our ill-chosen relationships while we battle so hard to assure them that they, at least, were wanted.

Sisters are something else entirely. In my own family we laughingly, and truthfully, speak of the psychic sisters and the psychotic sisters. Since there are only three of us in total, we need to take turns playing those roles.

Sisterhood can be a complicated bond. You can love your sister more than anyone else in the world, or you can try to eradicate her from your consciousness. You can trundle through the years of your mutual lives on parallel tracks, sometimes feeling the whoosh of her passing by, or you can weave yourself into the tapestry of her life, sometimes being the sparkling gold thread, and sometimes the olive drab.

A sister is an alternative self, a "me who might have been." You can believe yourself to be free of her or all bound up in her, deeply involved or not at all, and then one day you turn a corner suddenly and catch a glimpse of her in a reflection, and in that blink of an eye you realize that you are, after all, essentially each other.

KASLO, BRITISH COLUMBIA, SUMMER 1928

Margaret put the letter down on the table next to the hastily opened envelope and looked out at the snow-capped mountains. An active woman, it was unusual for her to be standing still and lost in thought.

Her brother's letter contained the news that her stepmother, Grace, had died, and enclosed a copy of the obituary from the *Haslingden Guardian*.

Reading the obituary, Margaret let out an audible harrumph.

She felt a surge of contradictory emotions: Grace had changed the course of her life. Margaret was just eight when her widowed father had married for the second time, and for a while it seemed to be a great relief to have another female again in the rough and tumble of family life at Meanley Farm.

But it was Grace's fault that within a year they had lost Meanley Farm, lost their happy life in Slaidburn, and ended Margaret's days of learning at the Quaker school in Newton.

It was because of Grace that she, Margaret, had to become a mill worker while she was still just a girl, slaving morning to night in the heat and the noise and the lint-filled air of a Lancashire cotton mill.

Certain things could have been overlooked or forgotten, because Grace had brought happiness to her father after he had been so sad and weary when her mother died. But Grace and her sister, Aunt Isabella, had brought shame to the family and made them all the target of sidelong looks and whispers and even hisses back in Slaidburn.

To Margaret, even after all this time, it still felt as if it was because of Grace that instead of continuing the girlhood life she had loved so much, perhaps one day marrying a farmer with prospects of a fine tenancy, she had found herself in a bleak mill town, married to William Whittaker, a bleacher. But she did love William. He had understood her horror at the lifetime in the mills that stretched out before them and, bless him, was willing to join her in doing something about it.

When Margaret and William decided to go to Canada in search of something better, father and stepmother had wished them well. With four children still to raise at home, John and Grace didn't need Margaret and William around to fill out their lives.

Now, here she was, almost thirty years later, still in exile in the Rocky Mountains, worlds away from Slaidburn, living a kind of pioneer existence. In the early years it had been very tough going, but these days when she thought about the prospects of her four children she knew that they each had a good education and a real opportunity to have the kind of happy, secure life she wished she might have had herself.

Yes, her children probably had reason to thank Grace, if only because of the accident of fate, but Margaret herself wasn't so sure she was even sorry that Grace was dead at last. She thought again about that old photograph, tucked away in her bottom drawer. It could still conjure up the same strong emotions.

She thought she ought to write to father and tell him that she was sorry Grace has died.

Maybe I will, after I pull some carrots for supper, she thought.

MONTREAL, QUEBEC, SUMMER 1975

The heat and the humidity of the Montreal summer were unremitting, and I felt trapped with my new baby in the apartment we had rented, sight unseen, on a busy downtown street. Meghan's birth had seemed perfectly timed, poised between my final exams and the job that would mark the beginning of my new professional life. I was delighted with my baby girl, but somehow the tasks required of my mind had taken a sudden lurch from the problems of business finance to those of baby constipation.

I felt like I had been accelerating steadily through my life toward some kind of goal, epitomized by the acquisition of higher education and a good job, and suddenly I had been physically snapped backward by the force of maternal gravity. Although, given the shape my body had taken on, *snapped* is too crisp a word for what had happened to me. *Smushed* or *soggled* was more like it.

I spent my milk-logged days in the miniscule furnished apartment, learning the intricacies of the plots of several soap operas and how to turn the pages of a book with one hand while breastfeeding a damp baby with heat rash.

There mother and tiny daughter were, sweltering in a

nondescript high-rise at Fort and Maisonneuve, where the police tore down the street every night, sirens blaring, at 2:39 a.m. I became convinced that what I was hearing was a nightly race to the doughnut store, and Meghan seemed to agree with me.

Her dad left us brightly every morning to go and play with the hyenas in the corporate jungle. Only the faint streak of mustard-coloured baby poo on the underside of his forearm, revealed for all to see by his unfashionable but at least more comfortable short-sleeved shirt, betrayed to his colleagues that he had another life as a relief nurse on the night shift in our sweaty little improvised nursery.

During that six-week period, which seemed to last a year, I had plenty of time for meaning-of-life thoughts. Where I got to, after some fevered thinking, was that the trappings of education, job, and even friends are ephemeral. Nobody in our extremely small playgroup of two, Meghan and myself, was impressed by my M.B.A. or my prospects as an executive. Our phone didn't ring with cheery calls from school friends, partly because we didn't have a phone and partly because my friends were all off starting their careers or taking vacations. And besides, most of them were back in Toronto.

Whatever the reasons, Meg and I found ourselves in total agreement that when you get right down to fundamentals, like a really dry bottom and birthday wishes on the actual day, the only people you can reliably count on are your beloved family.

Shortly after we reached that conclusion, Meg and I temporarily left her dad behind to continue playing on his corporate jungle gym while we went to stay at a pleasant cottage beside a cool, calming lake with Meghan's cool, calming grandparents. The soap operas had to lather on without me.

At that time the full extent of my beloved core family included the baby, my spouse, his two brothers and a sister, his parents, my two sisters and a brother, my dad, and my stepmother. Thirteen people, including lucky me.

WHAT WENT BEFORE

My mother died, after a long crippling illness, when I was eighteen. The echoes of that loss have ricocheted down the years with surprisingly little diminution.

She was called Tessie, and she fell ill with multiple sclerosis before I was even old enough to know her. So when I think of her name I feel a bit like Pip in *Great Expectations*, in the scene where he traces the letters on his parents' tombstones and forms an opinion of their nature based on the style of the lettering.

The name Tessie is pretty and curly and ends on an up note. In my mind the romance and tragedy of Tess of the D'Urbervilles is somehow intermingled with the fact that her given name, Theresa, appeared with no family antecedents.

In the full listing of her given names, Theresa was preceded by the stolid and rather severe pairing of the names Evelyn and Mildred, both already the names of virtuous and hard-working family members. But my grandparents doted on their only daughter, and before long their choice of Theresa had been tailored to fit her baby giggles, and she had become Tessie.

Dean and Tessie with Sheelagh.

And a Tessie she was. She had a light heart and a feminine manner. Evelyn Mildred Theresa Sadlier-Brown, hereafter known as Tessie Whittaker, was a woman who wore high heels with trousers and smoked cigarettes in a cigarette holder. Elegant to the end, she wore a triple-strand pearl choker and pearl earrings with her diaphanous nighties in her final illness.

Even though she didn't die until I was almost grown up, I can't remember ever having an actual conversation with her. Her illness robbed her of the power of speech well before she died, but I do remember smiles and sparkling eyes and warmth and caring.

In the story of my life she, sadly, has only a minor role, but she did infuse her part with a poignancy that made her stand out. She was a beautiful, blighted woman and I have always known that she loved me.

If this were a *Harry Potter* book, Tessie could appear in good health and radiating love, in a beautiful shimmering satin gown with her pearls on her ears and at her throat, in the Mirror of Erised, the magical device that enables one to see one's heart's desire. What I would give to own a mirror like that!

As it turns out, we have a bit of a history in my family of lost mothers. My maternal grandmother's mother ran away when my grandma, Evaline, was only eight, and my father's grandmother, Jane Isherwood, died when his mother, Margaret, was only seven. With feelings of loss and abandonment running generations deep, you would think that our family would have some genuine insight or ability to deal with such emotions. And I suppose we do, if you think repression an acceptable response.

From both sides, my generation inherited a tradition of active practicality, a no-nonsense reaction to being thrust unprepared into responsibility that I attribute, at least in part, to the tragically missing mothers. Neither of my grandmothers was particularly sympathetic: they were industrious women who "tidied as they went" and "sang while they worked." I have the vague impression that their husbands, my grandfathers, had sort of been "tidied" too, but that may just be because I was so young or they were so forbearing.

My sisters and female cousins and I are a capable and determined lot. As one of my cousins once said in an unguarded moment: "We do girls well in our family."

A LEGACY OF LOSS AND SADNESS

Ash Knott Farm, Forest of Bowland, 1874

All her life, it seemed, people had been dying around her.

Jane Bleazard's baby sister Ann had died in 1856, and three years later, when Jane was just seven years old, her mother died. Her big sister Margaret said that her mummy and little Ann were together now, but Jane wasn't sure how she felt about that.

She really missed her ma. No one had time to cuddle her in front of the fire in the evening before bed now that ma was gone. Jane still remembered how she used to giggle helplessly as her mother tickled her saying, "This little piggy went whee, whee, whee, all the way home." Jane didn't even like to look at her toes anymore.

And how was she ever going to find out what happened to the blue fairy? Ma was going to tell her if the fairy was found safe and sound in the bluebell wood, far from the grasp of the ogre, as she had hoped. But now ma wasn't here to tell her the end of the story. And silly old Agnes didn't even like the blue fairy stories.

"Who ever heard of a blue fairy?" Agnes had asked unhelpfully. "I'd prefer a yellow one."

When Jane was nine her sister Agnes, who was nineteen, died. When she was ten her sister Mary, who was sixteen, died. To Jane, the deaths of Agnes and then Mary felt like she was losing her mother over and over again. Her married sister Isabella moved in to help their father raise the rest of his family, but when Isabella died soon after, sister Margaret stepped in. In fact, Margaret went so far as to marry Isabella's widower and take on her children in turn.

But the misery wasn't over. Jane, by then the female head of the remaining household of Bleazards at Ash Knott Farm, was barely nineteen years of age when her brother James, twenty-one, died. Then, when Jane was twenty-one, her father Richard died as well.

Marriage to John Green Isherwood, just five months after the death of her father, offered Jane the chance of a new life. Despite her history of loneliness and sad loss, Jane brought love and hope to her union with John, and the expectation that together they would raise a large and healthy family.

John was living and working at Chapel Croft Farm, a long hilly walk from Ash Knott, and they took pleasure wearing in the fastest path between the two farms. Jane's surviving brothers liked John and they wanted her to be happy. So did her sister Margaret, now living over in Slaidburn, busily raising Isabella's children along with new babies of her own.

May 9, 1874, was one of the happiest days of Jane's life. While the certificate dryly noted the marriage of John Green Isherwood, aged twenty-eight, farmer, living at Chapel Croft, and Jane Bleazard, aged twenty-two, living at Ash Knott, solemnized at the Parish Church in Slaidburn, County of York, with Reverend Thomas Sturgess officiating, for Jane it was a hopeful new beginning. Now she had someone to care for, someone who would look after her and their children. Together they would build a new life.

TO LOSE ONE'S MOTHER

"I lost my mother" is a quaint expression. It suggests that she is simply misplaced, or that you are just temporarily unable to locate her. The senses of it somehow being careless as well as hopeless are amusingly captured both by Oscar Wilde, in *The Importance of Being Ernest*, and by Milne, in his little poem about James Morrison's mother. As the third verse of that charming work records:

> King John Put up a notice, "LOST or STOLEN or STRAYED! JAMES JAMES MORRISON'S MOTHER SEEMS TO HAVE BEEN MISLAID. LAST SEEN WANDERING VAGUELY: QUITE OF HER OWN ACCORD, SHE TRIED TO GET DOWN TO THE END OF THE TOWN — FORTY SHILLINGS REWARD!"
> — A.A. Milne, "Disobedience"

The sad truth, though, is that mothers who are lost are not simply mislaid, they are gone forever. You will never again be able to come crying to that lap for comfort, or to whisper your nightmares to her in the dark and have her make them go away.

For those who lose their mothers young, there is no one to help you choose your wedding dress while remembering her own, no one who can presume to talk to you about the fickleness of passion and the vital importance of honesty in a relationship.

There are lots of routine reminders, large and small, of the things you lost when your mother died. For example, you lose your roadmap for aging, the ability to estimate when your hair will go grey, or menopause will hit, or if your hands will be covered with liver spots by the time your reach sixty. Will your voice go whiney, and your children become embarrassed by you? Or might you develop a weakness for the bottle, turning the occasional drink into a series of empty bottles that, laid end to end or even side by side, fuse into a vast chain of misery?

If I only had her here even for a day I think that I would ask my mother what she hoped and dreamed and how she felt about her life. Everyone has always told me she wanted most to be a good mother and have lots of children, but we are real now, people not promises, and I would like to know if she is happy with us all. What would she have thought about John's difficult divorce and Terree's illness? Did she mourn all the responsibility that Penny was saddled with, or would she have been proud at how her first daughter rose so admirably to the occasion?

And what about me? Would she have understood me?

You can look at losing a mother in so many ways. Another meaning of the verb "to lose" is, of course, "to be defeated," which is quite apt in the case of the death of a mother if you think about it. If "losing mother" is a game with odds, then the odds are great that she will predecease you, but only by twenty or thirty years or so, not by almost an entire lifetime. But some of us get beaten by the odds. My mother predeceased me by forty-three years and still counting. That is too many years to be without the unconditional love and wise advice I imagine one might reasonably expect from one's mom.

I draw strength and understanding from the best children's writers. Robert Munsch wrote a wonderful children's book about mother love called *Love You Forever*, which contains the refrain: "I'll love you forever, I'll like you for always, as long as I'm living, my baby you'll be."

It is the "as long as I'm living" part that trips some of us up.

THE GREAT CHRYSANTHEMUM MASSACRE

I was at home by myself on a Saturday afternoon, getting ready for a night at the Delta Gamma House, when my father, Dean, called me from the University Hospital to tell me that Tessie had died.

I didn't even know he had gone to the hospital. We had taken to visiting more sporadically and only when in the neighbourhood of the hospital since, for some time, Tessie had seemed no longer to be aware of our presence at her bedside. By chance, though, I had visited that morning, after my classes, and the rasp of her laboured breathing and her still, blanched body had sent me running from the ward. I can still hear the slap of my sneakers as they hit the institutional granite of that long, long hospital corridor.

I learned later that the doctor had called Dean just a few hours after I had been there and told him to come right over. He knew what such a summons meant, of course, but after so many years of looking after her, he reacted painfully slowly to the information that suddenly Tessie was dead.

When Penny flew in from California a couple days later, one toddler clinging on to her skirt and a baby in her arms, she was met with a chorus of "Thank goodness you are finally here." No arrangements had been made for the funeral service or a wake; she was, as usual, expected to take charge of them all.

Guided by the funeral home, Dean had managed to provide something for my mother to wear. I am guessing here, but likely he chose the swirly pastel chiffon dress and coat she had worn to Penny's wedding because by then her only other clothes were nighties. He had also decided that the casket would be closed; in fact, locked.

Not surprisingly, we all behaved weirdly through the next week or so. We ate casseroles made by neighbours and the ladies of Saint Mary's Church Women's Auxiliary. Penny looked after her infant and helped the rest of us to put one foot in front of the other.

Penny must have looked after our sister, Terree (short for Theresa), too. I have no recollection of Terree or John or what they might have been feeling or doing during those dreadful days and nights. I know that, when I wasn't over at the university attending classes, I lay on the bed in my attic room listening to the song "Edelweiss" from *The Sound of Music* over and over. I do not even know if the sound carried downstairs.

Mainly I remember sitting with Penny in the living room on the day after the funeral, surrounded by the dreary floral tributes that were all a place like Edmonton could possibly muster in the autumn of 1965: rust coloured chrysanthemums, every one. Hardy flowers, chrysanthemums. They can last for weeks. Dean and Tessie were well-liked and there were morbid autumnal arrangements everywhere that you could see.

I do not know what galvanized us, but suddenly Penny and I began to gather up all the flowers, the newly arrived and the slightly worn, the golden-hued and the just plain dun, throwing them energetically into the garbage cans in the alley out at the back of the house. I think John happened by and joined in the frenzy, and that maybe Terree did too. All I remember for certain is that we kept throwing away flowers, many still in their vases, smashing the lids of the garbage cans down on their blossoms and snapping their stems, until there were no more of them inside the house.

When we retook our seats in the living room, Penny quietly commented, "Now that's better."

For my part, I never liked chrysanthemums in the first place, especially those in autumn colours, and I feel absolutely no guilt at having been part of the Great Chrysanthemum Massacre of 1965.

STEPMOTHERS ARE NATURAL VILLAINS

Three years after Tessie died Dean met and married Doreen in a whirlwind romance.

I was delighted for my father because he'd had no real adult companionship outside of work for many years, unless you counted our series of elderly housekeepers. Since I was already off living my own life, I expected Doreen to be a comfort to my dad in his old age.

My stepmother had a superficial resemblance to my mother. She was cool and elegant and had false teeth. But she did not love me and she never would.

To be fair, she never had a chance. I was already grown up and rarely around. And I was brittle and self-absorbed, and glib and secretive. In other words, hard to love.

Of course, my dad doted on me.

Doreen had an adolescent daughter, and a history of loneliness and loss of her own. She had suffered that most terrible of parental tragedies, the death of a child.

The story, as I was told it, was heart wrenching: Around 1960 Doreen had taken the brave step of divorcing her alcoholic husband and raising her two little girls on her own. Not long after, on a beautiful summer's day, she and the girls were at a family cottage and a group of people decided to go boating on the lake. Somehow the boat overturned. Doreen's four-year-old daughter, Cathy, was trapped underneath and she drowned.

The detail of adults diving and diving under the boat to find Cathy sticks in my mind, as does the terrifying picture of a beautiful day turning suddenly malignant.

Based on the photograph Doreen always kept on her dresser, Cathy was a classically lovely, fluffy little blond girl. Lesley, Doreen's surviving daughter, was a dark, sleek nine-year-old. The catastrophe not only affected Doreen, Lesley sank into a depression and had a very hard time recovering.

It was a decade later when Doreen met and married my father and Lesley became my stepsister. Poor little lost Cathy would also have been my stepsister.

Dean and Doreen had a whirlwind courtship, both of them eager for another chance at marital happiness. Suddenly Doreen found herself with four stepchildren, one of whom, my younger sister Terree, was still living at home. Terree and Lesley were both teenagers, and they liked each other. But Lesley was disoriented by her mother's sudden marriage, which entailed moving to a new city, and Terree was heading toward schizophrenia. For Doreen, suddenly being asked to cope with both of them was a nasty twist of fate.

Things still might have been all right if someone had taken the time to think about the forces that were at work. I am not suggesting that Terree could have been saved from schizophrenia — I don't think it works that way — but she might have been kept from being so disruptive to the relationship between Dean and Doreen.

Dean had recently retired and he was eager to share his life with someone who would appreciate what he had accomplished.

He had enough money to live, with occasional luxuries, and he was eager to enjoy them with Doreen. He liked her family, too.

Unfortunately, my siblings and I, at least the sane ones, initially were too self-involved to recognize that Doreen had value as an individual, not just as Dean's new wife. After her divorce she had been forced to earn her own living and she had built a successful banking career in Winnipeg before Dean suddenly arrived, married her, and took her away.

My siblings, Penny, John, and Terree, and I were all in the thrall of various forms of motherlessness, and we did not even stop to think what we wanted from Doreen. The truth was, we all wanted to be loved.

Doreen did not know we wanted to be loved. Even we didn't know the extent of our own need. And in the final analysis, all of that not knowing kept Doreen and her stepchildren from ever being anything very real to each other.

TRYING TO UNDERSTAND THE PAST TO GIVE MEANING TO THE PRESENT

I took a long time to become interested in rummaging about in family history. During the uncomfortable summer of 1975 in Montreal, I had concluded that while everything else in life takes a turn at seeming transitory or unreliable, your blood relatives are stuck with you, and you with them. But I hadn't done much to follow up on that notion in the years that followed, unless you count having more children as a way to ensure that you have more blood relatives to be stuck with.

In our family, like so many others, the Second World War played a very important role. I grew up amongst photographs and souvenirs of Dean's military service, and between my elder siblings and me the war was the source of the "great divide." Penny and John had been born before the war, while Terree and I were part of the baby boomer generation. Dean and Tessie's enforced separation during five long years of war inevitably changed their relationship. Dean's experiences as an officer in Europe had made him more worldly, while his return home meant Tessie had to play down some of her hard-won self-reliance.

My generation, saved from having such a devastating backdrop against which to play out our own lives, still managed, through diligent effort and considerable self-indulgence, to traumatize our children in new and different ways.

I spent my thirties and forties being a mother, a lover, a career woman, and a feminist, although not always in that order. It was not until I was approaching fifty that I began to think that I might be less "self-made" and more the result of genetics than I had previously acknowledged. Finally, I began to wonder where my family had come from and what kind of people they had been.

I knew surprisingly little. I did know the maiden names of both my grandmothers, and that all of my grandparents had come from England. I knew where they had settled in Canada, but nothing about where they had lived in England.

Unfortunately, I had begun my poking around in the family archives too late to obtain much help from the living. All of my grandparents were dead. My mother had been dead for twenty-five years, my father for ten. Undaunted, I decided to start with the Whittakers, because my sister Penny knew the name of the place in the north of England they had migrated from, and William and I were already in London on holiday.

According to Penny, the source of our Whittakers was Haslingden, a Lancashire town in the Rossendale Valley where my grandfather had operated a small side business repairing bicycles, called the Hazeldene Bicycle Works. Learning this, the fact that my grandparents had named their four children Hazel, Ivy, Ross, and Dean, suddenly struck me as rather touching. Either they were profoundly homesick, or they had demonstrated a remarkable lack of originality, or perhaps both. Mind you, my older sister's first names are Penelope Dale, which could suggest more nostalgia or simply that parents go a little crazy when they have their first chance to name a child.

Hazel, Dean, Ivy, and Ross Whittaker, in Kaslo.

Armed with a map showing the location of Haslingden, the names of my grandparents, and the naïve notion that it shouldn't be hard to find traces of people who had emigrated a mere hundred years ago, we set off to gather information on what I had no doubt would prove to be humble origins.

FROM A MILL TOWN IN LANCASHIRE

William and I rented a car in London and headed for the north of England. It took a lot longer to get to Haslingden than I had expected. Mind you, I am not much of a map reader and know very little about British roadways and distances.

My experience with former mill towns was non-existent. I had yet to encounter the evocative paintings of L.S. Lowry, so the blackened-brick bleakness of Haslingden was a little shocking to me. It seemed at first glance that there was little or nothing of the romance of history to be found in that soot-darkened, northern town.

After a night in a congenial hotel with a supper that included help with local pronunciations, "ossletussle" for Oswaldthistle for example, we set out with enthusiasm the next morning to explore and research. The trip to the local library was instructive, as was the local telephone book. Hundreds and hundreds of Whittakers had once called Haslingden home.

In Accrington we ran into the first of the many very helpful people who have made my research so interesting and exciting. By combining my husband William's journalistic skills with my bits and pieces of information, and the considerate help and guidance of the registry office staff, by lunchtime I had my Whittaker grandparents' wedding certificate in my hand.

To the uninitiated, the amount of information on an official British marriage certificate is a wonderful surprise. Suddenly I knew the names of both my great-grandfathers, the addresses of my grandparents at the time of their marriage, their occupations, their ages, who witnessed their marriage, and what religion they professed.

The year of the marriage was 1899. The certificate listed my grandfather as working in a mill as a bleacher, while my grandmother was described as a weaver. Although Haslingdon is an old mill town, the fact that they were both so representative of their community still somehow took me by surprise. It did seem obvious to me, however, how they must have met. Mill weaver meets mill bleacher. At least they should never want for sheets and tea towels.

In our own premonitory version of the new, popular television programme *Who Do You Think You Are?*, William and I drove immediately to the addresses listed on the marriage certificate, two humble stone row houses with two rooms up and two rooms down. Yet I found it fascinating that at the foot of my Whittaker grandfather's street were rolling hills that, if followed far enough, become the melancholy moors of Bronte country.

There was an old bench, clearly located to face the view, and I sat there for some time looking out at the verdant hills. I wondered, perhaps a little fancifully, if my grandparents had sat in this very place, talking about their plans. And I tried hard to imagine the situation in 1899 that led a young couple to leave that town, the mill, and the people they had known all their lives to emigrate to the Canadian Rockies. Of course, I didn't know much about work in the mills at that point, nor had I yet heard the extraordinary clattering racket of a mechanical loom.

Politely speaking, Kaslo, British Columbia, is an inaccessible town. You can take the plane from Vancouver to Castlegar and then drive north for an hour or two. Or you can come in through Cranbrook and then drive nearly the same distance, but with the addition of a car ferry ride, featuring excellent cinnamon buns, across Kootenay Lake. For those who like a bit of excitement, Castlegar has a definite edge. Because the airport is surrounded by mountains and weather conditions up there can be pretty dramatic, you never know for certain whether you're going to make it down between the peaks or if the pilot is going to decide, for safety's sake, to just fly on by. Food lovers prefer the ferry.

My grandparents emigrated over a hundred years ago, so getting to Kaslo from Haslingden must have involved a train, probably more than one, to Liverpool, an Atlantic crossing in steerage from Liverpool up Canada's St. Lawrence River to Quebec City or Montreal, a 2,500 mile train journey to Cranbrook, and a long steamship voyage up the Kootenay Lake to Kaslo.

Of course, it was not just the getting there that was so arduous and difficult, it was also the unlikelihood of ever getting back. You had to say goodbye to family and friends without any real idea of when you might see them again, or even if you ever would see them again. So I sat there thinking about the challenge of moving partway around the world to start a new life — the romance of the notion causing me to underestimate the inevitable hardship and feelings of loss that would be involved.

MARGARET ISHERWOOD, BORN APRIL 9, 1876

Jane held the new baby in her arms and smiled happily. Her first-born had been the son John wanted and needed, and he had proudly named his boy after his own father, Matthew. Now Jane had the girl that she too had dreamed of rearing, and she and John had already agreed to call her Margaret.

Matthew and Margaret, two fine names for two healthy children who could be a comfort to them in their old age. Jane wasn't much for imagining, but it really felt as if this bright little girl was going to find her life a great adventure.

Jane had the notion, wistful and yet hopeful, that she would be able to teach her daughter the things that she so wished her mother could have had the chance to teach her. She wanted to show her daughter how to cook and sew and wean baby kittens from their mother. Most of all, Jane wanted to watch her daughter grow into young womanhood, to help and encourage her to fulfill her dreams.

Being Jane's first girl, Margaret's name was full of family connection. Jane's own mother's name was Margaret, and Jane's beloved older sister was a Margaret, too. And though she may not even have known, both Jane's grandmother and her great-grandmother on her mother's side had also been named Margaret.

One reason that she might not have known about all of the other Margarets was that Jane's own mother, Margaret, had died so soon. She really never had the chance to tell Jane many stories about her life and the lives of her parents, stories about the choices life had presented to them and how those choices rippled down through the years to shape the lives of those who came after.

Jane's sister Margaret was sweetly flattered by the baby's name. She had held Jane's hand through her long labour, gently wiping her forehead. At one point she had even sung Jane a lullaby to distract her from the relentless pressure of her contractions. Though it was a longish trip from Slaidburn, through the Forest of Bowland, to the Isherwood dwelling at Mill Brook Farm, Margaret had already been around again to drop off clothes suitable for a little girl baby, including a lovely new knitted jacket with fancy work down the front.

"We'll have to call her Maggie," she happily admonished Jane. "Otherwise people will start calling me Old Margaret, and I've no need of that."

John's sister Mary and her husband, Tom Rushton, had also come around in their trap to see the new baby and to leave behind some freshly baked bread, but it was Tom's news of the neighbourhood that really had John and Jane most excited.

"I hear the tenancy on Meanley Farm may be coming up," Tom had told them. "What with Henry Harrison gone and John not well, they need a strong new tenant over there. Mary and I would dearly love to have you and Jane as neighbours."

"Do you think the estate manager would consider us for it?" asked Jane eagerly.

"Why not," said Tom. "That husband of yours has a fine reputation as a hard worker and an honest man. Everyone in Slaidburn knows that if you want a job well done, just go looking for John Isherwood."

Jane and John exchanged hopeful looks: The tenancy of Meanley was one of their dearest wishes. Growing up at Chapel Croft where Mary and Tom now lived, John had long admired Meanley's fine aspect and rolling fields. And there was family to consider. With Mary just next door, Margaret nearby in Slaidburn, Jane's brother Tom at Ash Knott, and her brother John in Newton, Jane would not lack for company and John would not lack for help when he needed it with the heavy work around the farm.

Once their visitors had gone home, the new parents shared their excitement quietly so as not to wake up the sleeping newborn, and just as she was slipping off to join the baby in sleep, Jane reached out and held John's calloused hand.

"Wouldn't it be wonderful if we can go to live at Meanley. With the school just over in Newton, the children can get a fine start in life. A farm like that is what I always hoped for us."

"Yes," replied John softly. "It would be a dream come true."

THE IMPORTANCE OF BEING MARGARET

As long as I can remember, I have known that Margaret Isherwood, my Whittaker grandmother, was born on April 9 because that is my birthday too. In recognition of our shared birthday, my father, Dean, Margaret's second son, with what was probably the resigned acquiescence of my mother, added Margaret to the front of the list of names they already had planned for me.

Margaret Sheelagh Dillon Whittaker is a mouthful, though it does at least have substance. But I was never Margaret. Instead I was Binkie until I could spell Sheelagh, which was quite late, and I have been Sheelagh ever since.

It was not until I delved into grandma's history that I came to realize the importance, the sheer immanence, of the name Margaret in my family. As a result of that ignorance, and because the computer age has made it increasingly difficult for people to list three first names, the Margaret part of my name had almost withered away.

However, I had not forgotten our shared birth date. That piece of information proved vital when, following that first excitingly successful genealogical venture in Haslingden, I went looking in London for my grandmother's birth certificate. I did not know the exact year, but I certainly knew the month and the day.

I went looking for my grandmother Margaret Isherwood's birth registration at St. Catherine's House in London, and from the records I learned that she was born in 1876 and her birth was registered in Clitheroe. I was surprised at the place name, Clitheroe, as I had been expecting her to be born in Haslingden. I was further surprised when I got the actual certificate and learned that Clitheroe was just the registration district for a birth that had actually taken place at Mill Brook Farm in the Forest of Bowland.

To a genealogical novice such as me, the various place names were both confusing and intriguing. Without much knowledge of or insight into Lancashire rural and urban life, especially in Victorian times, I really didn't know if the moves Margaret seemed to have made in her life were unusual or not.

Among the bits and pieces of information safeguarded by Penny, there had been some vague family story about grandma's father having "lost everything" in a big court case defending her stepmother from an unjust accusation over an accidental baby death. It was hard for either of us to make any sense out of it, and now both grandma and anyone else who might have known the facts were dead.

A more experienced researcher would have realized immediately that being born on a farm near Clitheroe but married as a mill girl in Haslingden implied a serious reversal of fortune. I simply did not understand that in the mid 1880s leaving a farm tenancy to find work in a mill town was wrenching, not a move one would make if there was a better choice. It was most likely an act of desperation or desire to escape the past and find a new place in a new community.

THE ABSENCE OF JANE

My searches were beginning to be peopled with gentle ghosts. People whom no one had thought about for many years were being resurrected by my queries. Their stories, their births and marriages and deaths, began to interweave with and be embellished by my discoveries. I had gone looking for antecedents and now they seemed to be whispering to me from the past, eager for their lives to be remembered.

I had learned our great-grandmother's name, Jane Isherwood, née Bleazard, from grandma's birth certificate, and I thought if I could learn more about Jane I could really begin to better understand Margaret's life. Penny's impression was that Margaret had lost her mother when she was still quite young, around six or seven years of age, so I went looking in the early 1870s for a death record for Jane Isherwood.

I looked and looked and looked, standing shoulder to shoulder with like-minded people engaging in a little genealogy research on their holidays or during their lunch breaks. The room at St. Catherine's House was full of so many shelves of large old books, usually four of them for each year, listing the names of the dead in copperplate handwriting. Like all of those around me, I heaved each book onto the high, long, chairless desk provided, hunted through the alphabetical listing, and then returned the book to its ordered place on the shelf. At times someone was standing there waiting for it.

I was somewhat confused in my geography and a little unsystematic in my searching, and I did not have much luck. After succeeding in my initial searches so quickly, this one was proving much more difficult.

I set Jane aside for a while in favour of hunting for a birth certificate for my great-grandfather Robert Whittaker. I was in a better position looking for him. Confronted with a neglected churchyard in Haslingden full of centuries of burials, William had mysteriously felt prompted to walk to a far corner of the graveyard, there discovering the gravestone of Robert Whittaker, his wife Ellen, my great-aunt Fanny, and her husband. Thus equipped with Robert's age and date of death, I thought that finding his birth certificate in the official records would be comparatively easy. Who would have thought that there would be so many men called Robert Whittaker living in Lancashire in the middle of the nineteenth century?

Finally, I had to give up and return to Canada. Despite the tedium of the search, and the physical discomfort of the surroundings, I was determined to go back and continue. I knew that the records just had to be somewhere in that building.

A SAD GOODBYE

Meanley Farm 1883

Jane wished so fervently for things to be different, better, for her and her dear Maggie than they had been for her own mother and herself. But in the end, they too had to face almost the same sad rituals of premature loss and death. It would take the resilience of young Maggie, raising children in a far-off dominion, to break the cycle at last. All Jane would ever know was that she was losing her life too soon and leaving her beloved daughter behind.

Matt and Maggie held hands as they filed solemnly into the room, nudging brother John in front of them as they went. Aunt Mary had told them to go and kiss their mother goodbye as she was going up to heaven to be with the angels, but Jane's laboured breathing and stifled moans only left the children convinced that nothing good or happy was going to come of all this.

Ma had been sick for quite a while, her legs swollen and her breath short. Da was drawn and tired, and he sometimes shouted at them now, something he had never done before. Aunt Mary was helping to look after the littlest boys, but she was tired too. The farmhouse had a neglected air, which was particularly hard on da because he always liked to have things clean and orderly.

Maggie missed two things a lot: her mother's laugh and her nightly stories. Jane had told them stories about a blue fairy that she said her own mother had told her, and Maggie just loved those stories.

In her heart, Maggie knew just what the blue fairy looked like — not too big with a long blue dress like a princess and lots of beautiful blue hair. Her mother laughed at her about the blue hair but then she helped Maggie make a dolly that looked exactly like the blue fairy ... almost. She had blue-dyed yarn for hair, a soft, long blue dress, and little wings made of real feathers sewn so neatly onto her back that they seemed to sprout through holes that had been cut carefully in the blue dress. Margaret adored that fairy doll and called her "Blue." When ma was feeling really sickly Maggie had tucked Blue into the bed beside her so the doll could keep her company.

Aunt Margaret came to visit as often as she could, trailing her mob of children and stepchildren behind her. Jane was particularly interested in how the children of sister Isabella were getting along, being raised by Margaret.

"Some other woman will be raising my littl'uns," Jane whispered to her sister, but Margaret would hear none of that kind of talk.

"You are going to get better," she ordered Jane. "There is nothing else for it. I have too many to care for already, and John and the children would be lost without you. Think about me for once, I've only two sisters left in the world and I need both of you."

Jane laughed at Margaret's posturing until she had a coughing fit. Margaret hugged her as tightly as she dared and then settled her gently back down into the covers.

"What this?" she said, finding the doll with blue hair in amongst the covers.

"That's Maggie's blue fairy. Her magic is supposed to keep me well."

"Let's hope it works." Margaret smiled, putting the doll back where she found her. "I always have been partial to the colour blue."

John went quietly into the front room for one last look at his beloved Jane. It was quiet now, the children asleep at last. His sister-in-law Margaret had washed and dressed Jane lovingly, talking quietly to her the whole time. Looking down into the wooden coffin, he saw a scrap of blue caught in the folds of Jane's soft white nightdress.

He gently lifted the little fairy doll out of the coffin.

"I think the living will be needing you, Blue," he whispered. "Especially my girl Maggie. Do you think you can look after her for now?"

The tiny doll stared up at him fixedly with her criss-cross-stitched blue eyes.

"I believe that is a 'yes,'" said John.

THE GARDNERS OF DALTON-IN-FURNESS

Grace Gardner was born into a life with few advantages. While New Year's Eve 1859 might have been an interesting date to be born, the prospects for a young working-class female in Dalton-in-Furness were pretty limited.

Her pa was an iron miner and her ma the vivacious local girl who had caught his eye. Grace was her parent's first child and she inherited her mother's slight beauty and magnified it with a gentle warmth.

Grace was a great favourite of her father's — her desire to please beguiled him just as it later would other men in her life. The sweetly toddling Gracie in her pinnie, growing into a surprisingly serious little scholar who was determined to learn to read and write, made him dream, at least for a moment, that she might marry well and even be the one to look after her ma and pa when they were old.

Then, as the years passed and he had to listen to more and more admiring comments about Grace from his mates, Ed Gardner began to worry instead. His advice to be careful of boys was gruffly delivered, and barely acknowledged by Grace ... or heeded.

Ed liked a pint and didn't mind spending a bit of time at the pub on a Sunday. His family was growing steadily and their house was noisy and crowded. Unlike those of his chums, the Gardner family were a healthy lot and most of his children survived.

After Grace, Edward and Isabella Gardner went on to have two more daughters at four-year intervals. Grace was eight and Jane four when Isabella was born. They were an interesting trio: Grace, the eldest, quiet spoken and acquiescent; younger sister Jane shared some of Grace's gentle loveliness, but with a bit of an artistic flair; and Isabella, the youngest, who was born solemn and matured somehow shrewd.

They all came to think of Isabella as the "smart one" and were probably right. She certainly was a fast talker and she had a quick mind. Yet there was also a kind of still intelligence in Grace's big eyes.

It was Grace's warm brown hair and soulful eyes, not the intellect, that attracted most men. Her gentleness and pliancy suggested that she might not put up too much resistance to a kiss and a cuddle.

In fact, Jane was the first Gardner girl to get pregnant. By the time Jane was eighteen her illegitimate son, Edward John Sykes Gardner, had been added to the rather full Gardner house at 9 Stafford Street in Dalton-in-Furness. She named him after her father, and maybe after the baby's father too, although no father was listed on little Edward's birth certificate. The name Sykes amongst his given names is the only clue to his possible paternity.

Perhaps to reduce the crowding at Stafford Street, but more likely just to help the family keep going, fourteen-year-old Isabella was not around to help care for baby Edward. She was already in service. Through some family connection, she and older cousin George Cartmell were working as general servants for a family over in Wesham.

But there were still three sons, two daughters, their parents, and the new grandson living in the little house on Stafford Street, all trying to survive on Edward's earnings from the mine and what little Jane could make as a dressmaker. Of course, Isabella was also expected to send some money home.

Then, within a year, there was yet another mouth to feed at Stafford Street. This time it was Grace's turn to bear an illegitimate child. She named him Thomas and described herself on his birth certificate as a domestic servant, making no mention of a father for the boy.

It must have been obvious to everyone in the Gardner house that there was no room for yet another child, fatherless or otherwise. Even before little Thomas was born, Grace knew that she would have to find a place to live and a job to support them both. Isabella seemed well set up and might be able to help her find work near Wesham. With a job in a new place, maybe Grace could start afresh.

December 15, 1882, was the beginning of Thomas Gardner's blighted little life. His mother looked down at his sleeping form and whispered, "Oh Thomas, what is to become of us?"

A DREADFUL PLIGHT

Seizing the chance to leave the stigma of unwed motherhood behind, at least for a while, Grace gladly went to a situation that Isabella had found for the two of them over at Crosshills, putting the baby out to nurse with a kindly Dalton woman named Agnes Creary and promising faithfully to send money for his care.

Even before she had any money to send, Grace wrote to Mrs. Creary, pestering her with questions about the baby. Sadly, Grace's letters had to be read out to Mrs. Creary by her neighbour's daughter, who was often too busy to write back, so Grace received little information on her son's progress. As she went about her new work, Grace often whispered a prayer for the health of little Thomas.

Despite starting out hopeful that she would find her feet and perhaps even be able to send for her child, Grace found that life away from her parent's home was lonely and much more difficult than she had imagined. Though Isabella had warned her, the heavy, demanding work of a farm servant still came as a shock, and Grace fell into bed each night exhausted. And the money that she earned was only pennies more a week than she owed Mrs. Creary. She spent very little, but her letters, while frequent, were increasingly filled with descriptions of her difficulties and empty of money for the care of the baby. Back in Dalton, Agnes Creary, while sympathetic, was becoming increasing impatient with Grace's excuses.

Isabella, by contrast, flourished in their new setting. She was used to being in service and she had long ago overcome homesickness. Never one to waste time or effort, she resorted first to her brain to devise ways get their work done quickly. While her sharp manner put off some of the other servants, Grace observed that if something wanted doing well, it was Isabella that they asked for advice or help.

Grace's money problems didn't ease, but her aching muscles eventually did, and she increasingly looked forward to going out on her afternoons off. By the time harvest came around, she was happy to join Isabella and the others for a night of dancing and good cheer. Unfortunately, the attention of a handsome young thresher and the beer and the moonlit haystacks were her undoing. Again.

As her stomach began to crowd her apron, all thoughts of reuniting with infant Thomas were driven out by the problem of what to do with the baby on the way. Isabella was furious with her, as much because she had foolishly undone Isabella's attempt to rehabilitate her as for her pathetic plight, and her parents back in Dalton felt completely helpless in the face of this new disaster.

To try to keep herself and this second child out of the workhouse, an increasingly desperate Grace obtained a place near Bolton-by-Bowland, where she could earn her keep until the baby arrived. The work was very arduous, especially for a pregnant woman, but Grace was relieved to have a situation of any kind.

Meanwhile, Mrs. Creary heard rumours that Grace was about to have another child, and fearing she would never see the money she was owed, hastily returned the child to Grace's parents, who equally quickly found a woman named Jane Gordon to look after him, promising that Grace would be good for the cost of his care. Fortunately for all parties concerned, except Mrs. Gordon, she and Agnes Creary were not acquainted.

MEANLEY WITHOUT JANE

They had so little time to enjoy their dream.

With the move to Meanley, John had gone out and surprised Jane and the children with the purchase of a horse, not just to help with the farm work and chores but for the children to ride on as well. There had been considerable debate about a name. Jane wanted to call it something silly like Dilly or Flo, and the boys favoured dull, obvious names like Grey or Stormy, but it was little Maggie who was let decide.

"Come sit on my knee, you bonny girl," said her pa, "and tell me what you would like to call this fine animal."

"Bonny," said Maggie, clapping her hands. "Let's call her Bonny."

So Bonny it was.

He should have known that all their cheery laughter was tempting fate. Jane's death came as a dreadful reminder that happiness is something you have to hold onto tightly, or it can just slip away.

In the exhausting and painful months after Jane died, John found it comforting to talk to her as he went about his farm work, or as he carefully fitted stones together for a new house for the squire's estate manager, sharing his worries about Matt's nightmares and Maggie's schooling. Sadly, as time went by he found that he was losing the ability to keep Jane in his thoughts. And at night his recurrent dream was of struggling through fields thick with mud to get home to her, throwing open the door at last, and looking about, only to find that no one was there.

Often he was trailed about Meanley by a gaggle of his children, in an unconscious imitation of geese following behind their mother. He was kind to them, even when they were underfoot, because he knew how frightened and disoriented they must all feel. Jane's sister and his own were doing the best they could for the littl'uns, but it was hard for everyone.

As he looked down at his children, solemnly throwing bits of dry bread at the ducklings, he realized that he must hire someone to help him run the farm and look after his family. He sometimes wondered how Jane had managed everything so efficiently, but he was past that. He would happily settle now for just another pair of hands and a woman's skill in the kitchen.

A SLAIDBURN WEDDING

It had been a difficult couple of years for both of them.

In his search for hired help, John had found that a farm widower with five children, no matter how well-intentioned he may be, did not have many applicants for the combined job of servant and surrogate wife and mother knocking down his door. He put out the word to his friends and acquaintances that he was looking for someone and waited impatiently to see who might turn up.

Meanwhile, though she found Grace irritatingly weepy and depressed whenever she stopped by to see how she was faring, Isabella kept on looking for a new situation for her, one that would take her with all of her baggage. And when Isabella heard of the job at Meanley, she felt relieved and hopeful. As she said to Grace: "That job might be your salvation."

Wisely, Grace agreed.

The chance to be hired girl over at the Isherwoods near Slaidburn sounded like hard work, but by then Grace had considerably less fear of hard work. She had learned to be afraid of other things, prospects she found much worse, such as a life in the workhouse with no hope of a reprieve.

Instead, Isabella had found her a miracle. In just months she had been transformed into an honest woman. She smiled at John across the room. There he was, standing up tall, almost afraid to believe his good fortune, and here she was, in love with a good man at last.

It was a joyful event for all involved, a new-year celebration and a wedding and a birthday all rolled up into one. Grace had just reached the age of twenty-five when she married John Isherwood on January 3, 1885, and it was clear that the two of them were very happy.

The fact that the bride was known to be pregnant did not even slightly dampen the celebrations — in fact, John was delighted that another baby was on the way and as he said to his mates at the Black Bull, "Why would such a sweet woman bother with an old man like me with five littl'uns, if she weren't going to have one of his herself."

When Grace first arrived to work at Meanley she already had a fatherless baby in her arms, so the locals knew that she had been no better than she had to be, but the combination of her quiet ways and John's need made most people happy to have her as part of their community. As Mary Rushton's mother-in-law was heard to remark, "That Grace does brew a fine cup of tea."

After the quiet ceremony in St. Andrew's Church, the Isherwood children and their cousins ran wild, full of excitement and wedding cake. Maggie organized the older children into a mock ceremony of their own, although no one could keep a straight face when Richard decided to wear the baby's shawl as a veil. Even Maggie's scolding about little James catching a chill without his shawl was interrupted by her own laughter.

Isabella had a fine time at the wedding. Not only did she attract the attention of one of the Robinson boys, but also she felt secretly proud that she had played such a big part in bringing Grace and John together. Her mother was too ill at the time to attend the wedding, and travel in the winter cold did take the stuffing out of you, but she was glad to see sister Jane again. It was Jane who needed cheering up those days, and Isabella felt that it was her responsibility to help Jane get over the news that Sykes had married a girl from Moorcroft.

Matt and Maggie were pleased to see their father so happy. He had been so careworn during those long months since their mother had died, and now he seemed his old self again.

Neither Grace nor John was a big talker, but as they sat by the fire that evening they shared a sense of deep contentment. While John believed he would never forget Jane, he felt he had his life back on track again and that Grace would make a fine wife and mother to his children. He hoped that the new baby would be a girl, perhaps a miniature of Grace in the way that Maggie was of her mother.

After the sadness and confusion of the last few years, Grace felt as if she could finally let out her breath. Ever since she had first fallen pregnant she had been frightened, frightened of what her friends and family would say, and frightened that she would end up in the workhouse where she felt certain she would die of shame. Isabella had been very impatient with her when she fell pregnant a second time, shouting at her that everyone would think that the Gardner girls were slatterns. Grace understood that Isabella feared for her situation as well as her reputation, but it still pained her to see the anger in Isabella's eyes.

Now she had a kind and loving husband. She had become a respectable farmer's wife, and that would make her respectable too. John had even suggested already that he might give baby James his name. What a good man.

Everything would be fine now if it were not for young Thomas, back in Cumbria. He'd been in the Ulverston workhouse for a bit, and maybe that was the best place for him. With the speed at which events had overtaken her and John, somehow the moment had not yet come to mention Tom's existence.

She hoped that Thomas would be safe and find his way in the world, but she just couldn't see how he could ever become part of her new life.

MURDERS LARGE AND SMALL

Once she retired from her job as a lawyer, my older sister Penny (the one with the middle name of Dale) caught the genealogical fever. Penny has been adept with computer technology since the sixties, when she worked as a programmer, so she took to hunting up things on the Internet as if it was second nature. Her proficiency with complicated spreadsheets and family-records programs belies her claim that she has no clerical aptitude.

Although we were raised in western Canada, we both love a change of scene. In the early southern hemisphere spring of 2001, I was living in Australia while Penny was living in New Zealand.

When she called me at my rented home in Canberra from her own temporary home in Wellington, on the evening of September 11, 2001, she was terribly excited. "You won't believe what I have found," she said in a voice filled with emotion. "I have found the family murder!"

Then came the modern day instruction: "Go to www dot Slaidburn dot org dot uk, forward slash suspected underscore child underscore murder underscore 1885 dot htm and read it! Our grandmother was even required to testify! It's amazing!"

I had to repeat the address back to her a couple of times and then I promised that I would look at the site immediately and call her right back. Our home computer in Canberra at that time required the use of the phone line to access the Internet.

"By the way," I asked, "how did you ever end up on a site called that?"

"Oh, I was just playing around on the Internet and I found it. "

"How many hours have you been on the net?" I asked sternly. Her answer was vague. It must have been another very rainy day in Wellington.

It was rather cold in the room in Canberra where we had set up our computer. Canberra is big on sun in the outdoors but, because it is inland, during the winter it can have very chilly interiors. Penny had called me on an evening that felt more like winter than spring, so it was dark, and I sat shivering and keyboarding away in the cold until I found the site and its amazing contents.

I quickly phoned Penny back to marvel together. It was the kind of family mystery you dream of finding as you plod through old records. Only part of it was there, of course. So after spending some time speculating about what she had discovered, we began to try to figure out how to learn more.

I had missed the 9:30 p.m. news in all the excitement, so I tried to combine watching the late night news with tooth brushing (it helps to have an ensuite near the TV) before going to bed. As I tuned in, Sandra Sully, Channel 10's blond late-night anchor, was announcing *Breaking News* and the coverage immediately went live to the scene. A plane had just flown into the World Trade Center in New York.

As I stood transfixed in front of the television, toothbrush drooping from my gaping mouth, a second airplane appeared on the screen like a car whose curious driver is slowing to look at the scene of an accident. And then it flew right into the second tower. In the Antipodes, the dreadful day that was America's September 11 was beginning to unfold through our night.

I called Penny in Wellington again, this time to tell her to wake up and turn on the TV.

Perhaps not surprisingly, it was some weeks before I really thought again about the 1885 Slaidburn Child Murder.

THE MORNING AFTER

September 12, 2001, was a very strange day in Canberra. It was beautiful and sunny, but most people were cheerless and bleary-eyed from exhaustion after being up most of the night trying to make sense of events half a world away.

I went to a lunchtime speech that I had previously been eager to attend because it was to be given by the clever and interesting Australian Senator Kate Lundy. But when I got back to the office I could not remember a thing that she had said.

I had spent an anxious period during my night of September 11 trying to find out if my son Matthew, a journalism student in New York, was safe. I got reassurances at about 4:30 a.m. through family in Toronto, although as it turned out, because of his own derring-do, they were a bit misleading. While Matthew had escaped any initial danger, he then tempted fate by using his newly minted press pass to head for Ground Zero and see what he could find to report on down there.

All over the world, friends and colleagues were facing the dawning horror of twenty-first-century terrorism, not to mention the massive dislocation and inconvenience that it brought in its wake. Some personal stories could be told with humour, like that of a friend returning from San Francisco to Hong Kong, who spent days on a hot, smelly jumbo jet parked amidst many other downed jets on the tarmac in Juneau, Alaska. Others, like that of our corporate doctor, scheduled for a presentation in the World Trade Center that day, who found himself literally on the ground at ground zero performing triage, simply reflected the shock of war.

Fearful of what the terrorist events might mean about the future, I turned away from the past. After printing out the information from the Slaidburn Suspected Child Murder site, I just put it aside.

Much later, as the world began to settle into a post–September 11 "new reality," and I began to consider resuming such previously ordinary behaviours as riding on airplanes, I remembered Penny's amazing discovery and returned to the Slaidburn site to reread its contents.

I found the site both amazing and tantalizing.

SUSPECTED CHILD MURDER 1885
These extracts were taken from the *Preston Guardian* of the time contained in a Victorian scrapbook kept in Clitheroe Library.
INQUEST PROCEEDINGS
Wednesday, 20th of May, 1885.
SUSPECTED CHILD MURDER NEAR SLAIDBURN.
ARREST OF TWO WOMEN. THE INQUEST.

Considerable commotion has been prevalent in the Slaidburn district since Monday, in consequence of a suspected case of child murder. About seven o'clock on Sunday evening the dead body of a child was found in a brook, close to the highway between Slaidburn and Bolton-by-Bowland, and about 1 mile distant from the former village.

Photo by Sue Burton.

Black Bull Inn, location of the inquest.

The discovery was made by a farmer's wife, named Bargh, who was walking alongside the brook with her husband. The child, which was apparently about two years old, was laid in the water with his head and shoulders under a curb stone. Yesterday, Grace Isherwood, wife of John Isherwood, farmer, Newton and Isabella Gardiner, her sister, were taken into custody on suspicion of being concerned in the murder. It is suspected that Mrs. Isherwood is the mother of the child, but Gardiner has made a statement to the effect that she had had the child to nurse the last four months, but gave it back to its mother, who was a stranger, on Saturday night, at Slaidburn. This statement, however, is somewhat discredited.

Yesterday afternoon, Mr. A. I. Robinson, coroner, opened an inquest at the Black Bull Inn, Slaidburn when the following evidence was taken:

John Bargh, Farmer, Field Head, Slaidburn, deposed: On Sunday evening, at seven o'clock, I and my wife went for a walk. We went up under Langcliffe Cross bridge, and in the fields along the waterside. About 30 yards distant from the bridge at the bottom of the pavement we saw a child lying in the water. My wife saw it first, and called my attention to it. It was lying face downward. Its head and part of its shoulder were under the edge of the pavement, and one leg was between the stones. After we had left the waterside we turned back to see whether the child was really dead. From the appearance of it, and the mud upon its legs, we saw that it must have been there some hours. I went for a policeman and returned with him, and saw him take it out of the water. I did not know the child. It is the same child that I have just seen. I had not seen anyone about there that day. My wife and Mrs. Camm, who are neighbours, and I met two women with a child on Saturday night, a little after nine o'clock, just above the bridge. They were going in the direction of Bolton-by-Bowland. They went up the hill in front of us, and then turned back and met us. It was dusk, and I cannot identify the women, nor can I say how they were dressed. One of them was carrying the child. They would be 40 or 50 yards above the bridge when we passed them. A conveyance was passing at the time, and drove between us just as we were passing it. There is no road down the brook side, and no one could get to the place where we found the child without getting over the wall. The water forms a pool at the end of the pavement of about a foot or 18 inches deep. The brook is the Easington Brook. I cannot speak as to the kind of shawls the women wore, or anything, except that they are nearly both of one height.

P.C. Sutcliffe said: a little before eight o'clock on Sunday night the last witness came for me. I went with him to Langcliffe Cross Bridge. In the water about 28 yards from the bridge, down the stream, he pointed to the body of a child. I examined it minutely, and found it was lying face downward; the arms were folded in front, and it was in a stooping posture on its knees. The right foot was under a large stone, but the stone did not rest upon it. The head was under the curb stone of the pavement, but was quite loose. The water was about 18 inches deep. The child had two petticoats and a shirt on and was without a hat. The clothes produced are the same as worn by the deceased. I went to Meanley Farm about ten o'clock that night, and saw Mrs. Isherwood and Isabella Gardiner, also John Isherwood were sitting each side of the fire. I said, "I suppose you have a little boy, Mrs. Isherwood?" She replied, "No." Gardiner then said that she had had one to nurse for the last four months, but had taken it to its mother. Mrs. Isherwood then said that they had had a letter from the mother of the child asking them to meet at Clitheroe on the previous day (Saturday), at twelve o'clock, with the child. They went there at twelve o'clock, but did not see her until four o'clock in the afternoon. Isabella Gardiner said she wanted £4 from the mother for nursing the child, but the mother said she must take the child back to Slaidburn and she would meet them there and pay the money. Gardiner further stated that they met the mother of the child at Slaidburn at ten o'clock the same night. She only paid her two shillings instead of the £4, whereupon they (Mrs. Isherwood and Gardiner) took off the child's frock, shoes, and stockings, but left its hat on. The mother, however put it a little coat on. They were waiting for more money, when a man came out of the Black Bull Inn and accosted them, and said if they were not off he would do for both the child and them.

Margaret Isherwood, aged nine years, living at Meanley Farm with her father and stepmother, stated: I have seen the dead child. I know it. It was named Thomas Dockrah, and has lived at our house for a week. Isabella Gardiner brought it. It was two years old, and could walk about. I saw it last on Saturday forenoon. Gardiner took it out of the house, and I did not see it again alive. She came back on Saturday night with my mother and my little brother James and the deceased child. They came back about five o'clock, but Gardiner did not come in. She was carrying a child, and went down the meadow to Slaidburn. My mother came into the house, and in a short time followed Gardiner toward Slaidburn. I was in bed when they came back. On Saturday morning Gardiner told me they were going to Clitheroe. I identify the clothes produced as those worn by the child on Saturday morning.

Jane Hayhurst, of Chapel Street, Slaidburn, deposed to washing the deceased and laying it out. She found a black mark on his forehead and a few scratches on his cheek. There were no other wounds. The child was healthy looking. The inquiry was then adjourned.

Saturday, May 23rd, 1885
THE SUSPECTED MURDER AT SLAIDBURN. THE ADJOURNED INQUEST. VERDICT OF WILFUL MURDER.

Further investigations made by the police into the circumstances connected with the suspicious death of a child at Slaidburn have resulted in disclosures which go far to indicate that a murder has been committed. The adjourned inquest was held on Thursday afternoon, at the Black Bull Inn, Slaidburn, before Mr. A.I. Robinson, coroner, and revelations were made which had justified the arrest in the earlier part of the week of the two women—Grace Isherwood, wife of John Isherwood, farmer, Meanley Farm, Newton; and her sister, Isabella Gardiner. The prisoners, it appears, are natives of Dalton-in-Furness, and the daughters of a miner residing in that town. Grace Isherwood was married to John Isherwood about last Christmas, after having been in his service for a short time as domestic servant, in which capacity she had been employed for twelve months previously in the neighbourhood of Bolton-by-Bowland. Prior to her marriage she had two illegitimate children, but it transpires that her husband was only aware of the existence of one, she having kept him in ignorance of the other by having it nursed at Dalton-in-Furness. The child which had been out to nurse was, however, returned to Mrs. Isherwood about a fortnight ago. Her sister, who was a domestic servant at Dalton-in-Furness, came with it, and the pair concocted a story with a view to deceiving her husband. They informed him that the child's name was Thomas Dockrah, that it belonged to a woman named Elizabeth Dockrah, and that the sister was nursing it. On Saturday they set out for Clitheroe with the child, and endeavoured to secure its admittance into the Clitheroe Union Workhouse. They were unsuccessful, as they were not in possession of the necessary admittance order from the relieving officer. The same evening they appear to have made a pretence that they were going to meet the child's mother, and they took the child and drowned it in a brook close to the highway some distance from Slaidburn village. The body was discovered on Sunday evening, and after due enquiries the prisoners were arrested on Tuesday.

The affair has created much excitement in Slaidburn and the neighbourhood, and during the progress of the inquest on Thursday the villagers congregated to await the result. In the course of the afternoon the prisoners were brought from the Bolton-by-Bowland Police Station to Slaidburn to be present during the inquiry. Mrs. Isherwood was in a delicate condition, seeming to feel her position acutely, and had to be supported by an officer when walking from the Slaidburn Police Station to the room in which the inquiry was held. She is 26 years of age and of respectable appearance. Her sister, who was only eighteen years old, wore a look of quiet unconcern, as she walked by her sister's side accompanied by two police officers. During the proceedings Mrs. Isherwood's husband entered the room and was accommodated with a seat. On his arrival both he and the prisoners burst into tears. The following additional evidence was called:

Jane Gordon, a widow residing at Dalton-in-Furness, said: I nursed a child belonging to Grace Gardiner for three months following Whit-week last year. It was a boy, and I identify Mrs. Isherwood as the child's mother. I do not know who was the father of it. I believe that the dead child is the same that I nursed. I identify the clothes worn by the deceased; some of which I myself made for the child. I did not receive anything toward the child's maintenance, and therefore took it to Ulverston workhouse. It was, however, taken out by the prisoners parents, for I saw it three or four months ago at the house of Mrs. Gardiner, at Dalton-in-Furness, when I went there for a sovereign that Grace (the prisoner) had sent for me.

Catherine Lofthouse, wife of Young Lofthouse, master of the Clitheroe Union Workhouse, deposed: on Saturday last, between two and three o'clock, two women came to the workhouse and wanted to leave the little boy. One of them had two children. She said she could not maintain both, and wanted to leave the boy. I told her Mr. Lofthouse was out, and she would have to get an order from Mr. Harrison, relieving officer, for its admittance. She did not give any name. The child she wanted to leave was about two years or 2 1/2 years old. It was dressed in plaid coat and round hat. I identify the two prisoners as the women who came. I believe the deceased to be the same child.

Dr. Bridgman, of Slaidburn, deposed to making a post-mortem examination of the body on Wednesday. It appeared to be a healthy and well-developed male child about two years old. There were no marks of external violence except the scratches about the face. He was of the opinion that the child died from asphyxia, or the prevention of air into the lungs. He thought death would be caused by drowning as the probabilities pointed in that direction.

Supt. Inman stated: about twelve noon on Monday last I went to John Isherwood's Meanley Farm, Newton. I there saw Isabella Gardiner and Grace Isherwood. Gardiner made a statement voluntarily in response to my enquiries as to the death of the child. She said: "I am eighteen years old, and a domestic servant, of No.3, Victoria Street, Dalton-in-Furness. I live with my father at that address. His name is Edward Gardiner, and he is a miner. I know Elizabeth Dockrah. We lived at the same village, Silecroft, near Bootle, Cumberland, about two years since. Dockrah was enceinte. She was confined at Dalton-in-Furness, at her father and mother's house who were then both living in Dalton. Her father and mother have both since died. When she lived at Silecroft she went with several men. She was a loose character. She lived at a farmhouse at Silecroft, but I don't know the name. I lived with John James Woodhead, Old House Farm. She left Silecroft before I did. I did not see her again until about four months since, when I met her by accident in the main street at Dalton-in-Furness. She had no child with her, but she asked if I would nurse her child until this Whitsuntide, but she said, "I will get you 4s.6d. per week for nursing it." About 8:30 p.m. Mrs. Cornish (since dead) brought the child to me. I met her in the street with it. Its mother was not with her and I have never seen Dockrah since then until I met her at Clitheroe railway station about 4 p.m. last Saturday. She was then in company with a man. Dockrah said, "His name is John Stables; we have been married about a month." I had the child with me at Clitheroe. The man that was with Dockrah never spoke. He was drunk. Dockrah asked me to meet her at the Black Bull Inn, Slaidburn, the same night with the child. I and my sister went, and soon afterward Dockrah and Stables came to us. Stables went into the inn, and Dockrah stood outside with us. At Clitheroe Station Dockrah gave me 2s. Stables, Dockrah, my sister, and myself all went down to Slaidburn bridge, and it was at this place that Dockrah took the child from me. It was crying at the time, and Dockrah took no notice of it. I asked Dockrah for some more money, and Stables said, "I will do for both you and the child." I got afraid, and left them. They said, "We will go to Bolton-by-Bowland."

Continuing, Superintendent Inman said: "She gave a description of Dockrah and the man Stables. I then came to Slaidburn and saw the deceased child, and I had taken from its body the little shirt, red petticoats, and her skirt. I proceeded to Dalton-in-Furness the same afternoon. From information I received there, I by telegram gave instructions for Mrs. Isherwood and Gardiner to be apprehended at once. About 12:30 on Tuesday I saw the prisoners in the police station at Slaidburn. I charged Grace Isherwood with having caused the death of her illegitimate child Thomas Gardiner, aged about two years, on the night of Saturday the sixteenth or on Sunday, 17th May, 1885, in Easington Beck, at Langcliffe Cross Bridge, Slaidburn. I cautioned her. She made no reply to the charge. I then charged Gardiner, and she replied, "I have not done it, sir." On Wednesday I received the letters produced, eight in number. They have been sent by the prisoner Isherwood at various times to Jane Gordon, respecting a child that the latter was nursing. I also produce from the Registrar of Births at Dalton-in-Furness a notice certifying that on December 15, 1882, Grace Gardiner, domestic servant, 9, Stafford-street, Dalton-in-Furness, gave birth to a boy named Thomas Gardiner. The reason they went to Clitheroe, from a statement made by Isabella Gardiner at the interview on Monday, was in consequence of having a few days previous to Saturday received a letter from Elizabeth Dockrah, the letter being dated from Rimington, asking for the child to be taken to the Clitheroe Railway Station at noon on Saturday. Mrs. Isherwood said Dockrah came off a train from the direction of Blackburn at 4 p.m. She also said that Dockrah had a ring on her finger. She knew her at Dalton-in-Furness, but was not much acquainted with her as she was a bad character and untidy.

Inspector Prosser deposed to receiving a telegram on Tuesday at 5.15 a.m. instructing him to apprehend Grace Isherwood and Isabella Gardiner. He went to Meanley Farm, Newton, and apprehended the prisoners. On Sunday

Afternoon he received from John Isherwood clothing which he was told was worn by the child.

Supt. Inman said that was all the evidence he had.

The Coroner said that before they proceeded to consider the evidence it was only right that the prisoners should have an opportunity of making any explanation they liked in regard to the matter. But he must inform them that he could not take any statement except upon oath, and of course everything taken upon oath would go upon the depositions, and might be used against them. The prisoners had better consider whether it was not more prudent for them to say nothing.

On being asked whether she desired to say anything, Isabella Gardiner said, "I am innocent of it." Mrs. Isherwood, who had her face buried in her handkerchief, did not seem inclined to say anything, but after being asked several times, uttered a feeble "No, sir."

The Coroner then said he was afraid there was no other course open but to find a verdict against both women of having wilfully murdered the child. He could see nothing in the evidence to bear out any other suggestion or to corroborate the tales that the women had brought forward in reference to the woman Dockrah. It seemed to him that Grace Isherwood had had the child; that she did not like to tell her husband about it, but desired to keep the matter quiet, and not knowing what to do with it, tried to get it into the workhouse at Clitheroe, but failing that, made away with it. It was not a case in which the jury could return a verdict of manslaughter. It must either be wilful murder or nothing.

The jury, after a few minutes' deliberation, returned a verdict of "Wilful murder" against both prisoners.

The prisoners, who had been removed whilst the jury were considering their verdict, were then called into the room, and the Coroner, addressing them, said: It is my duty to inform you that the jury have found a verdict of "wilful murder" against you. It is my duty to commit you both to take your trial at the Leeds Assizes.

Prisoners made no response, and they were then removed.

Photo by Sue Burton.

Stone under Langcliffe Cross Bridge.

CRIME SCENE INVESTIGATION: SLAIDBURN

I pored over the contents of the website, desperate to understand what had really happened on that Saturday in May 1885. Each time that I read the newspaper report, I noticed a new piece of information. It took a while for the significance of items like the eight letters from Grace about Thomas that Jane Gordon had kept to register.

Penny and I continued to discuss the case on the phone:

"How do you think they did it?"

"Did you see that our grandma called Grace her 'mother' and referred to a 'little brother James'? Was that her mother Jane's child or Grace's?"

"Did you notice that Grace is described as 'in a delicate condition'? That means she was pregnant again, of course."

"Poor John. Did you read that he and Grace and Isabella all burst into tears when he arrived at the inquest?"

"That Isabella was some piece of work! Or do you think she was just a teenager with no idea how much danger she and her sister were suddenly in?"

"Did you notice the details about the baby's clothes? Imagine being so poor that you would take the clothes off a dead baby."

"What happened to the baby's hat?"

"Did you see grandma was only nine? How scary was that, to have to testify at an inquest into a murder!"

Our speculations were lengthy and I was very keen to determine the outcome. Did my grandmother have a stepmother who was hanged for murder? Families are great places for secrets and maybe this one was ours.

Thinking about it all, I realized that my father had never spoken of grandparents of his own, and that, typically self-centred child that I was, it had not occurred to me to wonder why I had grandparents but he did not. Of course, my mother never mentioned grandparents either, but then, poor dear thing, she never really had a chance to mention much of anything to me.

MARGARET'S PLACE IN THE WORLD

When Margaret Isherwood had just started at the Quaker school in Newton, near Slaidburn, the year before her mother died, thanks to that mother she could already read and write. All through her life, Maggie remembered her disdain at being asked by the teacher to make rows of pothooks on her slate as a warm-up to learning to form letters.

While the children around her, tongues edging out of the corner of their mouths or just between their teeth, struggled with the strange shapes, Maggie defiantly wrote across her slate: SILLY POTHOOKS. Her pride in her ability did not diminish despite the punishment she got for her defiance.

Margaret was tough and resilient. She needed to be. As soon as she could comprehend responsibility she had been expected to help out, to keep the family going and to look after her little brothers. When her mother got sick, it fell to Margaret, as the only girl, to keep the boys fed and quiet so that her mother could rest.

Margaret was bright too. She was quick and observant and determined to make the best of every situation. It was a lot of work, but there was honour in being her da's big girl and the little boys had learned to mind her words. She loved them all fiercely.

Margaret had at first been a little slow to make space for another woman living at the farm. The baby was no problem, Margaret was accustomed to welcoming new little boys into the household. But where Grace, the hired woman, should fit into the family was a different issue.

Nobody but Margaret gave any thought to how she would get along with Grace. John Isherwood was simply relieved to have someone to help out and a little adult company in the evenings. His sorrow over the loss of Jane, mixed with fear of loneliness in the years ahead and worry that he wouldn't be able to cope, had left him feeling hopeless. Being with Grace made him feel almost contented again.

The luxury of worrying about the children's feelings was unimaginable to John. Besides, despite her human baggage, Grace was a real charmer, with rounded edges and an accommodating way about her.

The rapid changes in Grace's role at the farm surprised Maggie, but in her whispered conversations with Blue she admitted she was happy to have a grown-up woman around again. It was a relief to her to be able to relinquish some of the duties she had taken on. She hoped to be able to spend more time playing with Blue up in the loft now that Grace was there.

After the wedding, da had told Maggie that Grace was going to have a new little sister or brother for her to play with, and Maggie had her heart set on a girl. Grace thought a girl would be nice, too, and the two of them had begun a tentative discussion about what name might suit. Margaret favoured Jane or Primrose, while Grace wondered about a lofty name like Victoria. They both fell into fits of silent giggles at some of the names they made up, like Manura, which Margaret insisted was a great name for a farm girl.

As the months went by, Margaret began calling Grace "mother," a name that brought a deep smile strong enough to make it all the way to Grace's soft eyes.

A SURPRISE VISIT FROM AUNT ISABELLA

Grace stood speechless in the kitchen at Meanley, the letter John had brought still clutched in her hand.

A visit from Isabella would be a great treat and her mother's letter said that Isabella could be spared from her work long enough to wait with Grace for the new baby. The companionship and the help of another pair of woman's hands would be a wonderful relief, especially since the work to be done around the farm was steadily increasing as the days lengthened.

But what was her family thinking? Isabella, at least, knew that Grace had not told John about Thomas, and their ma had always been so accommodating before. Look how they had let Jane keep poor little Edward at the family home. Why the sudden need now to have Grace look after her own?

What was she to do with little Thomas? What was she to tell John? The pregnancy and the wedding had come upon her so quickly, she still hadn't found the right time to tell John about the little one she had left back in Ulverston. If she was honest with herself, she had to admit that she had been afraid to tell John about Thomas, afraid that even such a kind and loving man could be pushed too far.

With Isabella and Thomas almost due to arrive, she was filled with dread. She would have to head off Isabella and make sure that they both told the same story about why she was travelling with a child, and he would simply have to go back with her. Harsh as it seemed, Meanley could never be his new home.

John seemed very pleased that Isabella was coming to wait with her. Jane had always had her sister nearby in the village and John was glad that Grace would have a sister nearby too. For their part, the children were excited by the prospect of a visitor. Maggie and Matt were hoping that they would be allowed to stay home from school to greet their new aunt Isabella, but Grace was having none of that.

It was a cheerful pair who arrived at the station to be met by John, Grace, and baby James, and fortunately John scooped up Tom in his arms and hurried him to the trap, giving Grace a moment to whisper to Isabella that John did not know that Thomas was her child. Isabella, at first taken aback that Grace had not yet found the nerve to tell John about Thomas, quickly rose to the occasion. By the time she, Grace, and James had caught up with John and the toddler and bundled themselves into the borrowed conveyance, she had concocted a story about being asked to care for Thomas while his mother was indisposed.

On the way back to Meanley, Isabella cheerfully described their trip and gave fresh news of the family in Dalton-in-Furness. John was used to Grace's quiet ways so it was no surprise to him that she didn't say much, just busied herself feeding James and tickling Thomas with her feet. Thomas, unaccustomed to such attention, giggled softly and patted all the boots that he found himself amongst with his little hands.

Once they arrived back at Meanley, the waiting children ran off with Thomas to show him their horse, Bonny, while Grace and Isabella set about to preparing some tea for the family. Grace shushed Isabella in the kitchen. There would be time enough for talking about what to do with Thomas after John was off across the fields at work.

A WONDERFUL PLACE TO BE

Grace stood in the room flooded with May sunshine and fervently wished that something would happen to spare her telling John the truth about Thomas.

How can this room full of sunshine warm my skin when my thoughts make me feel so dark and cold inside? she wondered.

When Grace first came to work at Meanley, part of what seemed to have won John's heart was her enthusiasm for the house and the farm. From the start she had loved how the house flooded with light from the huge windows, which had originally been built to provide light for cottage weavers working at hand looms. Just standing in the yard looking at the vista out toward Slaidburn had enabled her to begin to hope that she was safe at last.

John had explained to her that his great-grandfather, a mason like himself, had built the walls of the farmhouse.

"Isherwood sweat is in the mortar of Meanley Farm," he proclaimed proudly.

At first he had told her frequently how pleased he and Jane had been to gain the tenancy of Meanley, but as the relationship with Grace deepened he mentioned Jane less and less often.

In their own way, the children loved Meanley as intensely as their father did. She could see their faces brighten when John talked about Isherwood sweat. The farm felt like a relative to them, a member of their own family.

Isabella, too, had been admiring of Grace's new home. To Isabella's way of thinking, her sister's situation was troubling but not impossible. Isabella believed that all that was required was the slow patient integration of Thomas into the Isherwood household, followed by a painful confessional evening of tears and requests for forgiveness, and Grace's life would be finally back on track.

"Isabella overestimates my charm and underestimates a husband's pride," Grace murmured sadly to herself.

OLD ENOUGH TO OBSERVE, TOO YOUNG TO UNDERSTAND

My grandmother Margaret was just newly nine years old when Isabella and Thomas arrived at the farm. I imagine she welcomed the diversion provided by the visitors, and the chance to break routine, not to mention the treats they might get to eat.

Nine years old can be an age of both wonder and premature wisdom. At nine you can do a lot of things on your own, but you still like to be cuddled and kissed goodnight by your parents. A dolly, especially one with blue eyes, a blue dress, and wings made of real feathers, can still hold an important place in a girl's heart, even when it is surrounded by real live babies.

At nine you can observe a lot, and adults often underestimate your acuity. And sometimes parents, because they want so badly to believe it, can convince themselves that you are comfortably handling emotions, even though you are not.

When you don't have the knowledge and the vocabulary for adult experience, you substitute words and ideas that you know for those that you do not comprehend. You do not even always know that you don't understand what is happening.

When I was nine a stranger tried to rape my sister. She ran into the house screaming, "Daddy, Daddy, a man just tried to raid me." Or so I thought she said.

My father immediately reached over, picked up the phone, and called the police, which struck me as a strange reaction to his daughter's cries of upset about a man trying to "raid" her. What was even more surprising, and scary, was that the police came over to our house right away and talked in serious voices with my sister and my dad in the hall outside my room. I remember hearing a policewoman's voice ask for a brown paper bag in which to put my sister's trousers.

Many years later, looking back on that confusing and frightening night, I realized that the word that she had been saying was, of course, rape.

Hardly any of us have the emotional experience or the vocabulary for murder, especially child murder. While life on a farm puts you closer to the animal experience of life and death, that doesn't help you with people, especially those closest to you. Nine-year-old Margaret's experience with death was centred entirely on the loss of her mother. Unlike in her mother's childhood, none of Margaret's siblings had died as infants, and her grandparents were all deceased before she was born.

In fact, it seems almost impossible to think what experiences could have prepared the nine-year-old Maggie for what was about to happen to her, including appearing as a witness at a murder trial and then departing forever from Meanley Farm and the life she had loved there.

BEWILDERING AND FRIGHTENING TIMES

It was all so bewildering. One day everyone was excited and having sweets for tea, and the next day her new mother looked sick and pale and their visitors didn't seem like fun anymore.

When the pretty young woman she had been told to call Aunt Isabella showed up at Meanley with a little boy whose name was Thomas Dockrah, it looked like they could all have a bit of a holiday, maybe even go on a picnic or something. Isabella didn't bother much with Thomas, but Margaret knew her way around little boys; her own brother Tom was much of an age with Thomas and they had lots of fun playing in the fields. Margaret found Thomas Dockrah to be a sweet little boy and so quiet you would hardly know he was there.

Still, the atmosphere of the visit was tense and strange. Isabella and Grace kept going off to whisper to each other, with Grace anxious and Isabella increasingly impatient. And her dad seemed surprisingly gruff.

Maggie was feeding the two Toms a slice of bread in the kitchen when she heard Isabella and her mother talking.

"I can't go back to Dalton with Thomas, our ma and pa said

it was time that you looked after your own. And I've got to get back to my job or I'll lose it," hissed Isabella.

"John will never forgive me for lying. I told him that James's father had deceived me with promises of marriage when it turned out he had a wife already. What will he think when he knows that I had a child even before I left Dalton?" moaned Grace.

"Ma's sick and she just can't take care of him and all the others," argued Isabella. "And you have such a good place to look after him here."

All week long Isabella and Grace held hushed conversations. Sometimes Grace would end up crying.

"He's such a mite, but he doesn't know me. How can I keep him? I have to think about caring for the little one that John and I will soon have," she sobbed.

Unbeknownst even to Maggie, many plans were developed and discarded before Isabella and Grace hit on the plan to take young Thomas and put him in the Clitheroe workhouse.

Isabella had insisted that she would not take him back to the Ulverston workhouse — her mam was just done taking him out of there. She had no wish to drag the child back to Cumbria, and she feared her parent's wrath if she arrived back at home with him still in tow.

They fixed on a plan. Grace was desperate to get the child out of the house, so on Saturday they announced that they were going to reunite Thomas with his mother at the train station and then do some marketing in Clitheroe. They knew there was a workhouse there and had convinced themselves that it was the solution to the problem of Tom.

The neighbours over at Chapel Croft agreed to lend the women their trap for the journey, and John walked over with them to help harness the horse. To Grace's horror, John suggested that he go along with them, but then he decided of his own accord that he had better stay near home and help his neighbour mend his barn door.

By the time she, Isabella, and the two children finally managed to set off for Clitheroe, Grace was shaking with anxiety. She felt weak and nauseated and had been too nervous to eat any breakfast back at Meanley.

When John suggested he might join them on their trip to the market, she had been horrified, then relieved when he changed his mind. She felt her emotions had been tied to the pulley in the barn, up and down they went. She had been touched by John's helpfulness in asking Tom Rushton if they could borrow the trap and in harnessing the horse for her, and she felt sickened by her deceit of such a kind, good, generous man.

Her little Tom was a good sweet child and he sat quietly on the floor of the trap as they drove along. He was silent and undemanding, as usual. Even at his young age, he was quite accustomed to unexplained changes in his life.

Isabella chattered incessantly as they drove along. Now that she had Grace alone at last, with a plan to get rid of Tom, she was full of questions about Grace's life: How had she got pregnant with Tom? Why didn't the baby's father marry her? How could she have let it happen again with James? What did she think about sister Jane and her little one? Why did the Gardner girls seem to fall pregnant with no husbands? Did John suspect that Grace was Tom's mother? Had she told him about Jane's little lost boy? Did he imagine the baby was actually Jane's or even Isabella's?

Grace's brief answers did little to enlighten Isabella. Made even more tired and ill by the new child in her womb, she seemed sunk into depression. She passed little James over to Isabella to hold so that she could manage the horse and she stared grimly at the road ahead.

The road to Clitheroe is hilly and lightly travelled, and the countryside can seem very bleak. The air was cool, especially in the shade, and they all moved closer together to keep warm.

The women had no plan for Thomas beyond leaving him at the workhouse. It was not Grace's intention to come and reclaim him later. She had never really lived with him and she didn't see how she could start now. He was going to the workhouse to stay until he was old enough and strong enough to find some kind of work to do. Maybe, some day, he could work on a farm. She had heard that some of the workhouse children were sent to work in the mills but she didn't know what kind of work children did in such places. Such prospects seemed a long way off right now.

A BIZARRE AND TRAGIC DAY

The long straight pathway leading up to the door of the Clitheroe Union Workhouse was bordered on either side with ugly gnarled and twisted trees. The scene was cold and forbidding. But then, so was the matron.

Little Thomas had been in the Ulverston workhouse for several months of the previous year, so it never even occurred to Grace and Isabella that there would be any problem leaving him here in Clitheroe. The news that he needed a bill of admission totally confounded their plan.

There was nothing left for them but to take Thomas back to Meanley and confess all to John. The prospect rendered Grace almost helpless with horror.

Still they had to get a grip on themselves; they had two little children to look after, goods to pick up, and errands to run. While they had set off early, the journey home would take some time, and John would be looking out for their arrival home.

The return trip was long and silent. Grace drove, lost in her own thoughts, sighing from time to time, while Isabella held tight to baby James, who was conveniently asleep. Little Tom travelled silently on the floor of the trap, in his nest of rugs.

At last, weary but somehow almost peaceful, they pulled up in the yard at Meanley. But when they began to unload the trap, Isabella suddenly told Grace that she feared Thomas was dead.

Immediately, the yard outside of Meanley was filled with rush and confusion. After a hasty exchange, Isabella scooped up Thomas, wrapped him in her shawl, and set off down the meadow toward Slaidburn. Grace went indoors, handed baby James over to Maggie to change and put to bed with barely a word of greeting or instruction, then went off over the fields in the same direction as Isabella. The trap and horse were simply left abandoned in the yard.

An hour later, John came home to find Grace and Isabella gone again, so soon after their return, with the horse and trap still standing in his yard. Shocked at their behaviour, he went looking for his wife and her sister.

Meanwhile, the two women were walking about the countryside in a state of near hysteria, trying to think what to do with the dead child. Desperate, they finally decided to leave it by the stream below the Langcliffe Cross Bridge. Isabella had to hoist herself over the wall, then Grace passed her the little body. She slipped several times trying to get it down to the water's edge, but they both felt certain that no one could see the little shape from above.

It was Grace's idea to keep some of the clothes, her need to look after the soon-to-be living overriding her sorrow for the dead.

Dusk was falling as they passed some people out walking, but the sisters hoped that they just looked like they were on a walk of their own.

To Isabella fell the burden of thinking up a story about where they had left young Thomas. Grace claimed she simply couldn't think at all and Isabella agreed rather waspishly that this certainly did seem to be the case.

It was late and becoming cold when John finally caught up with them. Isabella now had the shawl wrapped tightly around her shoulders and Grace was shivering so much her teeth were chattering.

The next morning Maggie asked where Thomas had gone. She had seen Isabella with what seemed to be a child in her arms in the yard, and she was curious about why the women had hurried off. The adults were preoccupied and paid her questions no heed, but that didn't stop her wondering.

Some of Thomas Dockrah's clothes had been brought back to the house — his jacket, frock, socks, and boots. It seemed very strange to Maggie that he had gone back to his mam without all his clothes.

Her dad seemed sad and that worried Maggie. Dad usually was the one to put on a cheerful face, even when things were grim. His manner was stern as he went about his chores, and mother and Aunt Isabella seemed to be avoiding him throughout the day. It was almost dark when, approaching the kitchen quietly, Maggie overheard mother and Isabella in agitated conversation as they prepared the tea.

"John insists on us telling him straight what happened," she heard Grace whisper, just before Dick came running in to ask, "When's tea?"

And it wasn't long after the tea dishes were put away that the policeman, Police Constable Sutcliffe, came walking up the lane.

A CONSCIENTIOUS POLICE CONSTABLE

P.C. Sutcliffe was respectful as he entered the Isherwood home at Meanley; he carefully wiped his boots at the door and held his helmet in his hand as he addressed farmer John Isherwood, John's wife, and his sister-in-law.

Sutcliffe immediately explained his reason for coming to the farmhouse. He was looking into the case of a young boy who had been found dead in the stony stream bed under Langcliffe Cross Bridge.

To John's surprise, Isabella immediately engaged the constable in conversation, volunteering that she and Grace had been wondering what had become of a child who had been in her care until the previous day. Her quick nervous intervention made John uncomfortable, while Grace sat stiff and silent on the other side of the hearth.

In response to the constable's further information that the child had been found drowned, Isabella remarked that she and Grace had just been wondering what kind of breakfast the child had had. At this comment, John looked at her sharply.

For his part, P.C. Sutcliffe found such a reaction to the news that one's charge, so recently relinquished, had been found drowned very strange, but he did not betray his feelings. And his continuing calm seemed to help keep Isabella at her ease.

Isabella needed little prodding to provide a detailed statement of their movements with the child the previous day, which the policeman took down in his fine hand. As he conscientiously recorded with his own spelling and punctuation:

> Isabella Gardiner of Meanly Farm in the township of Newton Late of no 3 Victoria Street Dalton, in Furness, states that she has nursed the Deceased Thomas Dockery for the last 4 months and came to Meanly Farm about a week since for the purpose of waiting of her sister, Mrs Isherwood, and brought the child with her to Meanley and on Saturday night the 16th Instant about 11 p.m. she gave over the Deceased to Its Mother Elizabeth Dockery while in the street opposite the Black Bull Inn Slaidburn. The mother then said that she was going to Bolton-by-Bowland the Child was then in good health and on Saturday the 16th Inst. about 11 p.m. Isabella Gardener by arrangement saw the Deceased Childs Mother, Elizabeth Dockery, on the Street near Black Bull Inn Slaidburn and there gave the child over to Its Mother. The Child then being in good health the Mother told Isabella Gardener that she would go to Bolton-by-Bowland. Discription of Elizabeth Dockery Age 26 years Dark Hair, rather tall and slender build Dressed in a Navy blue dress, a black cloth Jacket, a white straw Hat trimmed with blue Ribbon and fare worne Elastic side boots. Accompanied by a man who (crossed out) John Stables supposed to be her Husband. Discription about 5 ft 2 in.

A copy of Isabella's original statement, in P.C. Sutcliffe's own hand, located in 2005 by Cathryn and David Higham of Slaidburn.

High, Stiff build Complexion Fresh Dressed in Shaby dark Coat and Trousers, soft billerock Hat, White Tie around his neck and strong boots. Supposed to have been residing a Rimminton near Gisburn She had received a Letter address from Rimmington asking her to beet her with the Child at Clitheroe on the Saturday they went to Clitheroe at 12 noon but did not see them till when Elizabeth Dockery asked her to take the Child and meet her at Slaidburn and she brought the child to Slaidburn and give it over to Elizabeth Dockery and demanded soin … Money but she said that the man John Stables had said that If she was not off He would do for both her and the Child, she then went home with her sister.

P.C. Sutcliffe carefully folded up Isabella's statement and wrote on the outside, "Statement of Isabella Gardener." He then asked Grace and Isabella to come with him to identify the child who had been found drowned. Grace almost swooned at the prospect, and seemed weak and encumbered by her condition, and before she or Isabella could even answer, John replied firmly that he could identify the child who had been in his home.

As John was making himself ready to leave with the constable, Grace found her voice and said that she wished that they had taken the child to the workhouse.

"Happen it is as well as it is," was Isabella's quick reply.

Later, P.C. Sutcliffe regretted that he had not recorded those comments as well.

A BREAK IN THE CASE

Meanwhile, in Canberra, Australia, the partial story of the child murder continued to tantalize me. I returned frequently to the Slaidburn website in the hope that more information would appear. For some reason the simple act of leaving a query in the site guestbook never occurred to me. Looking back, I think I was in awe and amazement at what Penny had been able to discover and it didn't occur to me that more could be discovered by comparatively simple means.

Then I had what a detective-novel writer would call "a break."

In late October, while I was wandering about the Slaidburn site trying to glean more information, I saw a message on the notice board that made me think that I might at least find out more about my great-grandmother Jane and her family, the Bleazards. I sent off a tentative email to a woman called Elaine, who appeared to have Bleazard antecedents, asking her if she knew anything about a Jane Bleazard, who appeared to have died young.

Next thing I knew, I had the names of Jane's parents, the date of her christening, and the dates of the births of some of her brothers and sisters. Exhilarated by my easy success at gaining so much information from a stranger, I emailed my thanks and included this request:

> *I have one further favour to ask of you in regard to genealogy. If you look on the Slaidburn site, you will see that my grandmother's stepmother was accused of murdering her child. What it doesn't say is whether she was convicted or what happened. There is some suggestion that the Leeds assizes might have the info, but they do not seem to be on the net.*
>
> *If you are near Slaidburn could you call the librarian who did the work, or even email me the library's phone number?*
>
> *Maybe she was deported to Australia. Wouldn't that be a strange coincidence.*
> *Regards Sheelagh*

In response to my note, Elaine Buckley, an Internet-based fairy godmother, sent this message to David and Cathryn Higham in Slaidburn:

> *Sorry to bother you two but you might be able to help with this query from an Aussie. If you can't I will try Chris Spencer. Email me either way.*
> *Thanks Elaine*

And so began the twenty-first-century reinvestigation of the nineteenth-century Slaidburn alleged child murder.

THE SLAIDBURN CONNECTION

David Higham sent his response to Elaine's query early the next morning, October 30.

> *Subject: From the Slaidburn Website — Re the Child Murder*
> *Dear Elaine and Sheelagh,*
> *Thank you so much for forwarding such an interesting email. We never expected to have anyone contact us about the child murder.*
> *The librarian at Clitheroe, Mrs. Sue Holden, has given us various newspaper cuttings which we have turned into pages on the site.*
> *Sue does not have any further information on the source of the newspaper report or of the verdict. She suggested that the records may be in Leeds or possibly Wakefield.*
> *We will have to make further enquiries and make a visit to Leeds so it may be some time, still it is an excuse for a shopping trip.*

> *This matter has now gone to the top of our "to do" list.*
>
> *As soon as we can tell you anything we will be in touch.*

My own excited response was quickly sent. I tried to include some relevant background for the Highams without overwhelming them.

> *... I just read David's email and I am excited at the prospect of learning more.... I can tell you that my grandmother, who appears in the child murder write up as Margaret Isherwood, age 9, used to say that the family lost everything defending her step mother in a case involving child suffocation. We all had the impression that it was like a cot death or a careless accident, so my sister Penny, who is presently living in Wellington, New Zealand, couldn't believe it when she found the child murder site and when we both read actual testimony of our grandmother and the comment about our great grandfather bursting into tears when his new wife, now accused of murder, entered the courtroom....*
> *Sheelagh*

In the meantime, I had determined that transportation to Australia for British criminals had been discontinued by 1885, so the slightly romantic notion that I might find traces of Grace and Isabella in Australia had to be abandoned.

Meanwhile, though, the Highams immediately demonstrated the sensitivity and thoughtfulness I have since come to know as characteristic of them. Their next email reflected their concern that the interesting story they had selected for the Slaidburn website might have a negative impact on the descendants of those involved.

> Subject: More from Slaidburn
> Thank you for the family details. We hope that the report on the site has not been too upsetting for your family. Your email has really brought it home to us that the case involved "real people." We find it quite upsetting.
>
> David always saw the case more as an indictment of the Poor Law provisions of that time than an indictment of the individual. How different things might have been had she received the signature of the Overseer of the Poor at Slaidburn and that the child had received entry into the workhouse at Clitheroe.
>
> We will try to send a friend to the Public Record Office in London where we have found that the records of the criminal trials for the period should be kept.
>
> Fingers crossed that the records are intact and that we can find details of the case.
> David and Cathryn Higham

David and Cathryn, thorough researchers both, were also on top of the criminal trial lead.

> Subject: A little more from Slaidburn
> Dear Sheelagh
>
> We have checked with my friend in London this morning. She has a day off a week on Thursday and was wondering what to do, so she will now be visiting the Public Record Office at Kew....

If we manage to find out anything else in the
meantime we will let you know.
David and Cathryn

Within a day we had more information. As I came to understand over time, David and Cathryn are bright, well-educated, and curious, and this was a mystery that they, too, bless them, were keen to solve.

CONSIDERABLE COMMOTION

Slaidburn was in terrible turmoil. Jane's brothers, who had been quietly supportive of John finding a new wife, were shocked and upset. John Bleazard rued the day he had agreed to be a witness at John's wedding to Grace. His sister, Margaret, felt heartbroken that she had not been able to look after Jane's wee ones as she had done for their own sister Isabella, and that they had fallen into the hands of such a woman.

The Isherwoods were shocked and alarmed. Their centuries-old position as law-abiding people seemed to have been undermined by the actions of those two women — and outsiders at that.

Mary Rushton, living over at Chapel Croft, was deeply dismayed at the role her family seemed to have played in the tragedy. How she wished that her husband Thomas had needed to take the trap to town himself on Saturday. Then Grace and Isabella could never have made their disastrous trip to Clitheroe and things would be different today.

The Barghs had found little Thomas's body and summoned the police on Sunday. By Tuesday, the first day of the inquest, the reporter from Preston described the district as being in "considerable commotion."

In the carefully devised rotation of sites for legal proceedings, it was the turn of the Black Bull Tavern to host this inquest. Hark to Bounty, just across the road, had been the venue for such hearings for centuries, but in recent times the publican at the Black Bull had successfully argued for his fair share of the business.

Mr. Robinson, the coroner, had reacted quickly, calling together a jury of John Isherwood's peers, farmers and tradesmen from the area whom John had known all his life. In their work as stonemasons, John and his father Matthew had built or repaired homes or outbuildings for all of them.

Maggie was nervous and frightened by what she had been told would happen at the inquest. The policeman and her father had told her just to answer the questions slowly and honestly, but she was worried that Grace and Isabella would get angry with her. She had never had to answer questions in front of grown-ups before. Yes, she was bright and confident, but this was scary business.

Grace and Isabella weren't even at the hearing at the Black Bull that day. Maggie wondered where the policeman had taken them. By listening, she learned that the coroner, Mr. Robinson, was going to meet with people again on Thursday. Maybe she would see her mother and Aunt Isabella then.

That night at Hark to Bounty there was talk of little else. And across the road, the Black Bull regulars vigorously rehearsed the day's testimony with various embellishments of their own.

Poor Thomas, unwanted toddler, was buried on Thursday and all concerned hoped that they would attract little attention. Only John, Matthew and Margaret, P.C. Sutcliffe, and the Rector Halliday were there to see Thomas Gardner's tiny coffin into the ground. Passersby looking into the churchyard could see John's bowed head and shoulders, his normally strong, straight figure bent into a posture of despair. Matt and Maggie, joined by little James Rushton, stood by with childish solemnity, holding wilting posies of spring flowers for Thomas's grave.

Back at Meanley after the funeral, Margaret had taken Matthew out in the yard and made him swear an oath to never repeat what she was about to tell him. Once he had sworn his solemn oath and spit on the ground for good measure, she stood on tiptoe and whispered in his ear: "I saw it. I saw the dead baby when they came back from Clitheroe. It was all white and its arms and legs were hanging down."

Matthew drew back horrified, the image too much for his young imagination. "Don't you go telling that to anyone else," he said. "That's evil."

Maggie was a little disappointed in her brother's reaction. She had hoped he might press her for more details.

When the adjourned inquest reopened on Thursday afternoon at the Black Bull Inn, the two sisters were brought as prisoners from where they were being held in Bolton-by-Bowland. The neighbourhood was by now in a rare state of excitement, exacerbated by gossip and the funeral of the poor child. Sides were being taken and old secrets relating to inconvenient children were being whispered by a compassionate few.

Quite a crowd had gathered in the street outside the Black Bull to hear the inquest's findings. Those seeking drama were not disappointed — the jury returned a verdict of wilful murder against both prisoners and they were committed for trial at the Leeds Assizes.

PRESENT DAY — UPDATES FROM SLAIDBURN

All the background that I really had on Cathryn and David Higham was that Elaine Buckley liked them and found them very helpful, and of course, the fact that they had been so wonderfully responsive to me. They also seemed to be well-grounded in Slaidburn, especially since it was clear that the website was the product of their hard work. Hardly the thorough introduction most would prefer. Nevertheless, our joint pursuit of the outcome of the child murder charges, ably assisted by Penny, did cause us to coalesce into quite a hardworking and cohesive team.

> *Subject: Update from Slaidburn*
> *Dear Sheelagh*
> *An interesting and productive day.*
> *We revisited the Clitheroe librarian Mrs. Sue Holden today, principally to tell her your fascinating news and to thank her. She then showed us the fragile and tattered Victorian scrapbook where the original newspaper articles,*

which she had partially photocopied, came from. Turning the page, we realised that there was also an account of the Magisterial Court committal proceedings at Bolton-by-Bowland relating to the case. So more typing for the website! The articles came from the Preston Guardian and indeed confirm that the resulting trial was scheduled for the Summer Sessions of the Leeds Assize Circuit Court in July. Unfortunately no further reports of the trial in the scrapbook. In the immortal words of Homer Simpson ... Doh!

We then contacted the Public Records at Kew in London as this is where all records of Assize trials are kept. A most helpful gentleman is seeking to find the correct bundle (literally bundles of papers tied with ribbon) in which the records for that Circuit are kept, in preparation for the visit by our friend a week on Thursday. He did warn us that some records, eg. 1874, are missing but reminded us that the Leeds newspapers of the time would almost certainly have reported the facts of the case. We also found that the "alleged murderess" could not have been transported to Australia as this only occurred between 1787 and 1868.

We then contacted Leeds City Library who confirmed that they hold copies of several Leeds newspapers of the time and have them on microfiche.

So all in all we should be able to get to the bottom of the case for you in the near future.

We will email you when we have typed the Magistrates report on to the website, assuming that you have no objections. We meant to ask

*you whether you would prefer that we removed
the page from the site as we now see it as being
about "real people" and would not seek to distress
or offend in any way. Do let us know.*
David and Cathryn

As I read David and Cathryn's email, I couldn't help
thinking that it should be used as a teaching aid in a course for
investigative journalism or archival research. Their ability and
enthusiasm thrilled and reassured me. So did their dedication
to detail ... and their sensitivity.

With the story gathering momentum, the Highams and I
were keeping Penny and Elaine Buckley posted so that they
could marvel with us at their Internet discoveries.

> *Subject: Updated website*
> *Dear Margaret Sheelagh, Penny and Elaine,*
> *The typing of the magisterial proceedings is now
> complete and up on the website. You will also
> find that I have changed one of the photographs
> after re-reading the inquest evidence. I took some
> pictures from Langcliffe Cross bridge earlier in
> the year (foot and mouth disease restrictions
> have prevented me actually going into the field)
> and realized that the stream flows across a flat
> rock shelf before a pool approximately 30 yards
> below the bridge, which is more likely to be the
> "pavement" as was mentioned in the inquest
> evidence than I previously thought.*
>
> *I am also trying to find an old photograph of
> Meanley Farm for you. It was a 17th Century
> building with a long row of "weaver's windows"
> (for extra light) across the upper storey facade.
> As with many farmsteads in the area it was*

*pretty much as it would have been at the time of
the incident ...*
Best wishes, David Higham

David attached this remarkable post script:

*I have spoken to the Land-owner and I have
permission to take photographs in the field when
FMD restrictions are lifted which will show it
more clearly. Interestingly, although rather eerily,
she told me that her terrier always behaves most
strangely when they approach an ash tree right next
to where I think the incident took place.*

I thought his addressing me as Margaret Sheelagh was a
nice touch.

VICTORIAN TIMES — THE
MACHINERY OF JUSTICE

Mrs. Gardner arrived by train from Cumbria. She was not yet fully recovered from her illness, but felt compelled to make the journey in fear for her daughters' lives. She resolved to be a help around the house for John with the meals and the children. Her children had already caused him enough trouble to last a lifetime.

Compelled by necessity, John went to Clitheroe to find a lawyer for his wife and her sister. There was a firm his family had dealt with for minor disputes in the past, and it was there he headed, accompanied by his brother-in-law Tom for moral support.

"Thank goodness for family," he mused. "I can barely think straight at present, and I surely need help to explain our situation." Tom's quiet presence in the intimidating chambers in which they found themselves was a great help, and John was able quickly to secure the services of an advocate to appear with the sisters at the Magistrate's Hearing scheduled for the next week in Bolton-by-Bowland.

John's next job was to go visit Grace and Isabella in gaol and tell them what he had arranged. He had not yet been able to speak to Grace without crying, and he was irritated by Isabella's cool manner. He wanted to hug Grace and shake Isabella, both at the same time.

John tried not to spend their precious few minutes together recriminating Grace for failing to tell him about Thomas. It was clear from her floods of tears that she had been afraid and was full of regret for her failure to tell him all.

The truth was that it had upset him to realize that Thomas had been Grace's own child all along, although he had begun to suspect something of the sort during the lengthy visit. It wasn't that Tom had looked for mothering to Grace, or that she had sought him out, it was more that Isabella's story about being hired to care for the child just didn't ring true. He knew that Isabella was well regarded as a domestic servant, but he doubted that many people would consider her apt for childcare or that she would normally be willing to accept such a task. There had to be some special circumstance involved.

John had spent long hours pondering the morals of his new wife, even before he knew of this other child, and he had decided that she was more unlucky than she was corrupt. He simply couldn't think of her as a loose woman. Now, after demanding that she make a clean breast of it, he had concluded that in the first instance she had been young and trusting, and in the second she had been grievously treated. How he yearned to bash his solid mason's fists into the faces of those two men.

Grace had sworn to him there had been no others, and he believed her, at least for the present.

MAGISTERIAL PROCEEDINGS
PRISONERS BEFORE THE MAGISTRATES
Wednesday May 27th, 1885.
The prisoners, Grace Isherwood and Isabella Gardiner, were brought up before the magistrates at the Bolton-by-Bowland Police Court, yesterday.

Photo by Brian Dugdale

The Old Courthouse, Bolton-by-Bowland.

Considerable interest was manifested in the proceedings, and the space in Court allotted to the public was fully occupied. The prisoners when brought into Court exhibited signs of great distress and when walking had to be supported by police officers. Gardiner was quite overcome, and sank to the floor. She was raised by two officers and placed on a form, and immediately supplied with a glass of water. At the request of the Bench prisoners were accommodated with chairs, and they sat together in front of the prisoners' dock, which screened them from the gaze of the public. Gardiner seemed to realise her position far more than she did at the inquest. The husband of the prisoner Isherwood and the mother of both prisoners occupied seats in Court, and were visibly affected. During the proceedings prisoners scarcely looked up, their eyes being concentrated on the floor, and each held a handkerchief, which almost concealed their features. The case

Portrait by John Singer Sargent, 1902.

Thomas Lister, Lord Ribblesdale, master of the queen's buckhounds.

for the police was conducted by Supt. Inman. He first called John Bargh, farmer, Field Head, Slaidburn, who repeated the evidence he gave at the inquest on Tuesday as to the finding of the body of the child in a brook about a mile and a half from Slaidburn, on Sunday evening, and as to seeing two women at nine o'clock the night previous near to the place where the body was found. Margt. Isherwood, a little girl, and stepdaughter of Isherwood, also recapitulated her evidence as to the identification of the child and its clothing. On being asked if she had any questions to ask her step-daughter, Mrs. Isherwood looked up and replied in the negative, and added that what the girl had stated was true. Supt. Inman then informed the Bench that he did not propose to call any more witnesses that day. The full particulars of the case would have to be reported to the Public Prosecutor to see what course he would pursue. He therefore applied for a remand until Thursday next the magistrates then remanded the prisoners. They gave them the choice of either being sent to Armley or Preston gaol, and they accepted the latter. Yesterday afternoon prisoners were conveyed to Clitheroe in a conveyance and thence to Preston by the 3.15 train.

THE SUSPECTED MURDER AT SLAIDBURN.
MAGISTERIAL PROCEEDINGS
Saturday May 30th, 1885.
The hearing of the case against Grace Isherwood, 26, wife of John Isherwood, farmer, Meanley Farm, Newton, and Isabella Gardiner, 18, domestic servant, Dalton-in-Furness, for causing the death of Thomas Gardiner, aged two years, was resumed on Thursday at the Bolton-by-Bowland police court. The court was crowded, and many were unable to obtain admission. The magistrates on the Bench were Mr. John Howarth (chairman),

Lord Ribblesdale, Major Trappes, Mr. C. J. B. Trappes, and Mr. C. B. E. Wright. Prisoners were conveyed from Preston Gaol to Gisburn by train, and thence to Bolton-by-Bowland in a trap early on Thursday morning. When brought into Court, Isherwood had again to be supported while walking, and both were accommodated with chairs. Neither exhibited the same despondency as they did at the previous hearing, and they seemed to be more cheerful, the prisoner Gardiner being observed to smile on several occasions. The husband of the prisoner Isherwood, and the mother of the prisoners were in court, the latter of whom was much affected. The prisoners were defended by Mr. Baldwin, of Clitheroe, and Mr. Superintendent Inman conducted the case for the police.

The evidence given at the previous sitting by John Bargh, farmer, Field Head, Slaidburn, was read. Bargh found the body on the 17th inst. in Easington Brook, near to Langcliffe Cross Bridge, Slaidburn, in a pool of water about a foot deep. He went for the Slaidburn police constable, and returned with him to the brook, and the child was found to be dead. He stated that about 9 p.m. on the previous evening he had been walking by Langcliffe Cross road, and saw two women with a child walking a little in front of them. He afterward met the same women, but could not tell how they were dressed or who they were. They appeared to be about the same height. In reply to Mr. Baldwin, witness said: The brook flows westward, and runs into the Hodder. The place where the child was found was immediately below the bridge, about a mile from Whiteholme, Slaidburn. The child was on the Slaidburn side of the brook, and the nearest way to the place was over the wall, which was 5ft. high.

The evidence of Margaret Isherwood, aged 9 years, step-daughter of the prisoner Isherwood, was next read. She identified the deceased as Thomas Dockrah, who had been living at Isherwood's house for a week. The child was taken to the house by the prisoner Gardiner, and went away with the prisoners on Saturday week. Her mother said they were going to Clitheroe. She identified the clothes as those worn by the child. By Mr. Baldwin: I remember prisoners coming back from Clitheroe on Saturday week at night. I did not speak to the boy Dockrah. Gardiner was carrying him, and he was wrapped up in a shawl. I could not see his face, as he was turned to Gardiner's breast. He did not speak. Gardiner walked away with the child, which I did not see again. The same morning my father (John Isherwood) took the conveyance out of the yard, and the boy Dockrah was in the trap with him. My mother, Aunt Isabella, and the baby went across the field to Chapel Croft farm. My father came back directly. My mother, Gardiner, Dockrah, and the baby had gone to Clitheroe in the conveyance. When my father took the conveyance out of the yard, Dockrah was laid down on some rushes in the bottom of the carriage with a rug over him. By Lord Ribblesdale: I had breakfast with Dockrah that morning.

Mrs. Lofthouse, wife of Young Lofthouse, master of the Clitheroe Union Workhouse, repeated her evidence as to the attempt of Mrs. Isherwood to get deceased admitted into the Workhouse. Cross-examined by Mr. Baldwin, she said that Isherwood appeared to be taking every care of the child, as any mother would do. The prisoners went to the front entrance of the Workhouse and were visible to anybody about.

Edwd. Hanson, earthenware dealer, 22. Shaw Bridge, Clitheroe, stated: On Saturday, May 16th, the prisoners came to my house between 12 and one o'clock, and stayed about an hour. They had two children with them. They came about three o'clock up to my stable, and Mrs. Isherwood wished me to put the horse in the trap. They had the little boy with them, but had left the baby at our house until the horse was put in. Whilst I was putting the horse in Mrs. Isherwood said "The little boy's mother should have come by train but she had missed." She then got into the trap and arranged the seat and rugs, and then got out again. Isabella Gardiner then got in and sat down, and I lifted the little boy in. She placed him in the bottom of the trap.

Cross-examined: They had dinner at our house between 12 and one o'clock. The boy also had some dinner. They appeared to take every care of both children. They went away to do some shopping, and came back about three o'clock. After I had lifted the child into the trap Mrs. Isherwood took hold of the horse's head and went in the direction of our house, where they had left the baby. I did not see them start for home.

Walter Embley, shopman at the Co-operative Store, Lowergate, Clitheroe, said: On Saturday, the 16th inst., a little before twelve o'clock, I saw the two prisoners at the shop door, in a trap. They had two children with them, and after I came back from dinner, at one o'clock, they were in the shop. The children appeared to be about nine months and two and a half years of age respectively. I cannot swear to anything the children wore. They left the shop about 1:15 p.m. I saw them again about 3:30 p.m., when they came in the trap to the door for the groceries they had bought. I put the basket in the trap, and they drove off toward home. I saw the two children in the trap. Gardiner was holding the baby, and the little boy was sat in the bottom.

P.C. Sutcliffe recapitulated the evidence he gave at the inquest as to the finding of the child, and also to the statement made to him by Gardiner respecting the child belonging to Dockrah. In answer to Mr. Baldwin, he said anyone passing along the field where the child was found would have to be within a few yards before they could see the child as it lay in the water. He did not think it had been placed there dead, but thought the child had struggled in the water, from the position of the foot between the stones and the hands being partly clenched. When he was at Meanley Farm, Gardiner asked him what had become of the child, and he told her it had been found drowned. She said they had just been talking it over, and wondering what sort of breakfast the child had had that morning. She also said her sister, Mrs. Isherwood, was uneasy about it. He did not charge them with anything, but asked them to come with him and see if it was the child they had had. Mrs. Isherwood did not seem fit to go, but her husband said he would go; he would know whether the child was Thomas Dockrah — the child which had been at his house.

Jane Hayhurst, of Slaidburn, who laid out the child, and found no marks of violence on the body, repeated her evidence.

Dr. Bridgman again gave his evidence. He had made a post-mortem examination of the body, and found that death had been caused by asphyxia arising from immersion, the probabilities pointing to drowning. He did not use any test for poisoning. Cross-examined: Asphyxia might be caused by smothering, suffocation, or anything preventing the free admission of air into the lungs. It was quite possible for young children to be smothered accidentally when asleep by their clothing. But he knew of no disease, nor any other cause but drowning, that would cause the distension of the lungs to such an extent as to completely overlap the heart, as in this case.

John Walmsley, labourer, Waddington, stated that on Saturday night, the 16th inst., he was going from Waddington to Slaidburn. About half-past ten, as he was going on the carriage drive by Dunnow, near Slaidburn, he met John Isherwood and two women near to Dunnow Bridge. They were going in the direction of Meanley Farm. He did not know the women, but one was rather taller than the other. He did not see any child with them.

Jane Gordon, widow, Dalton-in-Furness, repeated her evidence identifying the child as one which she had nursed for the prisoner Isherwood; also identifying the clothing worn by the deceased.

Supt. Inman, after the repetition of his evidence, was cross-examined by Mr. Baldwin. He said he did not caution Gardiner before she made the statement at Meanley Farm. Supt. Inman was proceeding to put in a number of letters written by the prisoner Isherwood to the witness Gordon in reference to the nursing of the child, when Mr. Baldwin objected, and said they would first have to prove that the letters were in Isherwood's handwriting before the letters could be put in as evidence.

Inspector Prosser having given evidence as to the apprehension of the prisoners, the case for the prosecution closed.

Mr. Baldwin said he had no doubt the magistrates would send the case to a superior Court and he would reserve his defence.

Prisoners were then charged and they made no reply. They were then committed for trial to the Leeds Assizes which are fixed to be held in July. The hearing of the case occupied four hours.

SIGNS OF GREAT DISTRESS

On the day of the inquest, Grace was described by the *Preston Guardian* report as "in a delicate condition, seeming to feel her position acutely, and had to be supported by an officer when walking from the Slaidburn Police Station to the room in which the inquiry is held."

Isabella, on the other hand, "wore a look of quiet unconcern, as she walked by her sister's side accompanied by two police officers."

When John Isherwood arrived and was seated "both he and the prisoners burst into tears."

So much information in so few words. We learn that Grace was pregnant, and that she is overwhelmed by the dreadful circumstance in which she finds herself. We learn that Isabella, like many a teenager, may not yet have fully realized how perilous a position she and her sister were in and how unhappily things might all turn out.

Stalwart John — in that flood of tears we are reminded that he is faced with the prospect that the woman he loves will be tried for murder. An almost unimaginable plight.

That was Wednesday, May 20th.

The report of the first day of the magisterial proceedings on May 27th paints a picture of the sisters, their mother, and John all stunned by anxiety and distress. The sisters had been in gaol for over a week, and the gravity of their situation had almost certainly come home to Isabella. The entire family seems to be in the grip of an almost paralyzing fear.

In fact, the brief report of Margaret's testimony seems laden with subtext about the relationship between the nine-year-old girl and Grace, the woman she had only recently learned to call "mother":

> Margt. Isherwood, a little girl, and stepdaughter of Isherwood, also recapitulated her evidence as to her identification of the child and its clothing. On being asked if she had any questions to ask her step daughter, Mrs. Isherwood looked up and replied in the negative, and added that what the girl had stated was true.

Margaret Isherwood, a mere child, compelled to repeat a set of facts about a night that was clearly so fateful, and then required to stand there as her dejected stepmother was asked if she had any questions for Maggie. To Grace's credit, from her miserable position she supported her stepdaughter as best she could, underscoring, even if it might somehow be damaging to herself, that what Maggie had testified was the truth.

Between the beginning of the Magisterial hearing on Wednesday, May 27, 1885, and its continuation on the following Saturday, John seems to have engaged a lawyer to defend the sisters, and it appears that they now better understood the legal process that they were caught up in, and how things were likely to proceed. That in itself must have been reassuring for the two women. For Mrs. Gardner, the continuing prospect of two of her three daughters being hanged for murder left her as disconsolate as ever.

The witnesses called on Saturday painted a picture of two women going about their errands in Clitheroe while taking "every care" of the two children with them, including having dinner at Edward Hanson's home between noon and one o'clock. Surprisingly, not a lot was made of the fact that after feeding Thomas a nourishing dinner, they had then tried to commit him to the care of the Clitheroe Union Workhouse.

Dr. Bridgeman's testimony seems likely to have been the greatest cause for concern on the part of the defence, with his assertion that "he knew of no disease, nor any other cause but drowning, that would cause the distension of the lungs so as to completely overlap the heart, as in this case."

Perhaps prudently, Mr. Baldwin, the lawyer, saved the defence of the sisters for what he conceded to be their inevitable trial in the superior court.

COMMITTED FOR TRIAL AT THE
LEEDS ASSIZES

The prisoners were again taken back to Clitheroe in a conveyance, and then on to Preston on the train to be delivered to the gaol, only this time it was going to be at least two months before they saw another courtroom.

Grace gazed wanly from the conveyance as they left Bolton-by-Bowland, trying not to look back at her weeping mother, who was leaning all her weight on the equally miserable John.

Less than a year had passed since Grace had been living in Bolton-by-Bowland and had given birth to James, so she was well-known to the town and it to her. She had been sad and even desperate at times when she lived there, first when she discovered that she was pregnant yet again, and then when she began to fear that there would be nowhere to go but the workhouse for her and the baby. Indeed, it seemed then that nothing could be worse. But there she was, back in Bolton-by-Bowland, again in misery, again pregnant, and this time on trial for her life.

When their mother had arrived exhausted by her hasty journey from home, both sisters clung to her sobbing. Sadly, though, her own uncontrolled sobs offered Grace and Isabella little comfort.

John had tried to put on a brave face, with his news that the King-Wilkinsons had helped him to find a lawyer in Clitheroe. Mr. Baldwin, the lawyer, had been calming too, with his matter-of-fact style and his reassurances that the legal process might be slow but it would be fair.

If Grace had been a spiteful woman, which she was not, she might have been disgusted by the people of Bolton-by-Bowland who scurried to fill the courthouse. Where had they been last year when she had needed their help? They knew she had been cruelly used and abandoned, and many of them had their suspicions as to who was the father of young James, but they did little or nothing to help her and the baby.

Isabella's emotions were all over the place. If she'd been free to say what she liked, she would have shouted at the villagers who were pushing and shoving to get seats in the courtroom that she'd heard there were dancing bears in the circus, and shouldn't they be off to see them, not wasting their time on two women who never did anyone any harm. Mr. Baldwin, however, had told her in stern tones to quit talking, especially to policemen, and she had been affected as much by his concerned manner as she was by his words. He had told her and Grace that the police knew her story about Elizabeth Dockrah and John Stables was untrue and she would only make things worse by saying anything more.

It was late when they arrived back at the Preston gaol, and, of course, too late for supper. The cells were cold, the walls damp, and while Isabella's cell was close enough to hear Grace's disconsolate moans, she was too far from her to offer any comfort.

PAINFUL RECOLLECTION

The Preston Gaol was imposing and grey, draughty, noisy, and frightening. It looked like a rather squat Crusader fortress, and resolutely offered no comfort to those incarcerated within. The thick stone walls made echo chambers of the dreary cells. The routines of prisoner life, with the colourless but not odourless food and the menial tasks, only intensified feelings of hopelessness and despair.

Grace's pregnancy made her weary and nauseous, and the gravity of her situation simply terrified her. She was in a dreadful state of grief mixed with shock. She had been living a modest but very happy dream as the pregnant new wife of a respectable farmer, with five children to look after and one "little secret" whom she thought out of harm's way back in Ulverston. Now she was living a nightmare — her first-born child dead, her husband shocked by her lie, and her beloved sister Isabella caught up with her in a murder trial.

Many days passed before Grace found herself capable of useful thought. Her mind kept going over and over recent events, re-experiencing the shock and horror of discovering Thomas dead, seeing the faces of John and then her mother in the courtroom, hearing the words of condemnation from the magistrates. Her mind just seemed to keep going over and over every detail of the terrible day that Thomas had died, and of the subsequent hearings, in the hope that it could somehow find a way to save her sister and herself.

Slowly her tumbling thoughts began to shape themselves into a chronicle — the increasingly tragic story of her adult life. Starting with the discovery of her first pregnancy, poor little Tom, and the still cruelly painful recollection of how the man who was his father reacted to the news, she sadly considered the number of times she had tried to construct a decent life for herself and how each time it had all gone wrong.

Grace still felt a little surge of pride at how she had responded to the birth of Thomas. Determined to make a life for the two of them, she had quickly made arrangements to put him into care so that she could go into the countryside to work and try to find an employer who might take them both.

But for all Grace's effort and initiative, all that had come her way in the country, apart from hard, rough work, was another feckless man and another baby in her womb. When she first realized that she was pregnant and abandoned again, she had cried bitter tears. Later, when she heard the distressing news that Jane Gordon had put Thomas in the Ulverston Workhouse, she could only think that without the work as hired girl she had found at Meanley Farm she and James might soon be joining him.

In prison, memories of John made him seem like a knight of old, a man in shining armour who arrived to save her from disaster. First he gave her a job that allowed James to live with her, then when she again fell pregnant he quickly married her and made her a respectable woman. In marrying her, John had made it clear that for him baby James was simply part of her difficult past, and now he was welcome to be part of the Isherwood family's future.

There really hadn't been time in the hurried preparations for the wedding, just after Christmas and all, to tell him about Tom. She had been planning to tell him when the time was right, if ever it was, but convinced herself that Tom would be best left with her parents now that they had taken him in again.

Life was so busy at Meanley that thinking about Tom was something Grace had routinely put aside for another day. The prospect of his arrival at the farm with Isabella filled her with dread. Having grown to love John Isherwood, she now feared losing that love on account of her not having told him about Tom.

So sad. Tom himself had been at no risk of betraying her secret. He didn't call her "ma" or expect from her a loving embrace — he didn't even recognize her. When he and Isabella arrived at the station he was much more interested in the trains than in the people who met him.

Of course, he'd last seen Grace when he was just a few months old, and he had been through a lot of substitute mothers since then. Tom knew Isabella best, she had been around in his home in Dalton and had travelled with him all that way. Meanley Farm was simply a wonderful new place to him, with lots of kids and animals and even a baby to pet.

The week Tom and Isabella posed as caregiver and charge had been a nightmare for Grace. Whispered conversations and high tension between the sisters, Isabella insisting she wanted to get back home to find a new job, and Grace desperate to send Tom back with her or put him somewhere out of sight.

Time and again she had tried anxiously to imagine what John would say if she told him about Tom. He certainly was a kind and gentle man, and he wanted a woman around the house. And he seemed past grieving for Jane. But she had already surprised him with her new pregnancy, and before marrying her he had questioned her very closely about who might be the father of little James. To confess to him now that there was another child and another man back in Cumbria was too frightening to contemplate.

Putting little Tom into the Clitheroe workhouse had seemed her best alternative. She was able to justify the idea to herself by thinking that he was used to workhouse life, having already spent time in the Ulverston workhouse, and that Clitheroe was close enough to go and retrieve him if her situation ever changed.

In Grace's fear-filled reckoning, if John found out about her deception it could be the workhouse not only for Tom, but for herself, James, and likely their unborn baby, so sending Tom to the workhouse seemed no crueller than the alternative.

Standing just inside the big door of the workhouse waiting for the matron had felt strangely reassuring to Grace. The rhythm of the institution, with washing and cooking and cleaning going on throughout the building, made it feel as if life was going on.

The workhouse administrator, Mrs. Lofthouse, seemed to have no moral objection to having a two-year-old left in their care. The problem, as she had explained patiently to the sisters, was that they had no proof that Tom had been living in the county, and without that proof he could not be admitted. The rules were clear.

On the other side of the door again, the four of them had made a pathetic little tableau. There they were, standing lost and confused at the top of the walk, framed by gnarled and stunted trees: two young women, one with a babe in arms, and a two-year-old, who, tragically, nobody wanted.

Whenever Grace got to this point in her thoughts she retreated from the noisy chill of the prison around her into a bleak, silent stillness. At those times her mind seemed as empty as her eyes, but, sadly, it wasn't. She kept trying desperately to understand how it had happened that by the end of that day little Thomas, rejected first by his mother and then by officialdom, had ended up dead.

ISABELLA INCARCERATED

Isabella was frightened, confused, and chilled to the bone inside the dank prison walls. What had started out as a happy mission to deliver her toddling nephew Tom to his mother so that he could share her new life, had ended up instead in a dark prison cell. As well, she now had a hurtful, racking cough that kept her, and the other women on her corridor, awake in the dark and so tired in the light.

Isabella had really liked little Tom, a self-sufficient two-year-old with a ready smile and the ability to entertain himself for hours with the simplest things — a leaf or a twig or a piece of string. The Gardner family had felt the humiliation of his birth keenly, especially with Jane having already added to their family's burden with her illegitimate baby. Some of the local gossips had suggested to her mother, even in her hearing, that Isabella would surely be next. But she prided herself in the fact that she knew better than to blame little Tom for what the neighbours might say about her and her sisters.

Once Grace got married, it seemed that the problem of raising Tom was solved. None of the Gardners imagined that Grace had not told her new husband John about little Tom. She had always seemed so forthright, and he had accepted James, hadn't he? If he was willing to accept one transgression, why not two? Besides, he had a brood of five of his own for Grace to take on, plus the one on the way, so what difference would one more littl'un make?

Isabella still didn't really understand why Grace had not just told John about Thomas and been done with it. She saw how John looked at her sister, eyes all soft and warm, and she could see for herself how appealing Grace's soft manner and easy smile would be to a man.

Sometimes she wished that she was more like Grace, pretty and pliant, instead of being so quick and sharp. Her cousin George had often teased her about her manner, warning her that boys would not want to go out walking with a girl with a sharp tongue. Unless she got out of prison soon, Isabella feared that she was getting so weak and thin that no boy was going to give her a second glance anyway.

Ever since they first met with the barrister that John had brought to them in the prison in Bolton-by-Bowland, Isabella had known that it was going to fall to her to save herself and Grace from the noose. Since they had arrived in Preston, Grace had barely said a word. When they saw each other during meals or chores, Grace just stared at her with a hopeless expression, clutching her stomach and crying silently.

Grace's weakness strengthened Isabella's resolve. "I am going to explain what happened and everyone will listen and understand," Isabella promised her sister.

A PRISON LIKE A FORTRESS

In Slaidburn there is a charming tradition, at the end of each May, of choosing a May Queen and her court from amongst the children of Slaidburn and Dunsop Bridge. After a brief service at Saint Andrews Church, the queen and her entourage, and any other young people present, set off to see the squire, King-Wilkinson, who gives out coins to the eager children. The year that we were there my youngest son, Nicholas, received a pound from the hand of the squire. I am sure Margaret Isherwood would have been pleased to know of her great-grandson's participation in the ritual.

Having enjoyed the maypole celebrations, Nicholas, William, and I went on a field trip to look at the Preston Gaol. Since it was the end of May, our timing was right — I was hoping to be able to get some idea of what it had been like to be locked up in there, awaiting trial in the heat of the summer in 1885.

By car you can make the drive from Hark to Bounty in Slaidburn to the prison in Preston in about three quarters of an hour, if you don't get lost on the ring road heading into town. It would take longer from Bolton-by-Bowland.

The prison is still in operation, and the former governor's house is now a museum. The prison dates to 1845 and was built in what is described as the Victorian radial style. An aerial view shows the prison buildings fanning out like a misshapen star with points of unequal length from a central hub. Old photographs reveal a series of large cell blocks of blackened brick with small barred windows. In the photographs everything looks cold and wet.

Petty thieves, drunks, prostitutes, and the mentally unstable would have made up the bulk of the inmates of the women's wing of the prison in 1885. Female inmates tended to be rowdy, using rude language and raucous singing to maintain their spirits and undermine the authority of their gaolers.

Grace and Isabella had not been "gently reared," but they had come from a stable family home in Dalton-in-Furness and they certainly would have found the other inmates loud and frightening. But even in gaol female sympathies can be stirred, and Grace and Isabella were probably taken under the wing of some of the more toughened inmates and shown how best to get by. Grace's pregnancy would have heightened any desire to protect her, and she was likely given less-demanding chores and some assistance at mealtimes.

Visitors would have been terribly upsetting, reminding them of where they had come from and who they had betrayed. It was probably a relief when the frequency of visits diminished as John and Mrs. Gardner had to tend to the farm and the children back in Slaidburn.

Regardless of any help or privilege, the time in the prison must have been horrifying for the sisters. By day they had to work at menial but exhausting tasks like cleaning or laundering, and at night they were surely kept awake by the ravings and the nightmares of others, if not their own.

JOHN'S PLIGHT

John Isherwood was hurt, shamed, and frightened. One moment he had been a hard-working, contented, and respected farmer with a new wife, a healthy family, and a baby on the way. The next he had become the husband of an accused murderess, feeling broken-hearted, deceived, and horrified. Perhaps worst of all, he had no idea of what he could do to save his wife and his family's reputation.

Grace Gardner had entered John's life just when it had become impossibly hard; his beloved Jane had died, leaving him with five young children to raise on his own, as well as a farm to run. Matthew and Maggie were doing the best they could, but they were still just children and he needed adult help and company.

John had felt himself fortunate to learn that a young woman with a newborn was looking for a situation, and he sought Grace out where she was staying in Bolton-by-Bowland. Their deal was quickly sealed: Grace would work as hired girl and do her best to watch the children and tend the home, while John would provide a safe, warm place for her and her babe to live. He felt sorry for the agreeable young woman, left alone and pregnant by some lout, and resolved to keep anything like that from happening to his Maggie.

And John was grateful to Grace. Despite her difficult position she was not just sweet and pretty, she also threw herself into looking after his motherless brood and helping him run the farm. Grace's own gratitude was mixed with relief that she didn't have to return to Cumbria with another bastard and no prospects. With both involved so anxious, patient, and forgiving, it was no surprise to anyone that Grace was pregnant again by year's end, even with her James only six months old. John and Grace's January wedding was witnessed by Jane's brother, Tom, which seemed a good omen for at least as happy as possible a continuation of the life John had once planned with Jane.

And for almost five blissful months, John and Grace Isherwood and their family of six children seemed to be settled and even prospering. Maggie, Matthew, and John were back to attending the Quaker school in Newton, while Dick, Tom, and baby James got on with growing up ... until the day his new sister-in-law arrived at Meanley with little Thomas.

The days surrounding the death of Thomas were a blur to John. First of all, he couldn't make any sense of Grace and Isabella's explanation of why they had gone out again after coming home on Saturday night. Then there was a policeman at the door, with evidence that the child Isabella had brought to Meanley had been found dead.

And only then had he been told that Thomas was Grace's own child.

The speed and authority of the Coroner's Inquest and the Magistrate's Proceedings left John even more shocked and bereft. Not only did he have to find a barrister and someone to help look after his children, he had to make the long journey to visit the weeping women in gaol and try to keep their spirits up.

He couldn't believe that Grace and Isabella had killed the baby. But the case against them looked strong. He felt so hurt that Grace had lied to him. Yes, he would have been angry, and he wasn't sure he would have been willing to add yet another mouth to his house

Looking into Preston Prison from the old main gate.

Photo courtesy of Lancashire County Council.

hold. But nothing would have been as bad as the mess they were in now. Why hadn't Grace known that he loved her enough to forgive even this, and to help her find some place for Tom?

Once the Magistrate's Court in Bolton-by-Bowland had committed Grace and Isabella to trial, the Clitheroe barrister, Mr. Baldwin, told him frankly that the sisters' situation was dire, and that for the trial in Leeds they would need the best lawyer John could possibly find.

But how? In his desperation, John turned again to the family of the local squire, King-Wilkinson, for advice.

The King-Wilkinson family had long been involved in the practice of law, and knew well the reputations of many in the region's legal community. And so it was that John travelled to Leeds to plead for the help of a rising star of the North-Eastern Circuit, Edward Tindal Atkinson.

A LAWYER WELL-CHOSEN FOR A DIFFICULT TASK

In 1885 Edward Tindal Atkinson was thirty-eight years old and already well-established as a successful barrister. His practice was focused on the Leeds County Court and what was known as the Quarter Sessions, where he sometimes even argued cases before his father, Judge Serjeant Tindal Atkinson, with the apparent acquiescence of all involved.

The Tindal Atkinson family were prominent in British legal circles. While Edward's father was a long-serving county court judge in the circuit that included Leeds, his brother, H. Tindal Atkinson, was a judge of the Essex County Court.

At his public school, Felstead School in Essex, which is best known as the alma mater of the sons of Oliver Cromwell, Edward earned a first-class certificate. Following his call to the bar (Middle Temple) in 1870, he took chambers in Leeds, and was already a lawyer of some reputation and experience when he was approached by John Isherwood, diffident but desperate, to defend his wife and sister-in-law.

In addition to his reputation and experience, Edward Tindal Atkinson had some other very important attributes. As the

Yorkshire Evening News (15/12/1919) put it:

> Although he is physically well set up, and has a
> commanding presence, his method of conducting
> a case was of the quietest. His voice has a soft,
> lulling sound, and he was always persuasive rather
> than dictatorial toward witnesses.

The initial meeting between Edward the lawyer, and John the farmer, was a touching one. Edward soft-spoken and polite, John frightened and anxious. The fact that hiring such a well-regarded lawyer was way beyond the Isherwood's means was something that neither party dwelt on. Edward could tell immediately that John was a man who paid his debts. If Edward could lead his family out of this present horror, John felt willing to pay everything he had.

A THOUGHTFUL ASSESSMENT

Whether through luck, or, more likely, through wise advice and direction, John Isherwood had chosen well in selecting the defender of his wife and sister-in-law. Edward Tindal Atkinson was young, but not too young, and his demeanour did seem to match that of his two young female clients.

The strategy for handling the case was not easy to develop. On the evidence presented so far, Grace and Isabella looked guilty. There was motive: the need to hide the existence of yet another illegitimate child from Grace's new husband. There was the frustrated plan to leave poor little Thomas in the workhouse in Clitheroe, and then there was the opportunity for an expedient death: that long and lonely journey through the fells from Clitheroe to Meanley Farm with only each other and the two children for company.

Discussing the case over tea in his chambers, Atkinson and his junior decided that they needed to understand the state of mind of the accused and to gauge the kind of impression the two young women would make in court. Grace had managed to become a respectable farmer's wife, and Isabella sounded like a hard-working young woman, but would they seem so to a jury of twelve men? In particular, Edward was worried that Grace might seem a cold and cruel woman who had just abandoned her first child. There was also the impression of her moral character that having had two illegitimate children would create with the jury. And Isabella's wild stories about the child and the swarthy man who threatened their lives made her sound quite unreliable if not outright dishonest.

So the junior lawyer, Mr. Charles Morley, was dispatched to Preston Gaol to see what he could learn. When he arrived he found Grace too ill and too frightened to be much use. But he did get the sense that with her timid demeanour and slight figure she would strike a jury as more sinned against than sinning.

Slowly Mr. Morley began to piece together the details of the tragic life of little Thomas Gardner. The second illegitimate grandchild of the senior Gardners, whose small house was already overflowing, little Tom was given the Gardner last name at birth, and was left soon after with Agnes Creary while his mother sought work to support the two of them.

Grace had found a job at Crosshills, not far from where Isabella was in service, and began to work hard to make money to send back for the care of little Thomas. She sent funds back to Mrs. Creary for Tom's care whenever she could, and she wrote frequent letters asking after his health. But as the months passed, the letters became fewer and the funds less adequate.

Soon, Mrs. Creary was grumbling that she was not in the charity business, and gradually baby Thomas was passed from hand to hand. There was little room for sentimentality about the needs of small children in the crowded lives of the Gardners or their neighbours.

With the arrival of Grace's second fatherless child, there was little time left in her thoughts for the distant first one. Even the news that little Thomas had been placed in the Ulverston workhouse could not stir her to action on his behalf. She felt so sad about his plight but there was nothing she could do.

Mr. Morley thought the story, as he had heard it so far, offered him the beginnings of a possible defence. A meek and weak young woman, separated by circumstance from her child, sending money when she could, writing letters of loving concern, and then, as she is struggling all alone to support herself and her child, another man comes along and she is lost again.

Grace's inarticulate misery, combined with her history of care for the child, gave the defence a chance to make her the victim, rather than little Tom. Even the prosecutor would have a hard time giving Tom a voice in the courtroom, with only his salvaged clothes to mutely remind the jury that his only crime was that of being "inconvenient."

Eighteen-year-old Isabella was the perfect contrast for Grace's apathetic, head-hanging sadness. Though the younger sister by many years, she had been in service since she was thirteen, and was much more worldly than her meek sister. Isabella had to learn early how to handle dangerous masculine attention, and her position as middle child in a large struggling family had made her quick and watchful.

She also proved to be more capable of helping Morley with the defence. Prison life had already given her a hacking cough and a dreadful pallor, but she answered the questions put to her carefully and thoughtfully. She had observed a lot about different types of people and their ways. With the benefit of the experience of the other prisoners, she was dreadfully aware that if she and Grace were found guilty they could be sentenced to death. She paid close attention to the lawyer's questions.

For Isabella, Grace had at times been a stand-in mother, a loving older sister who somehow found the occasional moment to focus on her alone, in a home where people were crowded together and mostly paid each other scant attention. So sure was she of Grace's maternal instincts that she had felt certain that Grace would be glad that Tom had come to join her.

When Isabella learned that Grace's husband knew nothing about young Tom, she realized her terrible mistake. In the confusion that ensued she had only made things worse. In trying to make it up to Grace for her mistake in bringing Tom to Meanley, she went so far as to tell a ridiculous story to the police about his whereabouts. Of course that had just made their situation worse. Instead of admitting the terrible accident that had befallen them, her tale had made it look as if they were guilty of inept murder.

Carefully, the young lawyer extracted the details of Tom's last day from the sisters. While he had been encouraged to learn of Grace's many letters asking after Tom's well-being and the money she had sent for his care, there was still the problem of the drive home from Clitheroe and the dead body placed by the brook. How were they going to explain what happened on the trap ride through the fells?

SIMILAR PROBLEM, APPARENTLY
DIFFERENT SOLUTION

Penny and I have a third sister, Terree, whose official name, Theresa, makes her the bearer of our mother's name for our generation.

Despite the good fortune to be named after our mother, Terree has faced a number of disadvantages in life. To begin with, she was born when our mother was already seriously ill with the disease that killed her, although none of us knew, least of all Terree. And even though she was fourteen when Tessie, our mom, finally died, I doubt Terree has any real recollection of her. Even I, with my four-year age advantage, can't remember our mother as more than the gentle invalid with a dangerous addiction to cigarettes.

I imagine Terree's memories of our mother are probably like mine, only vaguer: a pleasant, sparkly-eyed woman with salt-and-pepper hair wearing earrings and a pearl choker, who lay in bed all the time in our parent's bedroom.

Unconsciously echoing two of the Gardner sisters, Terree and I went on to have our share of children out of wedlock. Naturally, I thought that in my case the decision to do so was modern and feminist, while, with an older sibling's innate right to disparage, I thought Terree was just irresponsible.

That wasn't true, of course — at least the part about Terree being irresponsible. Terree graduated from university and got a teaching job. She travelled around in Europe with our stepsister Lesley. She had a proper, although youthful, marriage, and I believe a proper divorce. But, in the background, while she was doing all those things, the schizophrenia that would come to define her was taking hold. She became increasingly whimsical, if not downright erratic. She heard voices, and sometimes she spun right out.

Although she spent some of her time in hospitals with locked doors, our family bought Terree a condominium to live in, and the state has helped keep the wolf from the door.

Well, sort of. I mean, Terree hasn't starved or anything, and she has the essential minimum of furnishings and of clothes in which to face Canadian winters. But a wolf in man's clothing did manage to find his way into her apartment and her life.

Terree had her first child out of wedlock when she was twenty-eight, I was thirty-two at the time, and Penny was forty-one. Dean, our dad, was still alive and he and Doreen cared about and worried over Terree's baby, little Joseph, from the moment he was born. Terree loved him ferociously, but her disease made it very difficult for her to give Joe the stable environment and consistent care that every child needs.

In those days, Terree was still in and out of institutions with some regularity, and Joe was sometimes cared for by foster parents and sometimes by Penny. In retrospect, none of us exactly knew what was happening with Terree and Joe all the time, and by the time we began to figure things out, Joe was already four years old.

At that point, on one of his and Terree's regular visits to Penny's house, Joe simply refused to leave. With the agreement of all concerned, Penny and her husband Dale adopted Joe.

That was our family solution for Terree's illegitimate baby boy number one.

Some years passed, five to be precise, and the same old wolf made Terree pregnant again. She knew by then that he had a perfectly good wife and several children, with whom he lived just across town. But I guess it is difficult to find a good steady male friend when you are mentally ill, so the wolf must have seemed better than nothing. From his point of view, Terree must have seemed a little strange, but she had a low-key sweetness, an apartment of her own, and boundless availability to recommend her.

So then our family had Terree's illegitimate baby number two to deal with, just like with Grace Gardner, except Grace didn't have rapidly changing moral standards in society and a middle-class family who thought they were modern to help her out.

By this point, our family understood the drill a little better. Actually, Terree made the decision herself when Daniel was twenty months old. She brought him over to Penny's house and left him there, saying she was concerned about her state of mind and thought she would go stay in an institution for a while. By then, sadly, Dean was dead, Penny was forty-eight years old, and John had a family of nine children to preoccupy him. As John so eloquently said at the time, "Sheelagh, this one's for you."

We felt very fortunate to be able to adopt Daniel. We had love to spare and then some, we had enough money, and we had a perfect space in the family, just after Matthew, in which to tuck him. Terree had given us a priceless gift.

But what would have happened to Terree and Joseph and Daniel one hundred years earlier? Terree and Joe would probably have lived with Penny and Dale, and Penny would have added the burden of care for Terree to the enormous burden the oldest daughter in a motherless family already has to carry. The wolf might have had a harder time getting at Terree a second time, especially if she was living with Penny. If he managed to find a way, the arrival of the second child would have been even more infuriating and demoralizing.

Or maybe Terree and however many children she had would have ended up in the workhouse. The rough work, thin rations, and segregated ages and genders would likely have made Terree rely more and more on the voices that are always there, waiting to talk to her.

CONTEMPLATING A DEFENCE

Back in Leeds, Charles Morley gave Edward Tindal Atkinson a concise version of what he had learned from his visit to Preston gaol. He had taken the time on the journey back to list what he thought of as the positives and negatives of the case.

"First of all," he told Edward, "both women are in a dreadful state. Grace is swollen with child and mute from misery, and Isabella coughs so hard she can barely breathe. Neither looks like a murderess, but they don't appear perfectly innocent either. It is going to be a tough case to make."

Edward looked thoughtfully at the young man. He liked a challenge, and this case certainly presented him with one. Infanticide was a common enough crime, but the two accused being comely, if distressed and ill, sisters who claimed they had no part at all in the child's death was unusual.

"How," he wondered aloud, "can we get a jury to believe it was all an accident?"

Steepling his fingers, he stared at the law books on his shelf as he listened for what else his junior had learned while in Preston. He was pleased to hear of the provisions for care that Grace had made for young Thomas, including her efforts to send money even after her marriage, but he furrowed his brow when he heard that Thomas's release from the Ulverston workhouse was at the instigation of Grace's parents, not of Grace herself.

He was surprised, but pleased, that the sisters could read and write, especially because it seemed likely that letters from Grace enquiring after Tom's well-being could be available as evidence of her motherly concern, however intermittent that concern seemed to have been.

The whole week of deceit after Isabella and Tom arrived at Meanley was quite problematic. He could certainly present Grace as sweet and meek and unlikely to intend harm to anyone, especially a child. But her sustained deceit of her new husband would make a jury uncomfortable. A way had to be found to ensure that she would be seen as loving and fearful, rather than dishonest and manipulative.

Isabella was a different problem. Her maturity and intelligence could work against her with a jury. He would have to be careful to keep the court from concluding that she, at least, was calculating enough to decide that Grace would be better off without the problem of Thomas.

He needed to present Isabella as a young woman who was devoted to her older sister. While she clearly wanted Grace to find happiness in her marriage, circumstance had saddled her with a terrible dilemma. She had been sent by her parents to deliver Tom to his mother, so she could scarcely come home again with him still in her custody. What was she to do with poor little Tom?

If Isabella was a murderess, her motive had to be love for her sister.

Could he convince a jury that it would be perverse to believe that sisterly love would extend to child murder?

Edward Tindal Atkinson, a barrister well-known in Leeds for his compelling arguments, did not feel at all confident that he had yet hit upon a defence that would save both the sisters.

IN HOPELESS CIRCUMSTANCES, SOMETIMES THE ABSURD SEEMS LOGICAL

Would I murder for Penny? Of course not — at least, not a child. A spouse, maybe ...

I have been in fraught situations, usually caused by romantic entanglement, when the world seemed reduced to a very small set of choices. I have, temporarily at least, lost sight of the greater world and the extraordinary number of options available when choosing how to live one's life. You don't need to be a fallen woman in late Victorian times to feel trapped and confused by the circumstances in which you find yourself. It can happen to any of us, any time.

In stressful situations all sorts of unthinkable notions can be entertained. For example, I remember once, for one night only, seriously contemplating a communal marriage, as described in the book *The Harrad Experiment*. In retrospect, it is hard to believe that I wasn't high on something that night. Certainly it was the sixties. But I know that I was just completely emotionally overwrought, if stone-cold sober.

We cannot know exactly what wild possibilities ran through Grace's mind in the days following Tom's arrival at Meanley.

But we do know that, under extraordinary pressure, ordinary people can do unthinkable things.

In trying to imagine Penny and me in the seemingly hopeless situation that Grace and Isabella were facing, I realize that in our case I would most likely have been the fallen woman and Penny the helpful sister. So maybe the question is, would Penny murder for me?

She and I have already proved that we would willingly raise a sibling's children if need be. We both did that for Terree without a backward glance. But what about an inconvenient child, a child who came along when we were too young, or too old, or just too tired?

I have confused attitudes toward abortion, and I suspect that Penny does too. I believe I am pro-choice, I certainly would vote that way, but I am not sure I could ever have an abortion myself if I believed I was carrying a normal, healthy fetus. But I can also imagine myself double-dealing with a female relative, hypocritically counselling abortion if I thought that her life would be made more difficult or her choices somehow greatly limited by the birth of a child. Or, more consistently, what about a child whose reappearance, whose very existence, would ruin everything?

Penny is saintly but pragmatic. For all her goodwill and generosity, I have occasionally seen flashes of a person who is fully capable of rationalizing actual bad behaviour or manipulating circumstances. Her how-can-we-get-out-of-this-one face is rarely seen, but it lurks in there behind her self-sacrificing demeanour.

Still, Penny is a genuine Christian, even if only of the Anglican variety. She doesn't have it in her to abandon a young child or to harm one in any way. Nor do I. So from a present-day perspective, the Whittaker sisters are not really like the Gardner sisters ... or are they?

Maybe the Gardner sisters just didn't have it in them to harm a child, either.

THE BIOGRAPHY OF A
TWO-YEAR-OLD

Edward Tindal Atkinson decided that in order best to defend the sisters, he needed to have a sense of the entire life of unfortunate little Thomas Gardner. He needed to be able to convince the jury that while Tom had not received the motherly attention one would have wished for him, reluctant neglect is not the same as murder.

First there was the question of Tom's birth, and the identity of his father. Tom was given the last name Gardner at his birth, but it seemed no accident that Isabella, in her initial story to the police, had said Tom's mother's name was Dockery. He also wondered about Isabella's choice of the name Stables for the villainous, threatening man in her story.

So Charles Morley was charged with the task of travelling to Dalton-in-Furness and Ulverston to talk to Grace's family and the women who had taken Thomas into their care.

Before going to Dalton-in-Furness, Mr. Morley reviewed the notes he had taken during his visit to Preston. Isabella had mentioned that a family called Dockery had lived next door to the Gardners on Stafford Street, and that a real man called John

Stables had lived in Dalton, although he no longer did. Perhaps he might learn something by pursing those bits of information.

A few difficult and tiring days later, Charles had spoken with or visited most of the people and places that Grace had known and he was more than ready to return home. Not much had been accomplished. He had found the Gardner family too anxious-to-please to be of much help, while the townswomen who had helped to care for Thomas were full of praise for their own efforts but very guarded about anything to do with Grace.

Charles thought it pertinent that no one sought him out with malicious stories about Grace, and that, apart from her obvious lapses, she was generally thought to be a kind and good young woman. Most had a good word to say about Grace's sister Jane, although there was usually a passing mention of her illegitimate son tucked in amongst the compliments about her skill with needle. Few of those he met could tell him much about Isabella: she was just a girl when she went into service and she had not been back with her parents for long before she had gone off to Meanley with the child.

Charles wrote out his notes while eating his dinner at a table on the grass behind the hotel, the summer's evening still bright and warm. Often, in working on a case, he was able to see the facts anew when he wrote them out on long sheets of foolscap. He hoped that would work for him now.

An Excerpt from Charles Morley's Notes:

Events in the Brief Life of the Child Thomas Gardner

Born December 15, 1882 at 9 Stafford Street, Dalton-in-Furness.

Mother Grace Gardner, a domestic servant, then living at 9 Stafford Street.

Dr Alexander Gray, Dalton-in-Furness, both delivered Thomas and told the Coroner that he had seen a child of around 2 years of age at the Gardner's house in Dalton in April 1885 when he was there attending Mrs Gardner.

Agnes Creary, wife of John Creary, Lower Brook Street, Ulverston, was visited at Whitsuntide 1883 by Grace with a child a few months old. Creary says that Grace told her that the child's name was James Thomas Gardner and that the father was a man named Dockray.

While the baby was registered only as Thomas Gardner, when leaving the child with Mrs Creary Grace seems to have added a "James" to his name.

A family called Dockery lived next door to the Gardners on Stafford Street. The Dockery boys, James Henry and Thomas Alfred, are reported to have been six and four respectively when Grace's son was born, while her own brother Thomas was seventeen.

(No obvious clue to paternity in choice of forenames.)

Mrs. Creary kept the child for 27 weeks but Grace failed to send funds on a regular basis so she returned the child to Grace's father's home.

Grace Gardner, the child's mother, was in service at Crosshills during this period.

At Grace's request, Mrs. Coward of Dalton-in-Furness retrieved Thomas from his grandparents' home and nursed him from November 1883 to June 1884.

On June 8, 1884, Grace Gardner gave birth to a sibling of Thomas, James Edward Gardner, in Bolton-by-Bowland.

(Why the fondness for the name James?)

Mrs. Jane Gordon succeeded Mrs. Coward in caring for Thomas Gardner in the course of the summer of 1884.

Mrs. Gordon did not receive anything toward the child's maintenance, so she admitted him to the Ulverston Workhouse. (She did receive some monies in early 1885 from Grace Gardner.)

At some point Grace Gardner asked Dorothy Dockray, an inmate of Ulverston Workhouse with a child of her own, to nurse Thomas Gardner. Grace told Dorothy that the father of the child was William Dockray, a miner. Dorothy declined to care for Grace's child.

(There had been a William Dockery aged about twenty living at Stafford Street around the time Grace fell pregnant.)

Some time later Thomas was taken out of the workhouse to live again with his Gardner grandparents.

Grace wrote many times to Mrs. Gordon from Meanley, including after her marriage, about the child and the payment for its care. (Supt. Inman offered eight letters as evidence at the inquest.) It appears she sent money in February to pay her debt to Mrs Gordon. Since she had a child the previous June and had started her new job in September that may have been her first opportunity to do so.

Mrs. Gordon saw the child at the Gardner's in Dalton around February 1885.

In her statement to the police, Isabella said that she had been looking after the child for four months, which would likely mean since January or February.

THE BIOGRAPHY OF A TWO-YEAR-OLD

(This may not be true as much of Isabella's story was a fabrication.)

Isabella Gardner brought Thomas to Meanley Farm on May 5.

Thomas Gardner was found dead on May 17, 1885.

Extenuating Circumstances

Grace sent letters and money to Mrs. Creary from Crosshills, although she never appears to have sent sufficient funds nor did the funds arrive on a regular basis.

In the summer of 1884, Grace was indisposed in Bolton-by-Bowland, giving birth to James Edward.

Grace went into service at Meanley farm in September, which was around the time that Mrs. Gordon put the child into the Ulverston Workhouse. Presumably, Grace knew that the child was no longer with Mrs. Gordon, but she still tried to pay her debt.

Grace sent many letters to Mrs. Gordon and she continued to send her money even after she knew that Mrs. Gordon had put Thomas in the workhouse. (Was she hoping to get back into Mrs. Gordon's good books so that she would look after him again?)

Since Grace was already pregnant again, this time with John's child, when she and John got married the prospect of telling John about Thomas must have been daunting.

(From where did Grace get the money to send to Mrs. Gordon, especially after her marriage to John?)

A jury might find that last point difficult, Charles mused on his journey back to Leeds. Indeed, so was the whole task of trying to organize the information he had gleaned about the life of Thomas into a compelling story for the defence. How could any reasonable man ignore the fact that Grace had never told her husband of the existence of another illegitimate child, and, even more damning, how could one be convinced that when the sisters found they were unable to commit that child to the workhouse in Clitheroe, he had so conveniently died?

He concluded, before drifting off into a fitful doze, that all of Edward Tindal Atkinson's considerable skill in defence would be needed in this case.

A QUESTION OF PATERNITY

The fathers, respectively, of Thomas Gardner and James Edward Gardner, villains both, received neither mention nor investigation in the proceedings that followed Thomas's death.

One is left to wonder: who were those men, and why did the legal system appear to be so indifferent to the fact that Thomas, in particular, had been abandoned by his father before he was even born.

One glimpse of possible paternity is the recollection by Agnes Creary, Thomas's first nurse, that Grace had told her that the baby's name was James Thomas Gardner and that his father was a man named Dockery, or Dockray as Agnes seems to have heard it.

It appears that Agnes was not a friend of the Gardner family, or she would likely have known that Dockerys were next-door neighbours of the Gardner's on Stafford Street.

At the time of Thomas's conception, the head of the Dockery household, Robert, a miner, was forty-five years old and his oldest son, William, also an iron miner, was twenty. Grace was a comely young woman and either man was a candidate to be father of the next-door neighbours' bastard grandchild, but, if so, why weren't they required to take some sort of responsibility?

There are strange inconsistencies to the various stories around Thomas. Grace told Agnes that his name was James Thomas, but the name on Thomas's birth certificate was just that, Thomas, and Grace gave the name James to her next illegitimate child. Spellings of course varied, as did pronunciation, but the name of Dockrah was used for Thomas when he arrived at Meanley and Isabella talked about Elizabeth Dockray in her statement to P.C. Sutcliffe.

So were the Gardner girls somewhat limited in their imagination, or was one of the Dockery men the father of young Thomas?

One wonders what Grace had told her parents about the child's father, or if, perish the thought, she had to admit that she was not sure who it was.

As the case progressed from court to court, no one queried Thomas's paternity. When Agnes Creary mentioned a Dockray in her testimony, no lawyer on either side seems to have followed up and asked Grace if what she had told Agnes was true. No testimony was heard about the man who had used her ill and left her to try to earn money alone for the child's keep. It appears to have been accepted by all concerned that the child was Grace's ugly secret and hers alone.

Perhaps the junior lawyer did try to elicit information about Thomas's paternity to use in defence, and Grace felt obligated to adhere, however dangerously, to whatever story she had already provided to John. Maybe the lawyer then decided that particular story would not bear close examination.

Most likely the cultural mores of the day were such that an illegitimate child was seen as the fault and responsibility of the mother and, unless the man involved was honourable, it was she alone who was expected to bear the burden of her sin.

Out of curiosity, I went searching for information on the most probable father, William Dockery, the young miner who lived next door on Stafford Street.

I looked for him on the 1891 census, thinking to find him somewhere in Cumbria, only to come up empty. I tried 1901 just to make sure I hadn't missed him. Not found.

It was only after some further search failures that I thought to look amongst the death records. William Dockery had died, I discovered, when he was only twenty-five. His son Thomas, if that is who he was, had only predeceased him by a couple of years.

ANOTHER CHILD LOST

Grace woke up to a terrible pain that started in her womb and encircled her heart. She had given birth twice before, of course. Indeed, one of those previous agonies had led to her present incarceration. But it was too soon for this baby, too soon and the pains were too harsh.

Her moans of anguish aroused the other prisoners who, in turn, shouted for help. It took a long time for anyone to come.

"What's all this about?" the wardress asked Grace harshly through the grill in the door before noticing the pool of blood that had already spilled from Grace's pallet onto the floor. Finally stirred to action, she hurried away to get help, returning some minutes later with a strong-looking male guard and unlocked the cell door. By then Grace was writhing with contractions and pain, and awash in blood. Taking in the details of her wretched condition, warders quickly bundled her up and took her to the prison infirmary.

In her cell down the corridor, Isabella was desperate to know what had happened to Grace and where they had taken her. When she found out that Grace had been taken to the infirmary, she begged to be allowed to go and help look after her.

"No healthy prisoners allowed," was matron's response, so it was nightfall before one of the wardresses was kind enough to tell her that Grace was still alive, but that the baby had died.

Days later, in broken whispers, Grace told her of the devastating birth of a tiny girl, no bigger than a puppy, who had briefly whimpered and then gasped for air and died. She didn't know what they had done with the little body, poor little mite born in a prison with no chance for life, but Grace whispered that she had secretly named the baby Victoria, and kissed her goodbye forever.

John thought that he could not feel more frightened and upset and alone, but the news of the dead little girl and his wife's dangerously weakened state left him sitting, head in hands, for hours by the empty grate at Meanley, tears of misery trickling through his fingers to the slate floor below.

Would he and Grace ever have the chance to share a bed again?

Maggie saw her father when she came down to make breakfast, but she didn't want to disturb him. She feared to learn whatever bad news had upset him anew.

As John was getting ready to go over to Preston for a visit to the gaol, he told her quietly that Grace was ill and the baby had died. This was the baby that Maggie had hoped to name, the little sister she had hoped for. She had been all set to beg Grace please to name her Jane.

Too late for that now, she thought sadly.

NO CHANCE TO "PLEAD HER STOMACH"

When they got word that Grace had suffered a stillbirth, Mr. Atkinson and Mr. Morley met briefly to discuss the legal implications of Grace's sad loss.

Grace was too ill to fully understand her situation, but the legal team were very aware that she had lost more than a baby; she had lost the opportunity to avoid immediate execution. Mr. Atkinson had consoled John with the information that women who were quick with child were not executed, but given a stay. With the latest news, the option for Grace to "plead her belly" was gone, and her fate had been cast into much sharper relief.

They decided not to remind their clients of the implications of this change in Grace's situation: it had always been a delicate issue since the extenuating circumstance left Isabella exposed to more serious punishment than her sister.

Mr. Atkinson decided it was still going to be important for him to stress the fact that, at the time of the arrival of Tom at Meanley Farm, Grace was pregnant with the legitimate child of a respectable farmer. He felt that the information, while it could be interpreted in different ways, could be argued by him to demonstrate the extent to which Grace had turned her life around and was therefore unlikely to cause herself new troubles by doing any harm to a child. It would take some skill to make that argument without arousing the issue of how much she had to lose if her relation to Thomas was found out, but he thought he had to take the risk.

Concerning Isabella, Edward and his junior spent some time trying to work out how best to portray her character. She obviously had not fallen into the unfortunate easy ways of her elder sister, at least not yet, and she had a clean record of industry and good behaviour. They agreed she had an air of intelligence, offset somewhat by a sharpish manner. Unfortunately, her maturity was a handicap. In order to deal with Isabella's original misguided statements to the police they had to find a way to portray her as young and foolish, not experienced and wise.

After lengthy discussion, the legal pair agreed that their best hope for Isabella was to show the jury how frightening the circumstance in which the two women found themselves had been, and how understandable it was that a very young woman in such a situation might make up a wild story. Here again, they hoped the jury would not be too observant, especially regarding the amount of fine detail in Isabella's statement, which betrayed a lot of careful thought.

As he rose to go over to the courthouse on another matter, Edward sighed and said, "I think the fate of Grace and Isabella hangs in the balance right now, and I just don't know what argument will tip it one way or the other."

A STRAW IN THE WIND?

As part of the defence preparation, Charles Morley had been assigned to follow a case that was presently before the court.

It was a trial for the murder of a child and, while the mother was much younger than Grace, elements of the situation seemed similar. On the morning the trial was about to commence, Charles hurried over to the law chambers to ask permission to attend in person so he could see and hear how the case was tried.

The facts of the case had many parallels: Sarah Elizabeth Dunn, aged seventeen, had been charged with the wilful murder of her illegitimate child, sixteen months old. It was claimed that she had left her father's home with her baby, Bertha, on May 8th and the body of the child was subsequently found in a hole filled with stagnant water. She had been committed to trial at the assizes.

While his junior took careful notes in the courtroom, Edward Atkinson was able to learn much of what he needed to know about the case from reading his morning copy of the *Yorkshire Post*.

A GIRL SENTENCED TO DEATH

At Durham Assizes on Saturday — before Mr.

Justice Wills — Sarah Dunn, aged 17, a domestic servant, was charged with the wilful murder of her illegitimate child, Bertha, aged 16 months, by thrusting it into a drain where a semi-liquid stream was flowing. The prisoner was left at the Birdhill Farm, near Shildon, her father's home with no one in the house but her child, on the morning of May 8th. The parents returned at noon after four hours absence from the house, and found it empty, and the prisoner was found the next day in Richmond, where she told her aunt that her child had been put out to nurse with a respectable widow. Her father, however, told the police he had suspicions, and the prisoner then admitted that the child was dead. The body was found buried in a hole close to the drain, and had been smothered with mud.

Mr. Milvain defended the prisoner and Mr. Skidmore and Mr. Liddell prosecuted. Mr. Milvain pointed to the prisoner's affection for the deceased; and the fact that the deceased required constant supervision. The child had fallen accidentally into the beck and was poisoned instantly, and the prisoner, fearing she would be blamed, and horrified at the accident, fled from the place. The jury found the prisoner guilty, but recommended her to mercy.

Mr. Justice Wills passed sentence of death.

— *Yorkshire Post*, Monday, July 20, 1885

Like many a skilled barrister, Edward Atkinson was a student of the moods and behaviour of judges. Having often appeared before Judge Wills, Edward knew him and felt certain that the obligation to sentence seventeen year old Sarah to death would have weighed heavily on him. It was all very well for the jury to recommend mercy when the judge had no choice on the sentence.

Edward hoped to be a judge himself someday, like his father and his brother, and he routinely tried to understand the range of alternatives certain arguments presented to a judge and the weight of judicial responsibility one might feel when complying with some of the harsher aspects of the law.

In the case of Sarah Dunn, Edward surmised that the responsibility to sentence such a young woman so harshly would frustrate the judge. He knew that an upstanding man like Justice Wills was likely to believe privately that the myriad of problems arising from illegitimacy were borne by women and children to a disproportionate extent. Natural justice was being thwarted by the fact that men could simply deny paternity or run away.

Days after the difficult sentencing of Sarah Dunn, Charles Morley knocked on the door of Edward's chamber without even having an appointment. He had come to report that Sarah Dunn had been pardoned. The explanation for her pardon was a surprising one. It seems that Sarah had been crying and moping around in the prison, as one who has been condemned to death well might, and that after a week or so she was granted a reprieve from being hanged on the grounds that she had "become despondent" following her conviction and sentencing.

How unusual. Edward and Charles concluded that Sarah's father and mother must have petitioned the Crown on their daughter's behalf, using the fact that her father had done the right thing by turning her in as grounds for leniency. Whatever the real reason, Sarah Dunn's reprieve was a good sign for Grace and Isabella.

Edward remarked to Charles: "Even the most ignorant of barristers knows that judges take it ill if their sentence is overturned. Let's hope for the sister's case that Judge Wills presides over the trial for the murder of Thomas Gardner."

WEIGHING NEW DEVELOPMENTS

Edward was thoughtfully stirring his tea when he heard the knock on his door. He had been sitting at his desk for some time, musing on what he had learned about child murder over the last several days.

The newspaper seemed tragically full of stories of murdered mites and their deranged mothers. There was the case of Isabella Hewson, accused of hanging her two-year-old son, Maurice, by a rope attached to a hook in the ceiling of her house.

In court she had sobbed and cried, "Oh, Maurice. Oh, Maurice. My son, my son," then fallen in a faint. Her reason for the deed, subsequently offered during the trial, was that she did not want him to be put in the street.

There was also the case of Emily Georgina Battersill, eighteen, accused of murdering her illegitimate male child by dismembering him and throwing him down a drain.

And, of course, there was the murder of baby Bertha by her mother, Sarah Elizabeth Dunn. The details and presentation of that case had become even more relevant to the defence of Grace and Isabella now it had been confirmed that Mr. Justice Wills would be presiding at the trial of the sisters.

He had also received a brief note from Mr. Morley informing him that Grace had not yet recovered from the stillbirth. Given her quiet disposition and weakened condition, it seemed unlikely that she would be able to offer much in her own defence.

Having nodded him in, Edward generously offered a cup of tea to Charles, as well as a seat. Almost as a continuation of his musings, he asked: "Do you think the younger sister, Isabella I believe is her name, could stand up in court and offer an explanation of their conduct? We do have her previous false statements to contend with — maybe the best way to deal with those is to have her give the 'true version' of events to the jury."

Charles looked thoughtful. "Were you thinking to have her read something out in court?"

"I am thinking to make them both pitiable and to somehow keep Isabella from cross examination. I think Justice Wills may have no appetite for sentencing young women to death at present, and if we can get the sympathy of the jury and give the judge some major points of contention with the prosecution's evidence that he can direct to the jury, maybe we can escape conviction."

The junior nodded. He was a great admirer of Edward's style, his soft-spoken arguments and elegant constructions. "I'm off to the gaol, then," he said, "to see what Isabella and I can write down in her own words. Let's hope she is more believable than with the 'truth' that she told to P.C. Sutcliffe back in May."

Edward smiled slightly. "I think we need to know more about the meal in Clitheroe. Justice Wills likes scientific arguments, and there is some talk in medical circles that the extent of digestion of food can suggest how soon after a meal a person has died. It looks as if the prosecution are going for drowning, not wilful suffocation. If the baby's stomach showed signs of an undigested meal, then we might argue that it had died before it was put in the stream."

"Perhaps a misdirected prosecution," he muttered to himself, "but who are we to complain?"

Mr. Morley, pleased at the prospect of a scientific argument, strode energetically down the street toward the Leeds prison where the sisters, their trial now imminent, had been moved.

PREPARING IN LEEDS

The journey from Preston to the prison in Leeds had been long and hot. Dusty and exhausted, neither sister had travelled well, although Grace's recent indisposition left her by far the worse off.

Mr. Tindal Atkinson paid them a very brief visit, but the young lawyer, with whom Isabella had begun to flirt feebly, worked hard with them to properly record what they claimed had really happened on that day in May.

He made Isabella write it all out, and it was a slow process. She had always been good at letters, but had never had much call to write at any length and her cramped handwriting was slow and sometimes not even legible. When he couldn't make it out, Mr. Morley made her write it again.

They had been carefully questioned about their dealings with all the witnesses, and had not a bad word to say about any of them. Isabella had never much liked John Stables, but that was because of his rough ways and reputation as a leaver, not a stayer. She regretted dragging her friend Elizabeth Dockery into things, yet also privately believed that the Dockerys had much to answer for, especially since she was convinced that one of them had ill-used her sister.

Isabella moved through defiance and into tears as Mr. Morley made her practise reading her written version of events aloud over and over. While he firmly reminded her that their lives might depend on how believable she was, his pressure on her to go slowly and articulate clearly put her under an unaccustomed kind of stress. It was only his entreaties that Grace was depending on her that kept her focused.

Trying to sleep the night before the trial, the sisters were glad to be together for a change and grateful for each other's company. They spent their time talking about what they would do when they got out of gaol, what special foods they would eat, and who they might see and where they might go. They agreed that they would prefer never to see Preston again. Grace cried for a while over the death of little Victoria, who would have been the first child of her marriage to John, and they prayed that little Thomas was happy in heaven.

Grace worried about the money John would have to find to pay Mr. Atkinson. She feared he might lose his tenancy. She also worried about those who had been their friends and neighbours. John was not very forthcoming during his visits about circumstances in Slaidburn, but she sensed that he was being shunned by some of the town folk.

Isabella shushed her rambling worries about the money. "John would pay anything to see you free," she said.

OH, GRANDMA, WE HARDLY KNEW YOU

Reading the magisterial proceedings had been a sobering experience for Penny and me. Suddenly a great gap had opened up in our knowledge and understanding of our grandmother. With our father long dead, and his brother and sisters now gone too, we had no one to ask about the family past. Nor were we certain that they had been told anywhere near as much about what happened to little Thomas back in Slaidburn as we now knew.

We began to ask around amongst our cousins for stepmother stories that they might have heard from grandma, but it turned out that while collectively we could remember hearing stories about a stepmother, none of us could remember any details. We had, however, been left with the impression that the relationship had not been a happy one.

My cousin Margaret, grandma's first granddaughter and official bearer of her first name, remembers her telling a story about the frustration of having to draw rows of J-shaped things that looked like pothooks on her slate at school. Grandma felt that those drills were for babies. Indeed, they were quite beneath her, because she already knew how to write.

Penny remembers grandma saying that she went to a Quaker school in York, but thought she meant the town of York, which was many miles east of her family's farm. Of course, to her Canadian grandchildren, born sixty years later than their grandmother, such distances no longer seemed so great.

Though Meanley Farm is in Lancashire today, it was in Yorkshire in the 1800s. We now recognize that grandma was most likely referring to the school in Newton, just walking distance from Meanley, which happened to be a centre for nonconformists, or Quakers. There is still a Quaker school there today, less than a mile from the farm, and the school's charter still allows for students of other faiths to attend as long as the number attending from their particular sect does not exceed that of the Quakers.

Cousin Margaret also remembers that, in later life, grandma tried to efface the description of her occupation as a mill worker from some official British document. The fact that she had worked as a weaver in a mill, while her husband was a bleacher, must somehow have seemed an embarrassment to her as she tried to find her place in the new world.

These days my brother, John, and his wife, Nancy, spend their summers in my grandma's little house in Kaslo, and one of the most prominent wall decorations there is a blow-up of the marriage certificate of our grandparents, William Whittaker and Margaret Isherwood. Sure enough, the enlargement magnifies the fact that someone has tried to scratch out the word *weaver* on the certificate. A sweet irony — grandmother's embarrassment now made larger than life and proudly hung on a wall by her grandson.

But that well-rehearsed piece of family history just seems to add to the confusion and mystery of Grandma Maggie's early life. How did she end up working in a mill in Haslingden? A settled life on a farm near Slaidburn, in the Forest of Bowland, in the late 1800s does not logically lead to working in a gritty northern mill town. So what series of events took the nine-year-old Margaret to Haslingden, and who went with her?

MR. JUSTICE WILLS PRESIDING

In the *Preston Guardian* of August 5, 1885, Cathryn Higham finally found the report of the Assizes trial in Leeds. Her husband, David, quickly put it up on the website so that we could all marvel at the outcome. Then she and David sent us an email to let us know that what they called "The Conclusion of the Story" was there for us to read.

Of course, even before I received their email, Penny Bent, tireless Internet investigator, had again phoned me at about 11:00 p.m. in Wellington, New Zealand, 9:00 p.m. in Canberra, Australia, to say, "Quick, go to the Slaidburn site, the trial outcome is there! Hurry!"

She had caught the Higham's posting of the trial result on the site before the electrons were even dry.

"Give me a hint," I said, never one for suspense. "Was our step great-grandmother hanged for murder?"

Penny has had a lot of experience raising children, including me, so she told me to look for myself.

"Give me a hint," I whined. "Will I be happy or sad?"

"You will be amazed," she replied.

MR. JUSTICE WILLS PRESIDING

And, of course, I was.

I phoned her right back. And there we were, again in the middle of the Antipodean night, although not so cold as previously because it was spring then, marvelling about events in 1885 and the impact those events eventually came to have on our own lives.

ASSIZE TRIAL REPORT
Preston Guardian, Wednesday, August 5, 1885

THE ALLEGED CHILD MURDER AT SLAIDBURN

At Leeds Assizes, on Monday, before Mr. Justice Wills, Grace Isherwood (28) married, and Isabella Gardner (18) single, servant, was indicted for the wilful murder of Thos. Gardner, on May 16th. Mr. L. Gane, Q.C., and Mr. Manisty, appeared to prosecute, and Mr. E.T. Atkinson defended.

Mr. Gane pointed out that the prisoners were sisters, whose home was at Dalton-in-Furness. Last September, Grace Isherwood went as housekeeper for a Mr. Isherwood, farmer, near Slaidburn, taking with her an illegitimate child. In January Mr. Isherwood married her. On May 5th, Isabella Gardner went to see Mrs. Isherwood, her sister, taking with her a boy some two years and five months old, stating that she had been nursing the child and that it belonged to one Elizabeth Dackray. On May 17th that child was found dead. In the evening of that day Jno. Barge and his wife were passing under a bridge which crossed Easington Beck, and as they did so they saw a child lying in a pool which was about 18 inches deep in the middle. Seeing that the child was dead, Barge left it and went for the police, and subsequently it was removed. When found, its head was about half way under the kerbstone of the pavement. The charge against the prisoners was that they

Meanley Farm (today).

had drowned the child, which the prosecutor alleged was the elder illegitimate child of Grace Isherwood, and which had been taken away by her sister on the previous Saturday. Before he married the elder prisoner, Mr. Isherwood was a widower, having one daughter, nine years of age. On the day in question, Grace Isherwood and Isabella Gardner in company with the two children went to Clitheroe in a neighbour's trap, arriving between 12 and one o'clock. They went to the workhouse there and saw the matron, Mrs. Lofthouse, to whom Mrs. Isherwood represented herself as a widow with two children, the elder of whom she wished to leave in the workhouse, being unable to support it. Having no order she was told that the child could not be left there. The two women then returned to the trap, and started for home with the children. They reached home about six o'clock, Isabella remaining outside the house with apparently the elder child wrapped up in a shawl. The mother entered, but Isabella moved off with the child toward Slaidburn; and Grace Isherwood shortly afterward followed her. About seven o'clock in the evening two women were seen to go on the bridge, beneath which the dead body of the child was found. The two women, however, could not be positively identified. About a quarter to eleven the same night, Mr. Isherwood was seen with two women going in the direction of his home. A Mrs. Tomlinson; about seven o'clock saw Isabella on that road, but she could not say whether she had any child with her. They did not speak, but the next morning — Sunday — Isabella told Mrs. Tomlinson that she had been taking a child to its mother. When the child was found dead a policeman went to Isherwood's house and asked Grace if she had a little boy. The other prisoner then said that the child they had had with them belonged to Elizabeth Dockray. Enquiries proved that although there were two women named Dockray who lived near, neither answered the description given. One had no child, and the other was in the Workhouse. When the child was alive it had on several articles of clothing; when found it had on two, and the remainder were found in the house of Grace Isherwood. They were given by her to the constable. This, and the fact of the non-existence of the woman described as Elizabeth Dockray, were two of the most important facts upon which the prosecution relied.

Evidence bearing out the above details was given. The court rose at half past five, at which time the case for the prosecution was not concluded.

The case for the prosecution was continued yesterday morning.

Dr. Alexander Gray, Dalton-in-Furness, deposed that he attended the elder prisoner in her confinement at her father's house on 15 Dec. 1882. She was then delivered of a male child. When attending the prisoner's mother in April this year he saw a little boy apparently just over two years of age at the house.

Agnes Creary, wife of John Creary, Lower Brook-street, Ulverston, stated that at Whitsuntide, 1883, the elder prisoner, then Grace Gardner, visited her at Ulverston, having with her a baby a few months old. She said the child's name was James Thomas Gardner, and that its father was a man named Dockray, living at Dalton. As she (Grace) was going to a situation she wished to place the child out to nurse, and witness undertook the care of it for 4s.6d. a week. She kept the child for 27 weeks. In consequence of not receiving her money regularly she returned the child to Grace's father's house.

Mrs. Coward, Dalton-in-Furness, gave evidence as to nursing a child named Thomas from the Gardners' house in November 1883, and kept it till June, 1884.

Mrs. Jane Gordon stated that she, in the course of last summer nursed the child known as Thomas Gardner. He was the same child whose body she saw at the Black Bull, Slaidburn, at the inquest. At that time some of the clothes which had been produced were worn by the child.

Further evidence was given respecting letters received by Mrs. Creary, which were afterward read by his Lordship. The writer, who was then in service at Crosshills, chiefly concerned herself in the letters about the welfare of the child, and the struggle she had to pay the money necessary for his maintenance. There were also several letters to Mrs. Gordon from Meanley, one or two of them after Grace

Gardner was married, and these also referred to the child and the payment for its nursing.

Elizabeth Dockray, aged 15, living at Dalton, said she saw Isabella on one occasion this year and she then told her she was going to see her sister and would take her sister's child Thomas. Did not know any other Elizabeth Dockray at Dalton.

Dorothy Dockray, an inmate of the Ulverston Workhouse, said she had a child — the only one she had had — which was in the Workhouse with her. Grace Gardner did on one occasion ask her to nurse the child Thomas Gardner, but she declined. Grace had told her that the father of the child was Wm. Dockray, a miner.

Evidence was called to disprove the statement as to Grace Gardner and Elizabeth Dockray having lived at Silecroft in service, and Thomas Thornton, landlord of the Black Bull Inn, Slaidburn, stated that on Saturday night, May 16th, neither Stables nor a woman calling herself Elizabeth Dockray was at his house.

Mr. H. A. Bridgeman, surgeon, Slaidburn, who made the post mortem examination, attributed death to asphyxia by drowning.

Mr. Thomas Scattergood, surgeon, Leeds, and lecturer on forensic medicine in the medical department of the Yorkshire College, said the evidence was consistent with death by suffocation by covering the mouth, but the probabilities were in favour of death by drowning.

Isabella here read a written statement to the jury, in which she said that John Isherwood had been very kind to her sister. He suspected that the child was hers, but she denied it to him, and said it was Elizabeth Dockray's. She being afraid that he would find it out, they arranged to get it into the Workhouse at Clitheroe, and, failing that, they agreed to take it home, her sister saying that she would tell John all about it. They accordingly wrapped it in the rugs, and it was quiet all the way home. She (Isabella) lifted it out of the cart and placed it on its feet, but it fell to the ground as though it were dead. They dared not take it into the house, being afraid that the husband would think they had done something at it. They agreed that she (Isabella) should take the child in the direction of Slaidburn, Grace following as soon as she could. She went and turned back again, then met her sister, and went with her along the Easington-road to Langcliffe Cross Bridge. There they decided to put the child into the water, Grace remarking that they must take the coat off. They did so, and Grace handed her the dead little boy. She decided to put the body where it would soon be seen, and carried it to the river. Neither of them did anything to it.

Mr. Gane, there being no witnesses for the defence, then addressed the jury, whose attention he called to the improbability of the suggestion that the child was suffocated in the rugs. Considering the size of the child, its healthy condition and the nature of the journey from Clitheroe, could it be believed that the child could meet its death in this way without the attention of the women being called to it?

Mr. Tindal Atkinson said the defence was, and had been throughout, that the child was dead when it was put into the water, and did not meet its death by drowning. He pictured the painful position in which the mother of the child was placed as the wife of a respectable man, who was unacquainted with the fact that she had more than one illegitimate child, and who, with the knowledge that there was another child, would possibly become estranged from her; and went on to argue upon the improbabilities which in his opinion were noticeable in the case for the prosecution. He pointed out that on the way from Clitheroe to Slaidburn there was every opportunity of disposing of the child had the women entertained this murderous design, and was simply inconceivable that having this idea, the child should have been brought all the way to the farm and then taken to a spot where any act of theirs was open to the view of anyone passing the bridge. He showed how the medical evidence came to no definite conclusion on the question of death by drowning, and urged the fact of undigested food, which had been partaken of at Clitheroe, being found in the stomach, as conclusive evidence that death must have taken place before the body was placed in the Easington brook.

His Lordship summed up to the jury in a most exhaustive manner, his address lasting considerably over an hour, and embracing all the facts of the case.

The jury retired to consider their verdict at five minutes to six o'clock, and were absent three-quarters of an hour. They then returned into court with a verdict of acquittal in the case of both the accused. The result was applauded in a crowded court.

THE RESULT WAS APPLAUDED IN A CROWDED COURT

When the jury retired, it was nearly 6:00 p.m.

Back in their cell, Isabella was a bundle of nerves; every part of her anatomy was in some form of motion. Her seated body shook from the hips, radiating down to her feet and up to her head, and she flailed both hands at the wrists as if to shake the tension from her body out through her hands. For once she didn't say much, just sat there, periodically shutting her eyes.

Grace was the same small, pale bundle of a person she had been throughout, eyes wide and terrified. John, still in the courtroom, was frightened too, but he felt it his responsibility to seem confident. He had put his faith and his fortune in the hands of Mr. Atkinson, and he would soon know if that faith had been misplaced.

For those still in the courtroom the waiting seemed interminable, punctuated as it was by moans emanating from Mrs. Gardner. No one blamed her, but the noise only added to the atmosphere of tension.

Mr. Atkinson had hurried from the courtroom and over to his chambers in Park Square, leaving Mr. Morley to monitor proceedings. As he walked briskly down the street, his thoughts on the outcome of the case veered from positive to anxious. He had become quite sympathetic to the plight of his clients, and certainly did not want them to hang for their crime. He had a suspicion that the judge had similar feelings, although he knew he was unlikely to be able ever to confirm that suspicion.

As the twelve jurors, city dwellers all, filed back into the courtroom, they worked at making their faces unreadable. They had been instructed that the audience in the court would be scanning them for clues of their verdict, and that they must leave that information to the foreman to read out.

A verdict of "not guilty" was delivered, first for Grace, then, to a hushed and crowded court, for Isabella. A collective sigh of relief was heard, followed by an instinct to celebrate, which the judge quickly curbed. The plight of Grace and Isabella — Grace's obvious delicacy and Isabella's girlish feistiness — had clearly aroused the protective instincts of those present.

On hearing the verdict, Grace and Isabella, both stunned, sank into their seats in the dock. Isabella had picked up her crumpled statement and was spindling it in her hands. A little dazed, she then looked about for the young lawyer to whom she believed she owed her life.

Grace focused on Justice Wills, her eyes filled with abject gratitude. She did not fully understand it all, but she felt certain that his lengthy and detailed summation of the case had moved things in their favour.

Grace didn't shift her gaze from the judge until she was jolted into movement by the clerk of the court intoning "All rise," and the judge left for his chambers. Only then did she turn to look for John.

Summoned by messenger, Edward Tindal Atkinson had hurried back from his chambers, managing to look poised and relaxed as the jury had filed into the court. He had been acutely aware that the outcome of the case was delicately balanced. He accepted the ensuing grateful tears and handshakes from the Isherwoods and the Gardners graciously.

"A fortunate outcome," he murmured softly to Charles as they gathered up their papers and left the court.

THE YOUNGEST WITNESS

Three times she'd had to stand up in front of old men with serious faces and tell them what had happened that evening. Three times her father and the men who asked the questions had assured her that all she had to do was tell the truth, tell what happened as accurately as she could remember.

She told what she had seen. Mother and Aunt Isabella had been away to Clitheroe all day and, when they got back, things were hurried and confused. She had run out into the yard when she heard the trap drive up, eager for her tea, but the women had barely noticed her there.

Aunt was already out of the trap and holding a bundle wrapped in a shawl. She said something in a low voice to mother, then she went off down the meadow. Mother came into the house, handed baby James to her with barely a word of greeting, and then went off out again herself.

James was in a sorry state, wet and cold, and she had to tend to him right away. Before she could even change his nappy, he started crying. The others were hungry. They'd had nothing to eat since midday, so she fixed them all a piece of bread and cheese while Dick dandled the dry and happy James on his knee.

The trap was just sitting there in the yard, the horse still in the traces and the groceries ignored in the footwell, when her da came in from milking. She could tell he was shocked at the state of things, but he said nothing, just carried in the groceries, asked Matthew to return the trap, and went off over the fields himself.

It was late when the adults all got back. She'd had to put the boys to bed all by herself. Matt had been no help at all. He claimed he was tired from taking the trap back and then stabling the horse. From below, she could hear Aunt Isabella talking fast and loud, loud enough to wake the children, and she could hear da speaking slow and soft. She couldn't hear mother saying anything at all.

After the policeman took mother and aunt away, she'd had to tell her story first at the Black Bull and then over in Bolton-by-Bowland. She had always wanted to visit Bolton-by-Bowland, where her friend Hattie was born, but the trip had been no fun. It was all driving and sitting around and waiting and da was very stern. She saw mother and Isabella in the room at the courthouse in Bolton. They kept shutting their eyes like they weren't listening, but when the man asked mother if what Maggie had said was true, she had answered "Yes."

After the journey to Bolton-by-Bowland, mother still didn't come back to the farm. Da seemed to be so upset and busy and he hardly ever joined the family for tea anymore. He was always off somewhere.

It seemed a bit like the time after ma had died. No one paid her and the boys much notice and they were able to run a bit wild. Grandma Gardner called them a bunch of little hooligans, but she was smiling when she said it. Aunt Margaret let them come to her house for tea whenever they wanted, as long as they promised to tell grandma where they were.

The kids who lived at Town End had a new game. They wrapped a straw doll in an old bit of rag and ran about shouting, "Hide it, quick." Then one of them would play the farmer and go looking for the wrapped up dolly. Maggie and the boys never got asked to play with them and Aunt Mary told them: "You take no notice of those ragamuffins. They don't know what they are playing at."

Maggie had been looking forward to the trip to Leeds. She and Grandma Gardner went on the train all by themselves while the boys had to go over to Aunt Margaret's to stay. Da was waiting for her and Grandma G. at the station, and he had found them lodgings in a public house. It was such an adventure that even the long faces of the adults couldn't dampen her excitement.

Sleeping at the pub wasn't at all the treat she had expected. There was a lot of noise from downstairs and she had to share the bed with Grandma Gardner. Grandma was soft and warm, but she snored so loud it shook the windows. Poor grandpa!

Grandma dressed her up for court. She even braided Maggie's hair, although grandma didn't quite pull the hair tight enough to make it tidy. At the courthouse, the bench she was left waiting on was hard wood and her feet wouldn't touch the floor, but it wasn't long before someone came and took her into the big room where she was asked to tell her story all over again.

She hadn't seen mother and aunt for a long time and they both looked quite ill to her. Still, she smiled bravely at them. Her muslin dress with the little blue sprigs had been made by mother for her to wear on May Day, and she thought it suited her well. She tried not to think about how small she felt alone on the chair in that big formal room with everyone watching her.

When she had finished telling about the clothes that Thomas Dockray was wearing when she saw him last, she got to go and sit on the bench between da and grandma. At the lunch break, da wanted her to go back to their lodgings, but there was nothing to do there and grandma said she did not want to miss any of the trial by journeying back and forth. Maggie promised to be very quiet so that no one would notice her and da just sighed and patted her on the head.

Da had told her before they left Slaidburn that what was happening was called a trial and that the people like herself who were asked questions were called witnesses. There sure were a lot of them. She gave a little wave to Mrs. Wilson when it was her turn to speak at the front, but Mrs. Wilson did not wave back. Luckily, no one noticed.

Late in the day, grandma took her back to the public house where they had a boiled dinner and went right to bed. More snoring!

The next day at midmorning they went over to the courthouse again, where lots of old ladies talked about caring for little Thomas and about mother sending lots of letters and some money, although it seemed that what she sent was never enough. At times grandma would quietly say, "Oh dear, oh dear," and one time the judge in his big white wig stopped talking and stared right down at her. That was scary, and afterward grandma was much quieter.

Lunch was a meat pie on the street, and it was after they had all settled in the courtroom again that she noticed Aunt Isabella had stood up to talk.

Aunt spoke very quietly so that even the judge had to lean forward to hear her, but her voice was clear. She told everyone that da had been so good to her sister that Grace didn't want to tell him about Thomas. That was hard to understand. Da was good with children: he often carried James in his arms to church and he surely had been upset to learn that Thomas Dockray had died.

After aunt had said her piece and sat back down, there was a lot of talk about whether Thomas had drowned or suffocated. She really couldn't understand why that mattered now. They had buried him even before summer had started.

Then they had to sit around waiting in the courtroom while the men called the jury went away, probably to get their tea. She sure wished that she could have some tea instead of sitting in the big hot courtroom.

When the jury came back, everyone looked at them, probably wondering why they got to go specially and have something to eat. Then the red-nosed man with the big ears who sat at the end of the row stood up and told the judge that they had found the prisoners "not guilty," and da and grandma jumped up and shouted, "Hooray."

The judge said "Order in the court" in a big loud voice, and then he looked over at mother and Aunt Isabella and told them that they were free to go.

Mother and aunt just stood perfectly still and then slowly lowered their bodies into their chairs as if mesmerized. They stood up again suddenly when the clerk sitting below the judge's bench called, "All rise!" and the judge swiftly left the room.

Grandma was all blown up with emotion, but she took a moment to explain that she and da had cheered because now mother and aunt could finally come home. Now her da was crying and he had gone over to put his arms around stepmother. Aunt Isabella, looking lost, walked over to them and laid her head on her mother's soft bosom.

For her part, Maggie wasn't sure if this turn of events made her feel happy or not. She needed to think.

COMING HOME

Suddenly they were free. After more than two months in gaol, constantly supervised and directed, the sisters were quite at a loss as to what to do.

The clerk of the court, sensing their bewilderment, reassured them that they were free to go. Mrs. Gardner offered to go and collect their meagre belongings from the prison, and John took Grace and Isabella over to lodgings where they could have a cup of tea, some fish and chips, and a bed for the night. A subdued Maggie followed quietly along.

Now they were no longer prisoners, getting back to Meanley Farm was no longer H.M.Q.'s responsibility but their own task to negotiate. Immediately after eating, the relieved John hurried off to buy tickets for their return on Wednesday's train to Clitheroe. He also sent a telegraph to his brother-in-law, Tom Rushton, asking him to meet them at the station.

Sadly, the news that the former prisoners were due home on the train from Leeds spread quickly and the general sentiment locally was that by their action the sisters had given the area a bad name.

As the train neared Clitheroe, both Grace and Isabella became almost feverishly excited. They were approaching their homecoming with relief and a fervent wish to disappear back into anonymous everyday life.

THE ALLEGED MURDER AT SLAIDBURN Grace Isherwood and Isabella Gardiner, the two sisters who were charged at the Leeds Assizes, last Monday and Tuesday, with the murder of a child at Slaidburn, and acquitted, arrived at Clitheroe on Wednesday night. As the women left the station they were hooted by the crowd.

— *Preston Guardian*, Saturday, August 8, 1885
(As posted on the Slaidburn website by D. Higham)

After the warm applause for the verdict in the courtroom, the hoots and jeers from the crowd at the station in Clitheroe came as a horrible shock to John and his companions. It was their first painful exposure to the fact that while a jury in Leeds may have found the two women not guilty, a local "jury" of their peers nearer to home remained unconvinced.

Both Grace and Isabella hid their faces, doing their best not to weep. Isabella started to cough and Grace distracted herself by making efforts to comfort her.

John looked about at the angry faces and felt a dreadful surge of hopelessness; he had lost his savings, and now his standing in the community too. What was going to happen to his wife and children?

It was such a great relief to see Rushton emerge from the crowd with the trap that the irony of their return to Slaidburn in the same conveyance that had carried little Thomas Gardner on his last journey was entirely lost on all present.

NOT GUILTY IN THE EYES OF THE LAW

Having read those shocking midnight revelations from the Slaidburn website and the note from David and Cathryn explaining exactly how they had found the trial report, I felt a little stunned.

As I wrote to the Highams after reading the report of the trial and its aftermath:

> *Subject: An Unexpected Outcome*
> *Dear David*
> *What a surprising outcome. I thought the two women were for the gallows for sure. I guess that is what the jury feared and that they felt that death was too extreme a punishment for young women who did not know where to turn....*
>
> *I wonder if the fact that Grace was pregnant played a role.*
>
> *So the story is the indictment of the Poor Laws that you thought it was, but in a different way. And the vague story of suffocation was not so far from the alibi after all.*

Thank you so much for the pictures. I imagined something much less picturesque.

Thank you for your part in this amazing story.

David's thoughtful response was a clear reflection that the story was not yet satisfactorily "finished" for any of us twenty-first-century sleuths.

Subject: Re: An Unexpected Outcome

Dear Sheelagh

Thanks for your email.

... Today we put a copy of the story with the original cuttings in Clitheroe Library. Sue Holden the librarian who drew our attention to the story in the first place was also surprised at the outcome....

Our thoughts on the case — we too thought they were "bang to rights." What struck us was the initial "vehemence" of the Coroner's summing up, perhaps with benefit of local knowledge. What seems bizarre is that the Easington Beck flows 300 yards from Meanley Farm at the bottom of the meadow in front of the house. There is a stream flowing into the Easington Beck in a ravine no more than 100 yards to the left of Meanley Farm and one wonders why they took the body of the child the best part of two miles up to Langcliffe Cross to dispose of it. They could have said that the child had wandered off and fallen into the Beck near the house — what a tragic accident — no questions asked.

It seems such convenient timing that the child suffocated on the way back from being rejected at the Workhouse.

Still people do very odd things when they panic. (Around 5 years ago an Asian man in

Clitheroe murdered his wife, dismembered her body and drove round to several local beauty spots, including the roadside of the main Clitheroe to Slaidburn road, set fire to the body parts in the midst of a summer drought, and thought that they would not be noticed !!! The grass fires were seen for miles around.)

At the Assizes trial there would not be the local knowledge element and I totally agree with your comments. The position where the child was found seems to vary with each trial report and if the policeman's statement is that the body was 28 yards down stream of the bridge the body would not have been seen from the road and it is only the fact that the farmer John Bargh was walking up the stream that he would have noticed it. To say that she said that she had put it there to be found quickly seems unlikely.????

We think that if they had been tried in Slaidburn that they would have both hanged.

However, on a lighter note — do you know if they moved away from Slaidburn or stayed at Meanley? We will have a look at the Slaidburn Church tombstone transcription record and the census if you don't have the details already and you are interested.

... Look forward to hearing from you.
David and Cathryn

Penny and I continued to marvel over the outcome of the trial. From her own experience as a trial lawyer, Penny informed me that what we had here was described in legal circles as a "perverse verdict." In situations of a perverse verdict, the judge or the jury or both make a finding that is inconsistent with what one would expect to be the most likely legal interpretation of the facts.

One of the most famous cases of perverse verdict in Canada was the Montreal trial of Dr. Henry Morgentaler, an alleged abortionist. While it seemed clear on the facts of the case that he was providing safe but illegal medical abortions to women in that city, the jury found him "not guilty." If, in the Morgentaler case, the jury was indirectly reflecting social change, what mood was the jury reflecting in the case of the murder of Thomas Gardner? Was it sympathy for the defendants, or a tacit recognition of the injustice of women and children "alone" having to pay the price, either in disgrace or in hardship, for the burden of illegitimacy?

ANOTHER TIME, ANOTHER PLACE

We took some time to digest what we had learned from the press clippings and the Higham research about the suspected child murder.

Christmas came and went, with visits from what the Australians call "rellies" and a wonderful trip to the seaside. On Christmas Eve, I was disconcerted to learn that the strong smell of smoke I thought was from neighbouring barbeques was actually wafting down from a bush fire on Red Hill at the top of our street, but I was beginning to learn that Australians generally take extremes of fire and drought in their stride.

Meanwhile, the new year brought with it a new angle on the story from David:

> *Subject: A recent article in the Times*
> *Dear Penny, Sheelagh and Elaine*
> *I was reading an article in the Times newspaper the other day. The headline "Victorian values let murderers go unpunished" caught my eye and reading it set me thinking. . . .*

Whilst of limited relevance to our researches, it does suggest to me that what might have been a "big deal" of a crime in a rural area would seem very much less important in a Victorian city such as Leeds where, if like Liverpool and Manchester, infanticide was a common and ignored occurrence. Perhaps this is part of the reason for what Penny described as a "perverse verdict."

One other passage in Dr. Archer's article also struck me as interesting: "Of all the Lancastrian murderers during the period, Fish was the only one who failed to generate any support for a petition of reprieve." Young women would have been viewed far more sympathetically by a jury as we have discussed in previous emails, even if they had been convicted it seems unlikely that they would have been hanged.

Hope this is of interest, all the best for the New Year....
David and Cathryn

The Times article made compelling reading. Of particular interest were the comments:

In Manchester only one person was arrested for infanticide between 1847 and 1859, and in Liverpool a very high number of "accidental suffocations" were recorded....

Dr Archer said that his work uncovered a world where guns were rife, wife-beating was unremarkable, the murder of infants regarded as a form of family planning and beat constables were routinely violent.

— *Times*, Dec 29, 2001

My own thoughts about the case had been put temporarily aside. Penny was moving back to Canada, to the immense joy of her extended family, who both love her dearly and rely heavily on her goodness of heart, and I was caught up in a very demanding business negotiation.

The outcome of the murder trial, while raising more questions than it answered, was known, and I had no spare brain-time to muse about the impact of those long-ago events on my great-grandfather, or even on his daughter, Maggie, my grandmother.

And I had not yet even begun to think about how those events had reached down the years to shape my own circumstance.

ISABELLA'S DILEMMA

Descending from the train in Clitheroe to a noisy, angry chorus of disapproval, Isabella, thin and blanched from incarceration and illness, realized that she was an outcast.

When the verdict of "Not guilty" was cheered in the court in Leeds, it had felt as if she and Grace would be free to resume their lives just where they had left off. But since that time, Isabella had slowly come to realize that there were still plenty of people who thought of her and Grace as murderers.

Much of the jubilation in court had, of course, come from family members and, she now realized sadly, from the sympathetic response generated by Grace's beauty and ill health. Outside of the family, even amongst their close acquaintances, none had come forward since to welcome them home or to wish them well.

During the trial, she had seen the judge looking at her carefully. She guessed he was wondering if she had it in her to do such an evil deed. He knew for sure that she was a liar, but were those serious eyes able to look into her soul and see if she was a murderer as well?

From the judge's thorough summation, it became clear that he had decided there was more than enough reason to doubt. Still, that didn't make her and Grace "innocent," just "not guilty."

John had been very kind to her through those endless days in gaol, probably because of her sister, but he was beggared now, and he had to worry first and last about Grace and the children and how they would all survive.

Waiting for the trial, Isabella had tried to keep Grace's spirits up — telling her that she'd soon be mistress at Meanley again. But that had been just to keep Grace from thinking about the gallows.

Left to herself at that terrible time, Grace would just stare into space, tears streaming down her cheeks, whispering, "We're done for." All her charm and winsome ways were wasting away in the lock-up.

There were moments when Isabella had even thought that if Grace didn't stop weeping she'd smother her ... but that was just her nerves talking.

The damp in the prison had begun to weaken Isabella's resistance. She felt chill all the time these days, even though it was still summer, and her cough had grown even worse.

She was free, but not needed here and with no prospects. Mum had said she could come home for a bit to Dalton-in-Furness, but she knew that she would have to find a job. The Ulverston workhouse, especially with all its tragic connections, would be no place for her.

So what would befall her now? An eighteen-year-old who'd been on trial for murder! Certainly a man like that young lawyer who worked for Mr. Atkinson wouldn't even have her as a servant, much less a lover. Working with the young barrister on her statement had given Isabella a chance to spend a considerable time with a different, more honourable, kind of man than those she'd known in Dalton-in-Furness — the men who'd got both of her sisters with child and then left them to fend for themselves. Those men were working men, miners mostly, who didn't have much to say to a woman and didn't have any use for her if she got pregnant.

Even when she was in service, Isabella had had no real contact with any men except for her cousin George and the field labourers. George had tried to get her to give him a tumble, but she was smarter than that, and the hired men thinking that she had "airs," with her independent ways, had not bothered her.

What man would want to marry her now and see her be the mother of his child?

Choking back her sobs, she began to cough so hard that it felt as if it would never stop.

THE COMPARATIVE COMFORT OF HOME

Alone at last in the privacy of what had once been Jane's marriage bed, John and Grace lay exhausted and silent, both lost in thoughts of how many months it had been since they had been able just to lie quietly together.

Grace had long been too overwhelmed by her fearful circumstance to think about how John might feel when she was back at home with him and the children. Now, as she started cautiously to think about their life going forward, she realized that she was afraid that the bond between them had been deformed by lies and confusion and that she was destined for a marriage that was no longer a joyous choice, but a different kind of life sentence.

John, secure in his own affection for Grace, was worrying about problems that were more practical and material. He was beginning to realize that the "not guilty" verdict was unacceptable to the morals of their community, and that many of his lifelong friends would no longer be comfortable sharing a pint with him at Hark to Bounty. His sister had tried to warn him that the women of the town had turned against Grace — an outsider who proved herself to be a liar and who had never been any better than she had to be, and attractive to boot. They feared her example and her possible influence on their men.

Some of his sister's warnings made him smile slightly. *Grace is an attractive woman, for all that,* he thought ruefully.

The sheer weight of the debts he had incurred made him frightened. While the case was proceeding, he had cared only about securing a positive outcome. Now he had to pay for all the legal work that had been done. Mr. Atkinson had been sympathetic, but it was going to take a long time to pay off all the legal bills, especially since local demand for his skills as a stonemason had dropped off since the trial. Matt and Maggie were going to have to earn their keep, and the others too, as soon as they were able.

John didn't like to bother the squire again, but it looked like he must. He needed some advice about how to repay his debt, and with the squire being of a legal family, he might have some insight into the feelings that flowed from a case like this, and how long it took to forgive and forget.

Although she had suffered a stillbirth and had scarcely eaten for months, John was convinced that Grace was made of sterner stuff than one would think at present, and he believed that she would be willing to have a go at rebuilding their life together. Despite all, he knew that he was. He also knew that he would have to make the first move.

"Good to have you home, Grace," he said as he blew out the candle.

"Good to be here," she said very quietly.

THERE'S A STORY HERE

Books have been my life. Work was just something I did to fill the spaces between pages. I feel anxious if I am away from home without a book at hand. I confess to retreating once in a while to read a few pages in the sanctity of the women's room during the most tedious of business meetings.

I have been an author in search of a story, and here at last I thought I might have found one. I really wanted to write about that long-ago child death in Slaidburn.

Having confided my goal both to my husband, William, and to Penny, they of course ganged up to make me get started. Like the lawyer she is, Penny recommended that I get a three-ring binder for my research findings, which I did. William just used his tried and true technique of implacable expectation and perpetual willingness to help until I broke under the pressure.

In addition to the binder, I needed to be back in touch with the Highams. The exciting possibility of a visit to Slaidburn to get the "feel" of the locality also began to emerge.

So, almost nine months after David's note about Victorian murderers, I wrote again from Australia.

Subject: At Work on the Slaidburn Murder Novel
Dear David and Cathryn
Inspired by the investigation done by the two of
you, I am trying to make progress on a story about
the murder and our communication about it....

 I am hoping to go to Slaidburn in November to
do some more research and I would be delighted to
meet you both.

 I don't know how busy you are pursuing other
interests, but if you are interested there are pieces
of research that would help me greatly. What I am
trying to do right now is to imagine what would
lead a woman like Grace Isherwood to do such
a thing, how it was that she returned to my great
grandfather and lived a life with him and raised his
kids, and possibly theirs, how my great grandfather
lost his farm and became a stone mason, and how
my grandmother felt being raised by a woman who
had "accidentally" smothered one of her children.

 I am finding the imagining challenging, but
interesting, and I have written some pages of the
proposed book.

 Please drop me a line and tell me how you are
and what you think.

David responded quickly.

Subject: Re: At Work on the Slaidburn Murder
Novel
Dear Sheelagh
... Since last speaking to you we have been to the site
of the "alleged murder" and have taken more photos
from in the field. We found that a ford under the
bridge has paving which continues down stream for

some 30 yards until it is edged with large blocks where the stream then drops about 10 feet into a pool. Most peculiar and suggested to us the possibility of a late or post mediaeval mill site. A difficult place to get to. The body was definitely not intended to be found....

Please let us know if you do intend to come over in November. We'd love to meet you and can probably arrange permissions to visit the relevant locations.... If you need a guide just ask.

Grace Isherwood's reasons for her actions seem to me bound up in the shame and stigma of illegitimacy prevailing at that time. Her good fortune in finding a good man to marry her might in her eyes have been threatened by the revelation of a child by a previous relationship. Indeed, the court case seems to revolve far more on the origins of the child than the evidence regarding the circumstances of the day in question. The farming community in this area still frowns on children born out of wedlock....

As for your great grandfather losing his farm ... perhaps legal fees? An agricultural depression? (There was a large migration from the Slaidburn area from the 1870s onward, particularly to the Liverpool area where many farmers became urban cow keepers and dairy men.)

As for my opinion, personally I think the difficulty in facing his neighbours in such a closed community where he would meet them at the Cattle Auction, agricultural merchants, pub, etc. or in the communal work that was a requisite of farming in those days would have led to him feeling "frozen out." His relationship with Grace would have become one of shared adversity which perhaps brought a sense of "us against the world."

... The other thing is I think he genuinely loved her ... and understood the pressure she must have felt in thinking she might lose her husband over an illegitimate child. Once things were in the open I think he must have trusted her with his children.

We are both well. I did a large web site for the Ulster Place-name Society during the summer (170+ photos) and then went and bought a "Boyne Curragh" (Irish coracle made of hazel branches with a woven willow gunwale, covered in a cow hide). I've been learning to paddle it on the River Hodder recently.

Sorry for my ramblings, but do keep us informed of how things are going. We are really interested.

Best wishes David (& Cathryn) Higham

Our plans began to develop apace. William and I needed to make a journey to Toronto in November, and if you hold a globe in a peculiar enough way you can find a justification for routing yourself from Canberra, through England and on to Canada.

Subject: Going to Slaidburn

Dear David

William and I would be delighted to have such a knowledgeable guide for our visit in November.

Could you help me out with a couple of locations? Where is Mill Brook, Bowland Forest, Lower Division, and do you know where Chapel Croft, Parish of Slaidburn, is? Also, do you know where Ash Knott is?

Finally, in any of the graveyards around is there a Jane Isherwood, died approx. 1884, or a John Green Isherwood, died near 1900 I guess, or a Grace Isherwood, died maybe in the early

1900s? They seem to have been members of the parish church of Slaidburn.

I loved the picture of you in your Boyne Curragh. Yours S

Subject: From Slaidburn
Dear Sheelagh
Just checked out the Ordnance Survey map. Mill Brook is approximately 5 miles from Slaidburn near Browsholme Hall. Chapel Croft is about 300 yards from Meanley Farm where Grace lived! There is a farm in the Slaidburn Parish called Ashnott or Ashknott (associated with lead mining from at least the early medieval period) about a mile from Meanley.

Also checked the Slaidburn Graveyard Headstone transcription re Isherwoods. There are a couple, but not the ones you seek.

If you could, tell us where you plan to visit, especially if it is a specific farm like Chapel Croft. We are happy to ask in advance of your visit for permission for you to have a look around, especially where there is no public access via a footpath.

Locals have been very generous when asked in advance. It seems a far better way than turning up unannounced. Since you are coming in November the likelihood in Slaidburn will be that it will be wet and cold, so pack your willies [sic] or buy a cheap pair whilst you are here, and a good coat.

May we ask your connection to Mill Brook?

How is the book going?

Look forward to meeting you.
Regards David and Cathryn

PS Here is a Slaidburn joke
Judgement Day
A curious fellow died one day and found himself in
limbo waiting in a long, long line for judgement. As
he stood there he noticed that some souls were allowed
to march right through the gates of heaven. Others
were led over to Satan, who threw them into a lake
of fire. Every so often, instead of hurling a poor soul
into the fire, Satan would toss him or her to one side.

After watching Satan do this several times, the
fellow's curiosity got the better of him. He strolled
over and tapped old Nick on the shoulder.

"Excuse me, there, Your Darkness," he said.
"I'm waiting in line for judgement, and I couldn't
help wondering why you are tossing some people
aside instead of flinging them into the fires of hell
with the others.?"

"Ah," Satan said with a grin. "Those are
folk from Slaidburn. I'm letting them dry out so
they'll burn."

David's note was my first indication that I was hopelessly
naïve in my notion that one could just drive up to a farm of
interest or traipse across a farmer's land to look at the brook.
Before then it had never occurred to me that one couldn't just
walk right up to a particular location like Chapel Croft and take
a look. City dweller!

As I came to learn, the country sense of one's property, and
who should be near or on it, is very important in the Slaidburn
area, and the notion is one of long-standing.

Reflecting on that information, I realized that back in 1885,
farmer Bargh's concern about what Grace and Isabella were
doing on his property on a spring evening probably played a key
role in the quick discovery of the body of poor little Thomas.

Chapel Croft Farm.

Having grasped the literal importance of respect for other people's property, I was very appreciative of David and Cathryn's efforts to make sure that we had permission in advance to tramp about on farmer's land and to walk up to their houses.

We had a little confusion over the kind of clothing William and I would need in the North. David sent a note telling us to bring our "willies" which I innocently interpreted as "woollies." When I wrote to him that we would certainly bring warm clothes, and arriving from Australia, could be counted on for woollies, he replied: "As for needing woollies ... I meant to put wellies (Wellington boots) and ended up typing 'willies' ... Freudian slip?"

A STRANGE COINCIDENCE

The social history of Victorian times seems to be enjoying a certain vogue right now, probably driven by all the Pennys and Sheelaghs out there on the 'net looking for their forebears. The long reign of Victoria, and the long reign of the present Elizabeth, have led to interesting comparisons about culture and government.

Both David in England and William in Australia came across newspaper articles about the latest theory concerning Jack the Ripper, the fascinating, unsolved, grisly Victorian serial-murder mystery that bears frequent reinvestigation. And David's proximity to the scene of our Victorian "crime" turned up an article about workhouses that was almost ridiculously close to home.

> *Subject: Re Slaidburn*
> *Dear Sheelagh*
> *… Another strange coincidence … Yesterday I was reading our local paper* The Clitheroe Advertiser & Times *and noticed an article about*

a new book about Clitheroe Workhouses. The author, Mr. Frank Lofthouse, is the great great grandson of Mr. and Mrs Young Lofthouse who were the first keeper and matron of the Clitheroe Workhouse (who refused entry to Thomas Dockrah because of the lack of a letter from the relieving officer).

… In the guestbook is an entry regarding the book which I reproduce here:

A colleague and friend of mine Mr. Frank Lofthouse has recently published a book entitled *Keepers of the House — A Workhouse Saga* which gives a detailed history of the Clitheroe Union Workhouse based upon board of guardian minutes and contemporary newspapers of the time. The Author Mr. Frank Lofthouse is the great-great-grandson of Mr. & Mrs Young Lofthouse who was [sic] the first keeper and matron of the Clitheroe Workhouse in a building which still stands and is currently occupied by Clitheroe Community Hospital. It was the family connection which first gave him the interest in the project and has finally published the book following five years of research and 120,000 words. It is a detailed fly-on-the-wall account of what it was like to be on the breadline in Clitheroe in the middle of the 19th Century. The book details how the decision by the Poor Law commissioners to group Lancaster and Yorkshire parishes to form the Clitheroe Union was a recipe for trouble. To begin with, the Yorkshire parishes deeply resented being governed from Clitheroe on the Lancashire side of the Ribble. At the time, paupers were considered to be an urban Lancashire problem and the Yorkshire districts saw no reason why they should be taxed to solve it. For more than 30 years after the Act, the Clitheroe Union defied the Government by refusing to build a new workhouse until the Government issued an ultimatum in 1869. Mr. Young Lofthouse and his wife had 11 children while they were in office at the workhouse. Two of the daughters became Assistant Matrons. Abandoned, orphaned or abused children entered the workhouse, only to be claimed by relatives when reaching a working age. Bear in mind that at this time the working age began at around 10 or 11 years of age. Trade in the cotton industry was in a constant state of flux and periodic strikes, fires and mill failures swelled the ever-increasing numbers of those seeking relief.... Order your personal signed copy of *Keepers of the House — A Workhouse Saga* by F.H. Lofthouse and published by Hudson History of Settle direct from the Author for the special price of ...

Best wishes David

Cathryn hurried to the Clitheroe library the next day to look up the Lofthouse book and quickly sent me a scan of an amazing photo from the book: Mr. Young Lofthouse and his wife Catherine Lofthouse — the very woman who refused to admit little Thomas into the Clitheroe workhouse on the day that he died.

The photo bears a remarkable resemblance to *American Gothic*, painted by Grant Wood in 1930. The Art Institute of Chicago's notes on the painting say: "Wood was accused of creating in this work a satire on the intolerance and rigidity that the insular nature of rural life can produce." In the 1880s, though, such a picture was not so much satire as it was a reflection of the state of the photographer's art and the rigid strictures of Victorian society.

The word *workhouse* is itself one to conjure with. The forbidding demeanour of the Lofthouses, although partly due to the requirement in those days to stay still for several seconds to be photographed, seems simply to underscore the sense of misery and dread the name evokes.

Some years earlier, Dickens had been horrified by the workhouses of Yorkshire. Through his fiction, he did what he could to try to bring their appalling circumstances to the attention of his reading public. If Dickens was horrified at the plight of a child like Oliver Twist, what might he have thought about poor little Thomas, whose first internment in a workhouse took place when he was not yet two years old?

DICKENS WOULD HAVE WEPT

The brief and tragic life of Thomas Gardner certainly had Dickensian undertones. The last of his hired minders, Mrs. Gordon, looked after little Thomas for roughly three months in the late summer of 1884. He was by then one-and-one-half years old. Having not received timely payment for his maintenance, she put the toddler, all alone, into the Ulverston workhouse.

Grace Gardner had written to Mrs. Gordon from Bolton-by-Bowland and then from Meanley, asking after Thomas and sending the odd bit of money. Given that she knew Grace's whereabouts, it is hard to imagine that Mrs. Gordon did not try to send word to Grace that she was putting the baby into the workhouse. At least his grandparents must have known.

As the matron of the Clitheroe Union Workhouse had made clear, admission was a process requiring the formal approval of a relieving officer. The master of the Ulverston workhouse would have had to assess Thomas's situation and to agree to his admission, so somebody must have had the opportunity to reflect for a while on putting Thomas into such a place.

Poor baby. In 1881 the UK census catalogued the 253 people who were inmates of the Ulverston workhouse at the time. Of the inmates, thirty were children five years of age or under, but only three appeared to be in the workhouse without other family members to watch out for them. Of the three, little Elena Livesey, a scholar aged two, did at least have her seven-year-old sister, Margaret, to look out for her. William Cross, two, and Charles McCann, four, seem to have been all by themselves in that harsh and desolate place. Just reading their names makes one want to weep.

In 1884, when Thomas was admitted, the situation would have been much the same. Who would have looked out for a child not yet toilet trained? Little children, even boys, wore petticoats, not breeches, to help deal with the problems of toilet, but there still must have been a lot of mess and bother. And who made sure they got food? One has to suppose that their fates rested entirely on the sympathies of others.

Maybe little Elena Livesey, six by then, or William Cross, who would also have been six, if they were still alive, tried to show young Thomas how to cope.

How did the baby eat and sleep, and keep from killing himself by falling downstairs or eating poison? Who got him up in the morning and put him to bed at night?

Workhouse food, consisting of gruel and boiled meat and vegetables, was probably well-suited to a child's digestion, but who would make sure he was served and able to feed himself?

In 1881 there were two women described as nurses and a matron at the Ulverston workhouse, but they would have had their hands full. In addition to the inmate children, there were a number of inmates described as imbeciles, as well as the deaf and the blind to look after. Men, women, and children were segregated, so perhaps one of the nurses looked after the children.

Toys were not allowed in workhouses until around 1900, so what did a little one like Thomas do to pass the time? Did anyone take the time to talk to him or to try to teach him anything? There

By kind permission of Peter Higginbotham.workhouses.org.uk.

Ulverston Workhouse Children's House.

was school for older children, so was a baby left even more alone while the older children attended classes? Was he left cooped up all day like those poor babies in the pictures of Romanian orphanages, with sad eyes and no residual belief in the value of tears?

The children of the poor were expendable. In all probability, nobody even really noticed Thomas, much less cared.

As for the demeanour of Thomas Gardner, he was probably a very passive little person. He was not wanted at birth, and nothing ever happened subsequently to make him feel otherwise. Even at two, he probably had a vocabulary of only a few words.

He had been serially abandoned. Looked after by a procession of different women, none of whom, including his mother, ever displayed any real attachment to him. He must have had a biological father, but that was the extent of his paternity. Only his Gardner grandparents seemed to care much at all whether he lived or died.

By any civilized standard, a lot of damage had already been done to Thomas. But, of course, that was nothing compared to what ensued.

COLD CASE INVESTIGATION:
1885 CHILD MURDER

During my trip to the Preston Gaol, I came upon a fascinating book in the gift shop called *Lancashire Lasses — Their Lives and Crimes* by Steve Jones. It is full of wonderful old photos and stories about the lives and crimes of women in Lancashire in the late Victorian period.

What particularly interested me was Jones's list of thirty Lancashire women sentenced to death between 1860 and 1914. In 1885, the year when Grace and Isabella went to trial in Yorkshire, two women were sentenced to death for infanticide, though their sentences were later commuted to penal servitude for life.

The facts were uncomfortably similar to those in the instance of the death of little Thomas Gardner. As Jones wrote in his book:

> Those unfortunate children born out of wedlock appeared to be at great risk. Elizabeth Lane ... from Ancoats told everyone she was going to take her illegitimate child to its father

in Warrington. It was found abandoned in mud by the edge of a canal.

21-year-old Margaret Higgins ... from Chorlton-on-Medlock murdered her illegitimate 14-month-old daughter Josephine when she took up with a new lover. The body was found in the river Medlock some 200 yards from the bridge in Cambridge Street. Margaret had a row with a new boyfriend to whom she threatened to drown herself in hopes that he would follow her and show some interest. When eventually she gave herself up to police, she told them that she had thrown the child over the wall into the river. The defence argued unsuccessfully that she'd accidentally dropped the child when climbing a wall near the river. (Page 89)

Elizabeth Lane was convicted and sentenced to death in July 1885, while Grace and Isabella were in Preston awaiting their trial, and Margaret Higgins was convicted in November. The parallels among the three cases, including all three infants being found at water's edge, suggest that Grace and Isabella were fortunate to be defended by E. Tindal Atkinson.

Thinking back to the article that David had found on Victorian values, I realized that it might actually be unsafe to generalize too widely about attitudes toward infanticide in the late 1800s. When and where you were tried, and who defended you, seemed to matter very much.

Sentiment in the locality undoubtedly played a big role in the pursuit of suspected cases of infanticide, and the Highams had found some important documentary evidence of the state of confusion that officialdom in Slaidburn had found itself faced with when the body of Thomas Gardner was discovered:

Subject: More from Slaidburn

On Sunday we discovered that the Parish Registers for both Baptisms and Burials (though not marriages) are still held in Slaidburn Church (rather than in the Public Record Office in Preston 20 miles away as we had assumed they would be)....

Our rector was kind enough to let us have a look at them this evening. We were given the keys to the Church AND the Vestry!! ... As someone said in the "Hark to Bounty" ... "You haven't lived here long enough. Even I 'avent seen in't Vestry."

The burial register starts at 8 January 1853 and ends on 20 February 1993.

In the burial register is Jane Isherwood's burial on 21 July, 1883.

There is also an entry for Thomas Gardner. He was buried on the 21 May 1885:

Thomas Gardner (Found drowned) Meanly, 21st May, Geo Halliday, Officiating Minister. No 841a

There is an entry underneath the taped entry for Thomas....

Thursday 21 May was the day of the inquest at the Black Bull in Slaidburn.

According to the Registrar at Clitheroe: "You can't issue a death certificate without an inquest verdict and you can't be buried without a death certificate." Slaidburn must have been a place in turmoil ... First the inquest then the burial, all on the same day.

Since the final words of the inquest report were that "the prisoners were then removed" I wonder if Grace and Isabella attended the funeral, or were they already out of the village on

the way back to Bolton-by-Bowland where they appeared the next day at the Police Court in front of Lord Ribblesdale....

The entry makes it clear that the vicar responsible for the burial was not the Parish's usual Rector ... yet another avenue to explore.

The Rector here was very surprised as Thomas Gardner's entry is the only one in 150 years or more which has been taped into the Parish records as a separate entry between other burial records. He wondered whether the Rector of the time had trouble bringing himself to carry out the funeral for some reason or that perhaps they waited for the result of the Assize trial before making the entry. Who knows?

We may be able to ascertain where Thomas might be buried by investigating the concurrent burials and using them to navigate to a spot in the churchyard. Thomas should be around 108 in the graveyard navigations numbering system....

Tragic little Thomas. Even his death record had no certain, natural place in the continuity of things.

No gravestone. Almost no life.

THE SLAIDBURN 1885 CHAT ROOM

It was all so thrilling! The more evidence we uncovered, the more determined David, Cathryn, Penny and I became not just to re-solve the case, but to find out everything we could about the people involved and their lives, both before and after the death of little Thomas.

Emails full of facts ferreted out from various sources began arriving with their electrons still hot from transport. It was from UK Census documents that we began to piece together more detail about the lives of John and Grace and their families.

The next message from the Highams contained freshly released 1901 UK Census information. They had found Grace Isherwood, age forty-one, living at 26 Lincoln Street, Haslingden. With her was her husband John, age fifty-five, whose occupation was listed as a stonemason; Richard, age twenty-one, reed maker; Thomas, age nineteen, cotton mill warehouseman; and James Edward, age sixteen, apprentice barber. Matthew, Margaret, and young John were no longer living at home.

Grace and John had several new children listed on the census: William, age fourteen, apprentice barber; Elizabeth, age nine; and a little Isabella, age seven. William and Isabella were both listed as born in Haslingden, while Elizabeth had been born in Dalton-in-Furness.

According to David Higham, Haslingden is about twenty-five miles from Slaidburn (forty minutes by car). I had known that Margaret Isherwood was working in a mill as a weaver and living in Haslingden when she married in 1899, but when or how she had gotten there was unknown to me.

Slowly, the facts of the family's relocation were beginning to emerge, but we still faced a gap as to where they were between 1885 and 1901. Still, if William Isherwood was fourteen and born in Haslingden, then the family most likely had been in Haslingden since at least 1887.

Even before I could form my questions, David and Cathryn were back to me with information from the 1881 census that we could use to piece together more of the lives of those long dead people we all found so fascinating:

> We have had a look at the 1881 Census tonight ...
>
> John and Jane Isherwood are at Meanley with their children Matthew, Margaret, John and Richard.
>
> Grace Gardner is 22 years old and living at Stafford Street, Dalton-in- Furness (the street is still there) with her parents Edward age 52 (iron miner) and Isabella age 52. Also in the house are Jane age 18 (dressmaker), Thomas age 16, Edward age 12, John age 8 and Edward John Sykes Gardner age 3 month, grandson.
>
> Next door at 11 Stafford Street are Robert Dockery age 44 (iron miner) and Hannah age 40.

Also in the house are William age 19 (iron miner), Richard age 16 (iron miner), Anthony age 13, George Andrew age 11, Elizabeth Jane age 10, John Edward age 9, James Henry age 5, Thomas Alfred age 3, Joseph age 1.

From the newspaper Grace had two children before her marriage. Thomas was born 15 December 1882, and that child's father was called "William Dockray."

I wonder if the grandchild Edward age 3 months in the summer of 1881 is Grace's first illegitimate child? Or the illegitimate child of her sister Jane?

… The newspaper says that John and Grace married around the previous Christmas, i.e. December 1884.

As for the child that she was carrying at the time of the trial in summer 1885, it should have been born in late 1885 or early 1886, but the first child born in Haslingden (William) was born in 1887. I can only conclude that either:

1. She lost the baby.

2. The child is not on the 1901 census in Haslingden because it was about 15/16 and away from home. Grace wouldn't be the first "housekeeper" to have taken an as it is still called "all found job" and ended up pregnant and marrying her employer.

I wonder if Jane Isherwood (nee Bleazard) died in childbirth giving birth to James or did Grace give birth to James before she married John? It would be good to find his birth certificate or do you already know the answer?

I was gripped. It was wonderful to be able to share the investigation with people who were as obsessed with the murder as I was. And there was more:

> This is fascinating. Where is Isabella in 1881 if she isn't at the house in Dalton-in-Furness? She would have only been 14 at the time. Was she already in service?
>
> According to the trial, Dr Alexander Gray said that he attended Grace on December 15, 1882, when she had the child who seems to have been called James Thomas Gardner. It is interesting that she named her next child James as well, although she seems to have called the first one Thomas.
>
> It would be interesting to see if the birth certificate identifies a father. Was it permitted to have no father listed? It would also be interesting to see who was Edward John Sykes Gardner's mother. Maybe Grace had actually had three illegitimate children !!! I wonder who Sykes was?
>
> I also wonder if Jane died in childbirth, but I think that the child would have been Tom. We need to find Jane's death date. Could the local parish records tell us anything?

David quickly found the young Isabella, working as a farm servant whose employers had a possible connection with Slaidburn:

> Yes. Isabella Gardner is listed as 14 years old, unmarried, general servant, born Dalton, Lancs, dwelling: Medlar, census place: Medlar with

Wesham, Lancashire. (Wesham is between Kirkham, Blackpool and Fleetwood on the Fylde coast 40 miles from Slaidburn).

The head of household is Leonard Mason born Wyresdale, Lancashire who is married to a Dorothy Mason of Quernmore. Two of their children were also born at Quernmore, Wyresdale borders on Quernmore; Quernmore borders on Tatham — Could there be a link with the Tatham Bleazards either by family or friendship? Getting a job is often who you know not what you know ... Wyresdale is 12 miles from Slaidburn just across the fells of the "Trough of Bowland."

And other pieces of the puzzle steadily came electron-ing in from Slaidburn.

We have found that in 1891 the Isherwood family were living at 9 Helmshore Road, Haslingden. This information came courtesy of Thomas Isherwood's granddaughter — we found her on the web via the Haslingden family history website!

In 1901 Grace's brother Edward is at 24 Devonshire Street, Dalton-in-Furness with his wife Helen, age 24, and their children Isabella, age 5, Samuel, age 3, and Helen, age 1. Living with them is Isabella Gardner (Edward's widowed mother) by now aged 73.

I cannot find any of Grace's other brothers and sisters, the grandchild Edward John Sykes Gardner, nor the rest of the Dockery family. Maybe I just haven't looked well enough. As for Grace's sister Isabella, there are 4 Isabellas in 1901 who were born in Dalton-in-Furness at the right date. None are called Gardner so either Isabella is one of them and by 1901 was married or had died between 1885 and 1901. I can't tell without a more detailed search.

Cathryn

The members of our Slaidburn 1885 Chat Room were working overtime. David's last email was sent at 4:00 a.m., and with my location in Australia nine hours ahead of the UK, I was able to read and respond while he had a decent hours sleep, although David often seemed to get by on only a few hours. In his next note he began by apologizing for being inaccurate, a totally unnecessary apology. He then went on to provide some important information about hiring fairs:

> *Subject: Hiring fairs*
> *... Isabella Gardiner probably went to a hiring fair to find HER OWN job at Wesham with the Mason family of Quernmore near Tatham. Whilst working for that family she might have heard in discussion "over the kitchen table" that a friend or relation of her employers had just died and her husband was looking for a live-in housekeeper. At this point she might have suggested/recommended her sister Grace who was seeking a position. If Jane Isherwood nee Bleazard died at a period far removed from a hiring fair (usually Michaelmas and Whitsuntide) her husband might have needed somebody "a bit quick" to look after the children and could have written to Grace and hired her "un-seen" on the basis that Isabella's employers had found Isabella's work acceptable and that presumably Grace would have been brought up with the same work ethic. Pure speculation.*

He might just as easily put an advert in the newspaper. Who knows?

Here are some odds and ends from the internet which might be of interest:

In Victorian times (and for many years afterward) the "Hiring Fair" was a routine way of finding a job. These fairs were held in most towns twice a year, in May and November. Usually held in the market square, they were a bit like a livestock market, except that it was work, not animals that were being traded!

People looking for jobs, including young school leavers, would meet with local employers including farmers and the agents for large estates belonging to the gentry of the district. Anyone hired as a "living in" servant for up to a year at an agreed sum of money would be legally obliged to stay in the job for that period. Many were stuck with bad employers and terrible working conditions until the end of their "contract." They were also times for people in work to change their employers in the hope of better conditions.

Hiring or Statue Fairs were normally held annually, in major market towns (minimum six and two thirds miles apart). The dates varied, but round about Michaelmas was favoured.

The spare labourers wanting a job stood in line, indicating any special skill: shepherds had a crook or sheep wool; carters had a bit of whip cord; maid servants held a little mop (hence the other name of Mop Fairs); ordinary agricultural labourers smeared themselves with manure and hoped for the best.

The employers walked down the line, prodding to test for sturdiness and even temperament. If they recognized a man as son of one of their good workers, they might hire or recommend him to others as good stock. If they spotted a member of the notorious XYZ family, they warned the others. (Could Grace's illegitimate child have given the family a reputation locally leading to Isabella having to find work some distance from Dalton-in-Furness?) If they fancied the look of a workman, they offered a small amount for the year, bargained up by the man. When they agreed on a wage, they shook hands and the "hiring penny" changed hands (6d in the 1700s).

The labourer then went off to enjoy the fair and went home with the master. He lived in at the farmhouse (as a "farm servant" for the next full or half year — no nonsense about days off.) Completed service and the full payment of the agreed 4 or 5 guineas at the end of it gave the man a right of settlement in the parish. If he broke the hirings, even by one day, he had to start again and build up a second full year (and would not get paid for work already done).

Draw a six mile circle round a market town — this is where the men would normally be drawn from. Good workers got hired easily, at the nearest fair, so probably stayed close to the home parish (in the closest group of villages between home and fair), and probably in the quarter sector of the circle nearby. Sickly men, or those with a background of stroppiness or drunkenness, might be hired further away, say 12 miles, by farmers no one else wanted to work for. The worst case was that no one would take you and you had to go to the next further away fair. And the next. The fairs were slightly staggered

*in date — but hiring at a secondary fair till the next
Michaelmas might give a less than a year contract
— no settlement....*

Best wishes, David

What an informative but merciless glimpse into rural sociology David had provided. He had also discovered, from an ad in the Penrith Herald of 1877, that "best men" earned £20 for a year plus board and lodging, scaling down through "good men" to lads and second-class lads, through first and second-class women, ending in girls who might be paid between £5–£7 for the year.

Imagine standing at a fair holding a little mop, or worse yet, smeared with manure, trying to attract an employer! Although I must admit that I have had interviews for jobs where I would have been quite glad to have some manure on hand.

JUST DO THE MATH

David's salary information provided me with my first glimpse into how large a piece childcare would have taken from Grace's wages.

Grace had agreed to pay Agnes Creary 4s, 6d a week, and while my ability to add up old money is poor, I think that there were 20 shillings in a pound, which would mean that Grace owed around £11 per year for childcare for Thomas when her own wages were likely to be £10–£12 at best. In other words, Grace was in a hopeless position. No wonder she never was able to send enough funds to pay for Thomas's various caregivers. And there was no point in her telling the truth of her financial situation. All that could flow from that would be the speedy return of Thomas to her parents or the workhouse.

When Grace left her baby and went into service, she had never worked away from home before, and she had little experience of how a servant earned money and how they might spend it. Her complaints in her letters probably reflected her dawning realization that she could not earn enough even to pay for the care of Thomas.

Grace's second pregnancy was a complete disaster. She would lose wages while she delivered and suckled the baby, and suddenly she was faced with another child to maintain. It was a measure of Grace's fortitude that she did not give up completely at that point, and kill herself, directly, or indirectly by entering the workhouse. Instead, she found another job, one that would let her bring her new baby with her. John Isherwood had been the answer to a desperate woman's prayers.

A LETTER TO MRS. CREARY

July 27, 1883

Dear Agnes

I am sorry that it has been some time since I last wrote.

I am still trying to accustom myself to life on a farm. We begin our work days in the early light of dawn. The animals start their crying and crowing while it is still dark and the chores never let up until it is dark again.

I imagine Thomas sometimes wakes early as well.

How is little Tom? Does he have any teeth as yet? Is he eating gruel or does he still cry for milk?

I hope you are able to put him out for air when the weather is fine.

Enclosed you will find 7/6 which is all I have at present. Money is very short. We are paid only fort-nightly and I have had some unforeseen expenses.

I will send more as soon as I am able.

Sincerely, Grace Gardner

SOME QUESTIONS, SOME ANSWERS

We were all having a fascinating time positing theories and chasing down facts.

I wondered about the child referred to by Maggie in her testimony as "my little brother James." He seemed too young to be one of John and Jane's children, since he was just nine months old at the time of the alleged crime. Was he Grace's second illegitimate child (or her third)? Or was he, in fact, Grace and John's first child?

Cathryn ordered up the birth certificates for the children we thought to be Thomas and James from the registrar in Cumbria.

To everyone's surprise, the registrar's office phoned to check with Cathryn because the Gardner birth certificates she had requested showed two different mothers. Cathryn, bright as always, asked, "Does it seem the mothers were sisters?" An affirmative answer led her to request both certificates, guessing that Grace's younger sister Jane had given birth to the other child.

The next email from Slaidburn gave me some answers and raised new questions:

Subject: From Slaidburn

I have received the birth certificates from the Registrar at Barrow-in-Furness and they are as follows (as you can see there is no mention of a father for either child):

Certificate 1

Date	Born 11 December 1880
Name	Edward John Sykes
Mother	Jane Gardner a Dressmaker Informant Jane Gardner mother, Stafford Street, Dalton When Registered 26 January, 1881 Registrar James Dickinson

Jane would have been 17 or 18 when he was born. I cannot find a "Sykes" living locally who might have been the child's father, but at least we know who his mother is.

Certificate 2

Date	Born 15 December 1882
Name	Thomas
Mother	Grace Gardner a Domestic Servant Informant Grace Gardner mother, 9 Stafford St. Dalton When Registered 23 January, 1883 Registrar James Dickinson

Grace would have been 23 or 24 when he was born.

I am sure that we can assume that it is likely that Thomas's father was William Dockery. After all, he lived next door to Grace, was an "iron miner" and would have been 20 or 21 when Thomas was born and seems to coincide with the entry in the paper that he was the father of the child.

I have also had a look today for George Halliday the Minister that officiated at Thomas's funeral ... I haven't had any luck in finding him on the 1881 census around either Slaidburn or Dalton-in-Furness....

Bye for now Cathryn & David

It was all becoming quite addictive.

Subject: Relief
Dear Highams
I was crestfallen when I logged on this morning and there was no note from you. I've grown accustomed to our correspondence.

My husband William still thinks it was the Dockery senior, who was in his forties with a worn out wife, who was the dad of Grace's child. Why else would the parents not have married, since they were both young and employed?

Cathryn, I was thinking yesterday that I don't remember Grace ever being quoted as saying anything. She let Isabella do all the talking. Interesting to speculate as to why. Maybe they thought Isabella was a better liar.

The response from David came quickly:

Dear Sheelagh
Nice theory. Perhaps father Gardner didn't have a shotgun....

The information that we had found out about Grace and her sister Jane made me think again about Isabella. Sometime around the birth of Edward John Sykes Gardner, Isabella went off to work as a domestic servant on a farm. There might have been some family connection, but one wonders why she was sent away to work. Maybe with the arrival of sister Jane's baby the house on Stafford Street just seemed too small for all of them, or maybe Isabella was already showing a desire for something different from the way her sisters' lives seemed to be heading.

PRACTICALITIES

David, Cathryn, and I were also engrossed by the practicalities of the "crime." I started to wonder what a horse-drawn conveyance called a trap looked like, and how the four travellers, Grace, Isabella, little James, and Thomas, would have been arranged in the vehicle.

I also wondered about the rug in which Thomas had been wrapped. Was it rough and thick and heavy, like a horse blanket, or something more comfortable?

While there was regional variation in the design of pony traps, they all had certain characteristics in common: they had two large wheels, a bench to sit on, or possibly two short benches facing each other, and some sort of footwell. Space would have been quite tight for two women, a babe in arms, a toddler, and their purchases.

The Highams took the opportunity to go to a Lancashire textile museum and look at a fulling mill in action: a process that converts woven wool cloth into heavy worsted rugs. The products of such a process were very heavy rugs that were often used as horse blankets.

Having looked at the heavy, dense rug material, David mused in a spirit of fairness: "Who knows, it may have been possible for Thomas Gardner to have smothered accidentally if he was wrapped in such a heavy blanket."

The type of rug the sisters had used to wrap up little Thomas played on my mind. Was it possible to wrap a two-year-old up in such heavy blankets that he would suffocate without one noticing? As I wrote to the Highams:

> *Is May very cold in Slaidburn? I wonder if you would wrap a two year old in a very heavy blanket (32 oz) on a May day? Especially since we know he had a hat and coat on (and a sweater I think) since they took them off....*
> *Yours in curiosity s*

Not to be outdone, David wrote back "in curious fascination."

> *I have seen snow in Slaidburn in June ... but I agree, wrapping a child in a heavy felted horse blanket does seem unlikely and somewhat excessive....*

But a few hours later he was back to me with further reflection on the topic of blankets in May.

> *I was thinking more about hot weather in May. I remember driving old Fordson Major tractors without cabs during hay-making at little more than walking pace on blazing hot days in June and July and being absolutely frozen. The inactivity and*

lack of movement soon makes you cold. You would always put a pullover and often a coat on....

In retrospect, maybe wrapping a child in heavy blankets wouldn't seem such a strange notion, and the trip to and from Clitheroe involves a climb over a relatively high fell (400 m?) I think temperature drops by one degree Celsius for every 100 m increase in altitude ... or something like that.

Further research with a pony/trap/carriage, driving/rug, agricultural history specialist led to these further helpful nuggets of historical information:

In 1885 a trap was probably a gig, Ralli car (sp. not Rally cart) or Whitechapel cart. Some of these can be seen in Marylian Watney's Looking at Carriages *or Sallie Walrond's* Encyclopaedia of Carriage Driving.

And as to the type of rug found in a trap and likely to be used to cover a child:

Depends on the context. A horse rug was a thick woollen cloth; the better quality ones were "Melton" cloth which was nearly waterproof. It was shaped for the horse to wear while standing waiting during travel, or at night in the stable, and had straps at the neck and round the girth to hold it in place. A driving rug or apron was intended to keep the driver warm while driving in bad/cold weather and again may have been of Melton cloth if it was a good quality one. Usually (in England) the cloth was a "drab," beige-y colour. It had one

set of straps to hold it in place round the wearer's
waist. It was nowhere near as big as a horse rug,
unless it was a double rug to cover both driver and
passenger; in that case it had an extra bit let in at
the centre so it could be tucked under the rumps of
both humans and horses and keep out the elements!
In summer it was lighter and intended to keep dust
off the clothes — may have been linen or cotton.

Grace and Isabella borrowed the neighbour's trap and likely the blanket. But I would have thought they would have brought their own wrappings for the children, although the rug may have simply been stored under the seat. It seems unlikely that one would wrap a two-year-old in a really heavy blanket, immobilizing him. The two-year-olds I know would protest vigorously. But then, the two-year-olds I know haven't spent any time in a Victorian workhouse.

Penny pointed out a key statement about the rugs that I had previously overlooked. At the Magistrates Proceeding, Edward Hanson, the earthenware dealer in Clitheroe, described Grace as getting into the trap and arranging the seats and the rugs, then getting out. "Isabella Gardiner then got in and sat down and I lifted the little boy in. She placed him in the bottom of the trap."

In Penny's opinion, Grace arranged the rugs to make a little nest for the two-year-old. Hanson then lifted him up and Isabella placed him in the nest. Thomas was wearing a coat and a hat and he would be sitting up but warm and protected from bouncing.

The sisters then drove over to the co-operative store, where Walter Embley brought out the basket of groceries that they had bought and put them in the trap as well, presumably on the floor beside Thomas. It sounds as if the floor of the trap was quite full at this point, and that little Thomas was tucked up in his little nest.

When we next hear of Thomas, his seemingly lifeless body is wrapped in a shawl in Isabella's arms.

A TIMELESS TOPIC

Subject: Yet another one from Slaidburn
Dear Sheelagh
Your husband's theory on the parentage of Thomas,
i.e. the next door neighbour with the worn out wife
... A totally unconnected conversation last night
in the pub:

> *"Bloody disgusting! ... 67 year old and he's*
> *gone and got the next door's 17 year old daughter*
> *'up t' stick' (pregnant)"*

> *As they say around here 'nowt's fresh!' (there*
> *is nothing new)*
> *David*

I must admit, I did appreciate David's accompanying translations.

A LESSON IN EFFECTIVE RESEARCH

Back in Slaidburn, the Highams were following up on the details of poor little Thomas's burial. We had worked out that the burial and the second day of the coroner's inquest were on the same sad day, but it was confusing to note that the usual rector did not conduct the service for Thomas.

Dear Sheelagh
I have found the rector who buried Thomas Gardner.

The current Rector, Mark Russell-Smith, told us that there is something called "Crockfords Clerical Directory." It is an annual publication which lists all ministers ordained within the Anglican Church and the Parish that they are the minister of for a given year.

"Crockfords" was in existence when Thomas Gardner died. In 1885 there were 3 Halliday's (one in Australia and one in County Durham) the third was Ezra Halliday (rather than George as we took the entry to be). He was the minister at Dalehead

Church which is the next parish to Slaidburn. (Now disappeared under Stocks Reservoir built in the 1920s/1930s.)

Looking at the Burial Register for May and June 1885 the Slaidburn Rector buried someone on the 7th of May and the next entry is for the 16th of June. Maybe he was simply away from the parish when Thomas Gardner needed to be buried, hence it fell to the Rector of Dalehead to do the job.

Mid-May is a bit of an unusual time to be on holiday, but of course there are many things that might have kept the rector from performing the service. Could the Slaidburn rector have been on the coroner's jury, I now wonder?

AN OFFICIAL EXPRESSION OF OUTRAGE

The Church of Saint Andrew, an ancient building with ancient traditions, had recorded the burial of Thomas Gardner in its ledger with a hiccup. The entry had been carefully written on a page from elsewhere in the ledger and then hinged into the record over the space where it ought to have been. But that strangely appended record only suggests confusion on the part of the church. The detail of the official registration of Thomas Gardner's death reveals scarcely controlled wrath.

Thomas Gardner's death certificate was sent to us on the green registration paper also used to record death by natural causes. But this record was dramatically different to those of other leave-takings. Since he was only two, Thomas's occupation was described on his death certificate as "Illegitimate child of Grace Gardner, wife of John Isherwood." Under cause of death, the official had written, "Wilfully drowned in Easington Brook by Grace Isherwood and Isabella Gardner."

The source of the information was noted as Arthur Robinson, the coroner.

We were all shocked by the seeming harshness of the death certificate, but Penny found the best way to put it all into words. First, she called the document an "utterly amazing death certificate," then she went on to say:

> I appreciate the bald statements of the 1800s as shown in the "occupation," but the "cause of death" entry reminds me of the time in my family years ago when the neighbour's dachshund killed my children's kitten. My three daughters and a bunch of neighbourhood children had an elaborate burial, and created a headstone that said, "Here lies Snowball, murdered by Fritzi." There was real anger there, and I read that in the coroner's language too.

WORLDS APART

Once they understood what had to be done, Grace and John moved quickly. Trying his best not to look backward, John gave up the tenancy to Meanley and gathered up their beds, linens, pots, and tables and chairs. Then, with the help of Tom and Mary Rushton and the older children, they were off.

The squire had listened to him thoughtfully when he had gone for advice, and the advice that he had received was that he needed to find a way to start afresh, somewhere where the family's history and troubles were not known and where he and Matthew and Margaret could find work. The King-Wilkinson family had contacts over toward Rochdale, and the squire felt that there was plenty of work to be had in the surrounding towns, now full of mills.

He was not happy to see an Isherwood move from Slaidburn, but the squire was realistic and he knew that the taint of the death of a child could last for generations. The mill towns, while not that far away, were worlds away from the closed society of his village, and he felt certain that the struggle and comparative anonymity in a mill town would help protect John's family from the stigma of

Grace's trial. Mill workers had too many immediate problems of their own to worry about such things.

John went over to the area to assess his prospects, found the family some rooms in a house at 3 Deansgrove, and suddenly they were on the road to Haslingden.

A week earlier, John had been surprised when young Matt sidled into the barn to talk to him while he was grooming the horse for the man who had bought her. Matthew was a quiet boy, and he didn't often initiate conversation. It turned out that Matthew didn't want to make the move, he wanted to go to find work on a farm nearby, and he promised that he would send every penny of his earnings on.

John had felt sad and rueful. He wouldn't be needing a strong young man around in their new town life in the same way as he had on the farm, he wasn't even sure what work would be available for himself, but he thought he just might be able to find work as a mason. Matthew had no talent for masonry; he was a good farmhand.

"Well, son," John said solemnly, looking down, "you are almost at leaving-school age, and while we will sorely miss you, I can see you need to be allowed to work at what you think you can do best. If you promise me you'll go to school in Newton after the harvest and until spring planting, I'll see if Tom and Mary would give you a bed in exchange for chores."

Standing up slowly from where he had been bent over, cleaning Bonny's hoof, John put his hand on Matthew's shoulder. "When you get yourself hired at the Spring Fair, best be sure to keep some of your money back for a drink and a pie with your mates," he said gruffly, in an attempt to cover his embarrassment, "but Grace and the littl'uns and I will surely be grateful for any wages you can spare."

The deal was quickly done, and Matt went to live with his aunt and uncle at Chapel Croft, the farm where his grandfather, also named Matthew, had tenanted before him.

On arrival in Haslingden, Maggie and the younger boys were full of the excitement of change, trying to take in the darkened buildings and smokestacks that made up their new landscape. The children ran in and out as Grace and John set about trying to sort their new home. In no time they realized that they would have to send some of their beds back with Tom to Slaidburn. They just didn't have enough room for all that they had brought.

Just as well Matthew didn't come, John thought. *Where would we have put him?*

Maggie was full of curiosity about her new school. The next day she was going to lead John and Dick over and see when they could start. She earnestly hoped they would not seem too countrified in their new surroundings.

Young Tom was trying to entertain baby James with sticks he was using to build a pen for his little carved pony. Ironically, it was little James, born James Edward Gardner, who was the biggest beneficiary of the move to Haslingden.

"He's an Isherwood now and no one need ever know different," John assured Grace.

TWO MORE BOYS

For some reason, while the Highams and I had consulted the 1881 UK census and the 1901 census, we had yet to find our Isherwoods in the census of 1891. We knew that at some point the family had moved to Haslingden, but we had no idea how quickly they might have felt the need to move. Influenced by the "not guilty" verdict, we underestimated the extent of the social ostracism they would have been exposed to in Slaidburn by those who had been their friends and neighbours.

When we did track the Isherwoods down in Haslingden through the 1891 census, many questions were answered, only to be replaced by new ones.

The record, sent to me by my friends at the Lancashire Family History Society, revealed that by 1891 the Isherwood family was living at 9 Helmshore Road, Haslingden, and that the family had grown.

John Green Isherwood, then forty-five, gave his occupation as farm bailiff, while Grace was thirty-two. The oldest child still at home was Margaret, fifteen, whose occupation was listed as cotton weaver. John, fourteen; Richard, eleven; Thomas, nine;

and James Edward, seven, were all there, and there had been two new additions: William, five, and Joseph, four.

Interesting choices of names for the two sons born after the trial, William and Joseph, neither the name of any close Isherwood or Gardner relative. The Dockerys from next door in Dalton had sons called William and Joseph.

Hunting up William's birth certificate, we were able to learn that he was born in August 1886, twelve months after the end of the trial in Leeds. At the time of his birth, the family was already living in Haslingden, on Deansgrove, and his father John's occupation was listed as a cowman.

What a world of information and speculation can be entered through documents like birth certificates and simple census entries. By 1891 John had progressed from humble work as a cowman to being a farm bailiff. Grace and John were living together and steadily producing more children. Matthew, although only sixteen, had left the family. And Margaret had become a mill girl.

If Maggie had gone into the mill to work just after the school-leaving age of twelve, she had three years seniority by then. Thinking back to her 1899 certificate of marriage, where her occupation was listed as weaver, she likely worked in the mill for eleven years. Eleven years of deafening racket and inhaling cotton lint.

Between them, John and Maggie were supporting the family, although Matthew would have sent some of his earnings home as well. Home, a simple two up, two down, was full to overflowing. The boys probably slept in one room, although the very youngest likely shared with John and Grace, and Maggie may well have had to sleep in the kitchen. The front room was for "best."

None of grandma's grandchildren, nor, to my knowledge, any of her children, ever were told stories of her life in the mill, and now that I realize how long she worked there, I also realize that we must not have heard about it because it just caused her too much embarrassment. Like the dreadful experiences suffered by my husband's great-grandfather, who, at eighteen, was transported from Wales to Tasmania, where he was systematically starved and then whipped for complaining by the farmers to whom he was assigned as free labour: for those closest in time to the actual event, such information is often something to be obliterated from family history, hopefully forgotten and buried — at least, until a later generation finally digs it up.

CARRYING ON AS BEST SHE COULD

Isabella feared she would be a jinx, but Grace insisted, so Isabella again set off from her father's house in Cumbria to wait with Grace for the birth of her next child. This time, as she journeyed to Haslingden, Isabella felt awkward about John, though he was always kind and friendly toward her. Maggie was a bit put out that her place as "next in charge" was being usurped by Isabella, but they did enjoy giggling together about boys while they did the washing up.

The relief over the live birth of a little boy was shared by all, but his birth had special meaning to Grace, John, and Isabella. He had a lusty cry and a fine royal name. "Fit for a prince, I'd say," said the neighbour next door but one, and it seemed as if little William had sealed the pact. They were all going to have a new life.

Back home in Dalton, though, Isabella found it hard to get going again. In her whispered talks with Grace they had agreed that for her to find a new situation she needed a story about the "accident" and the misunderstanding and confusion that had followed. Between them, they agreed that the troubles she had suffered with Grace had to be left in the past, but she had yet to find anywhere where ugly versions of the crime of which they had been accused had not preceded her.

She found it hard to summon up the will to look for work away from her parent's home. For one thing, the cough that had started during her time in Preston Gaol just would not go away, and at times her slight frame seemed barely able to withstand its force. For another, she was thought too peaked to seek new work as a farm domestic, and had been reduced to taking the few odd jobs she could find around home in Dalton. She tried to help Jane with her dressmaking, but Isabella had never been very good with a needle and now her eyes often refused to focus properly.

As Isabella's mother whispered to her sister Jane, "The life has gone out of her. She used to be so quick and bright. Now she just coughs and sighs and looks out the window."

Isabella rarely left the house, and there were no young men to walk out with. She realized she had no interest in the young sons of her parent's friends, boys who were already working long hours in the mine. When she did venture out, she saw prettier, livelier girls who would be happy at the music hall and the pub, but the men that they were flirting with had rough hands and even rougher accents.

Only news of a visit from Grace could bring a sparkle to Isabella's eye, and Grace did try to go to see her as often as she could. While they had always been close, that dreadful summer had created a bond between them so close her mother joked, "You'd need one of Da's biggest chisels to break them two girls apart."

LIFE IN HASLINGDEN

As time passed it almost began to seem as if Meanley Farm had never really existed. Their new reality was defined by the bleak and sooty buildings of Haslingden. The people on the street looked tired and grim as they dragged themselves home from work in the thick twilight. Seeing them made you feel tired yourself.

Grace and John did slowly realize, however, that the hard lives and fatigue of their neighbours strangely helped their family. Their new friends and neighbours had no energy to inquire in detail about how the Isherwood family came to be living in a mill town. Their story of tough times on the farm and the need to find work for the family was readily accepted. With Grace being a miner's daughter, people found it easy enough to believe.

Maggie found it particularly difficult to adjust to her new home and new school. Da seemed strained and weary. Stepmother was very quiet and often ill. Maggie had to herd the little boys to school in the morning and back in the afternoon. Then she had cooking and darning to do. She was grateful that the teacher let her take home a book to read in the evenings.

When her da came to talk to her about working part time, Maggie was excited at the prospect of such a big responsibility. She welcomed the chance to work in the mill and bring home money to buy better food for her brothers. Matthew was already at work on a farm and doing his best to send money home, and Maggie was proud that she would get a chance to contribute too.

But she still felt a little sad. She liked the feeling of mastering her lessons in arithmetic and learning history. She was really sorry to be leaving school early, and knew already that she would miss it. Father had told her that she was a big girl now, and didn't need much more schooling. He said he was plenty proud of how well she could read and write and do sums. But back at the school in Newton there were girls and boys as old as fifteen, at least for parts of the year, and she had always thought she would go to school there for at least that long too.

On the other hand, it would be good to get out of their crowded house, even if it meant going to a noisy, cold, and damp mill every day. At home the cooking and washing seemed endless, and there was no place she could go where there weren't little boys wanting her attention. She had to wait until everyone had gone to bed at night before she could lay out her pallet in the kitchen, and sometimes she was so tired that the waiting seemed endless. She would sit over her darning by the fire and try to will the boys to settle down so that she could lie down in turn.

At work she was small and quick and very useful to the foreman. When she started he could send her scuttling under the looms to help twist up broken warp, certain that she would be nimble enough to not get caught by the machine when he started it up again. She sensed it was dangerous, little Lilly got a bad knock on the head that made her permanently silly, but she took pride in her proficiency and agility.

Maggie missed Matthew. He was never much of a talker but they used to have good fun when they played in the barn. Now that she was working in the mill she discovered she had no time to see her new school friends. Some of them, like her, were starting to work at jobs in the mills, and she had quickly learned that if you didn't work in the same mill the long hours meant there was very little chance to see each other.

Grace wasn't much company for her either. Grace never talked about what had happened during that scary summer, and Margaret was still confused about what Grace and Isabella were supposed to have done with the child. She had overheard some of her relatives gossiping about Grace when they thought Maggie was out of hearing. As a result, when Grace had tried to act like a mother and tell her about growing up, and what the boys would be wanting to do with girls, Maggie had smirked at her in an ugly, knowing way, and said, "Just who would you be to be warning me about boys, I wonder."

Still, Grace was the only other female in the house, and she genuinely tried to help Maggie, warning her about the arrival of her monthlies, and scrimping and saving so that Maggie would be free to spend some of the money she earned at the mill on some worsted to make herself a nice dress for best. While repeated pregnancies sapped Grace's energy, and the boys often refused to mind her, Grace did make an effort to get along with Maggie, especially since she felt that it would please John.

ANOTHER LOST BOY

Originally, I had obtained William Isherwood's birth certificate to see if he could by any chance have been the baby Grace was carrying when she was taken into custody. From it, I had learned that the family was already residing in Haslingden by the time he was born. The 1891 census information listed a brother, Joseph, four, but I could not find him mentioned anywhere subsequently.

I decided to try to obtain the certificates for Joseph's birth and his death, to try and see what had happened to that little half great-uncle of mine, and I was surprised at the difficulties I encountered in tracking him down in the records. Finally, I went to the original census document, instead of the transcription that I had used earlier, and, at last, found clarity. There had been a transcription error — Joseph was not four years old at the time of the census, he was only two months old.

Knowing Joseph had only been born in 1891, it was comparatively easy, though very sad, to find that his death had occurred only a year later. Yet another lost little boy for Grace and John to mourn.

Then the implication of the birth of Joseph in 1891 struck me. Clearly Grace was no practitioner of any kind of birth control, so why were there no new Isherwood babies between the birth of William in 1886 and the birth of poor little Joseph in 1891? I could only guess that Grace and John had conceived other babies during those five years, and that they had not survived.

Next, I went looking for Isherwood babies who had died in Haslingden in the time between William's birth in 1886 and the birth of Joseph in 1891. I found three: Mary Ann Isherwood, dead at the age of zero in 1888; Mary Isherwood, dead at the age of one in 1889; and David Isherwood, dead at the age of zero in 1889. Poor little mites.

Surely at least one of these children belonged to Grace and John, if not more. I know John's mother's name was Mary Ann and his sister was named Mary, and that John did like to keep names in the family.

How much loss and pain had there been in the Isherwood household in the years that followed the trial?

Grandma never mentioned dead infants — perhaps they were part of the past that she and her husband William had tried to leave behind by going to Canada.

THE INHABITANTS OF GRAVE C 999

Rita Hirst of the Lancashire Family History Society is a resourceful woman who has lately become famous in her community for her pivotal role in the installment of BBC's ancestor search program *Who Do You Think You Are?* that features Sheila Hancock.

Well before the BBC recognized her talents I had met her online, and I had the good fortune to spend time with her in person in the Haslingden Library.

Rita came up with the next important piece of information in our quest to learn what happened to Grace and John. Through our queries and her reading of the Slaidburn Child Murder site, she had been drawn into our web of investigators, and her on-the-spot knowledge proved invaluable.

On my very first trip to Haslingden I had looked for Isherwood graves at the site of Saint James Church, where my grandparents had married, but had been unable to locate any. As it turned out, Rita knew that a fellow member of the Lancashire Family History Society has an index to Holden Hall, another Haslingden cemetery, and in that index she hit pay dirt (if it's appropriate to use that phrase where graves are concerned).

What Rita uncovered was that in the Holden Hall Cemetery in grave C 999 — a portentous number — are buried six people:

James Edward Isherwood, died age twenty-nine, buried July 24, 1913

Mary Isherwood, died age five months, buried October 11, 1913

Grace Isherwood, died age twenty-three, buried July 18, 1927

Grace Isherwood, died age sixty-eight, buried June 5, 1928

John Green Isherwood, died age eighty-three, buried January 15, 1930

Ada Halstead, died age fifty-two, buried March 5, 1947

All in all, a fascinating list of occupants.

Sadly "my little brother James," as Maggie referred to him, Grace's second illegitimate child, died an early death at twenty-nine. And, some months later, a tiny baby called Mary died — was James her father?

Then we have a namesake Grace, also tragically young at death. At twenty-three, she was of an age to be the last child of Grace and John, but she could possibly also have been the daughter of one of their boys.

Grace Isherwood, once described in a newspaper as the wife of a respectable farmer, lies in this same grave, dead at sixty-eight. My immediate reaction was that, despite bearing so many children and the awful early stress of being imprisoned and on trial for her life, Grace lived a fairly long life, especially for one of her generation.

The information about John Green Isherwood made me smile. By all reports, he was a good, hard-working man, and he lived a long life. You could also say he lived a full life, although he could very well have done without some of the things that filled it.

My great-grandfather John outlived two wives, and by the time he died, in addition to his British descendents, he had four healthy grandchildren — two teachers, one scientist, and one engineer — living in North America. I wonder what he knew about them all, and I wonder what they knew about him. Much too late to ask, I'm sorry to say.

And who on earth, I wondered, was Ada Halstead? And why was she interred with all those Isherwoods?

In our online discussions about Rita's most recent fascinating information, David declared that the story became more like a cross between D.H. Lawrence and Catherine Cookson all the time. Personally, I had been thinking more along the lines of Thomas Hardy, even if it was the wrong end of England.

DAVID SAT BOLT UPRIGHT

Now that we had the details of the cemetery and the gravesite, Catherine and David wasted no time in going over to Haslingden to see what they might learn. I think we were all hoping for tombstones with inscriptions that would reveal attitudes toward the deceased.

I wondered about who had attended the funerals and the various causes of death. My heart went out to James and Grace the younger, and little baby Mary, and I tried to let them live a moment or two again in my thoughts.

The Higham's report of their field trip and its aftermath was very thought-provoking and a bit funny.

> *Subject: From Slaidburn*
> *We had a trip to Haslingden Cemetery today to look at grave C 999. Looking at Rita Hirst's email there are 6 burials in the plot.*
>
> *UK graves usually hold up to three burials so they obviously bought a "double plot."*
>
> *Holden Hall is a small cemetery about a mile*

from 9 Helmshore Road.

We found the grave in no time (the grave digger scraped the grass back to show us the plot number) and had expected to see a tombstone. However, as you can see there isn't one, just two "empty plots" with a small flower vase marked "In Loving Memory." ...

You mused a while ago: How could John stay with Grace and allow her to raise his children after what had happened? David couldn't sleep last night, musing over the case, and suddenly sat up and said "It was Isabella."

After finishing the chronology today we are both drawn to thinking that if any malicious act was carried out it was done by Isabella. Perhaps she smothered Thomas in the back of the trap just to resolve the situation.

After all, Isabella had "brought the problem to her sister" and she wouldn't want to take Thomas back to her parent's home (just another mouth to feed, etc.) It is only our (and perhaps the Court's) assumption that Grace had most to lose and would therefore be the most likely person to carry out any criminal act. Who knows what went through Isabella's mind as she sat in the back of the trap whilst Grace would have been driving the horse. John seems to have stood by Grace, maybe because he knew that she hadn't done anything.

Also, it appears that Isabella is the one who seems to have "lied through her teeth" to the police in her statements....

We still feel that if nothing else, they were guilty of concealing a body and the story of placing it where it would be found quickly is a complete fabrication.

The spot where Thomas was found is invisible from the road and it seems pure chance that Farmer Bargh's wife happened to be walking up Langcliffe Brook side. Hopefully a visit to Langcliffe Bridge when you come will bring it to life….
Cathryn

The image of David sitting bolt upright in the middle of the night and proclaiming, "It was Isabella" is both endearing and enduring. Even though I identify slightly with Isabella as the younger, less lovable sister, I suspect that he is right.

MY TURN TO WONDER

While still busily fulfilling the requirements of my day job, and trying to meet the needs of my far-flung family, I was much preoccupied with what really happened that day in Slaidburn.

Like the Highams, I had constructed a chronology of events from the newspaper reports and information we had gleaned from various sources in the hope that by looking at all of those events in sequence something new would be revealed.

Then it was my turn. After long hours puzzling over what I knew of the events that took place in May 1885, I sat up one night with a thought bubble over my own head. It related to the two places in the reports on the crime where it says that John Isherwood was seen with the two women walking home, presumably from the area of the bridge, at 10:00 or 11:00 p.m. on Saturday night. Suddenly I wondered if John was implicated after all in the cover up of the murder. Maybe they had needed his strength to carry the toddler's body down to its rather inaccessible hiding place. Grace and Isabella were described as being of similar slight stature and a two-and-a-half-year-old child can be heavy, especially if he is "dead weight."

Rereading the testimony, it seemed to me that the child was dead when the sisters arrived home at 5:00 p.m., since they had not entered the farmhouse with him. Instead, Isabella had whisked the child off across the fields in her arms.

In her testimony, Maggie said she never saw the child "alive" again after the morning, despite the fact that she was there when they got home and saw Isabella head off across the fields. I wonder if there was something subconscious reflected in her choice of words or if she was just responding in kind to a lawyer's question.

I was beginning to fear that my genes were more involved in the crime than I had at first thought. Maybe John had helped the sisters hide the body.

My sister Penny had a slightly different theory. She felt that my concern about John's strength being need to place the body didn't fit with what had happened earlier. In her words:

> Isabella trucked off across the field at 5 ish. Is she just going to drop the kid in the field and wait until later. I want to believe that perhaps JGI wanted to know what was going on and they snapped and told him and he wanted to walk to the site. Or, they could be creating an alibi by walking as a trio down the public road with not a care in the world. The farmer and his wife who found the baby were doing that. You would think that people who worked so hard would want to sit at home in the evening, but they probably didn't have comfy furniture. You notice that there is no problem leaving Margaret in charge back at the farm.

For his part, David felt that since the place where John met the sisters was nearly back at Meanley, he had simply become concerned because of the hour and had gone looking for them. His theory on why Grace and Isabella returned through Slaidburn was that they wanted to provide an explanation for John as to why they were not returning with Thomas, such as meeting a woman in Slaidburn who took him. But that leaves us with a couple of troublesome hours.

Upon further reflection, I think that David had a good point. Grace and Isabella needed some sort of explanation as to what they had done with the child since Margaret had seen them come home with him.

I do still wonder, though, what the sisters told John when they met him in the dark on that disastrous day.

LOOKING FOR ISABELLA

As our dossier of documents grew, and the story of the crime and their lives began to have shape, the sisters, Grace and Isabella, became more and more real to me. Thanks to Rita Hirst's research and the stories that I half-remember being told by my grandmother, I had begun to have a fair picture of what happened next for Grace, but I still had no idea what kind of life the teenaged Isabella went on to have.

Although she'd been in service before she was fourteen, it seemed most likely that Isabella had gone back to her father's home in Dalton-in-Furness after the trial. But, somewhat strangely, she hadn't returned to Dalton from Leeds with her mother immediately after the trial, because we know the sisters journeyed back together to be hooted at by the crowd at the railway station in Clitheroe.

Eighteen years old, marked as a villain, where could she go, what could she do, how would she be treated? I began to feel worried about Isabella's welfare, even though I knew her fate had so long ago been resolved.

Somehow, it felt unlikely that she shared the comparatively good fortune of her sister. There was no loving husband and gaggle of children waiting for Isabella to get out of prison. Her mother and father back in Cumbria were the best she could do and it was likely that they felt she and Grace had brought shame on the family.

One of my notions was that she had ended up in the workhouse, perhaps even the one from which little Thomas had at first been retrieved. She and the witness Dorothy Dockery could have become fellow inmates, struggling to find a way to get out and have a chance at a better life.

Pursuing the Ulverston workhouse idea, I located the workhouse on the 1891 census, and found Dorothy Dockery still an inmate there. She was then thirty-one years old, still single, and with the occupation of domestic servant. The child she had with her in the Workhouse in 1885 was no longer an inmate. Instead, she was registered alongside her own illegitimate child, a boy named James, who was one-year-old. Born into the workhouse, I hate to imagine what life had in store for little James Dockery.

In Thomas Hardy's novels, character determines fate, and I wondered if Isabella's quick intelligence and capability, especially when compared to her sister's uncomplicated charm, tended to isolate her. Grace appears to have been very warm and maternal. People responded to her, males especially. Isabella, on the other hand, was a bright but sharp adolescent, and might have been rather more uncomfortable to be around.

The 1901 census added further to my curiosity about Isabella's fate. In the still-growing family of Grace and John Isherwood in Haslingden, there were now two additional daughters: Elizabeth Isabel, and, somewhat surprisingly, a second called Isabella.

Grace's mother's name was Isabella, an obvious source of daughter's names, yet somehow I felt that in this particular case it was not her mother but her sister whom Grace was seeking to memorialize. These particular echoes of Isabella seemed to speak of a deeper sense of gratitude, or perhaps guilt.

Isabella shared Grace's burdens and her secrets. She might have even killed for Grace in a misplaced act of sisterhood. Only the two of them knew what had really happened during that ride in the trap. From the names of her children, I felt that Grace was determined to acknowledge Isabella's importance to her.

But was there a further meaning to Grace's daughter's names? Where was Isabella in 1901, six years after their trial? What was happening in her life?

Had Isabella found someone to marry her after all? Had the chill of the prison weakened her health? Was she living out her life as a spinster with a stain of shame, or could she already be dead?

The 1901 census seemed to contain no record of an Isabella Gardner of the correct age and place of birth. Finding out if she had married was a more difficult task.

As usual, Cathryn helped me, putting Isabella's first name and place of birth in the 1901 census in the hope that we might find her under a married name. There were a couple of possibilities, but long hours searching through the old books of marriage entries in the Public Records Office failed to confirm them.

I became increasingly preoccupied with "looking for Isabella," as I privately styled my sad search through old records. And I began to wonder if I would ever know her true fate.

A CAREFUL READING OF THE REPORTING AT THE TIME

The main library in Leeds is a fine old building in the centre of town. My husband and I first went there to try to find additional newspaper reports of the trial of the sisters, and I went there again later to learn more about the distinguished career of Edward Tindal Atkinson.

Logic suggested that the *Yorkshire Post* of 1885 would have covered the trial and, hunting through the microfiche, we confirmed that the Leeds Assizes received regular and thorough coverage from the *Post's* correspondents. More interesting was the fact that the story had even made it into the *Times* of London, in a somewhat abbreviated but very informative and well-written synopsis published on August 5, 1885.

Careful reading of each of the newspapers — the *Preston Guardian*, the *Yorkshire Post*, and the *Times* — yielded little snippets of additional information, as did the rereading of the Guardian's coverage of the inquest and the Magistrate's Hearing.

Worrying away at the details of what had happened on that May day, each rereading seemed to add a tiny piece or two to the puzzle.

For example, I noticed that at the Magistrate's Hearing the man from the co-op said that he had put the groceries on the floor in the trap. Having just come from poring over photos and drawings of types of trap used in the 1880s, I was struck by that information. There was not much space on the floor of a trap, and with the feet of two grown women and a bundle of groceries, I realized that the floor space was much more crowded than I had previously imagined.

For me, the lack of space on the trap floor made the accidental suffocation story much less likely, especially since the child could have been in a partial sitting position in his nest of rugs on the floor of the trap. Presented with the same information, however, my husband immediately offered quite a different theory: "What if the co-op man, knowing the outcome and fearful that he might be accused of putting the groceries on top of the blanket-wrapped child, simply lied?"

In the *Times* story I noticed that it said Thomas spent one month in the workhouse, a fact I had never seen before. If he only spent August in the workhouse, he must have been cared for by his grandparents from September to May. The doctor saw little Tom at his grandparent's home when he was there attending Mrs. Gardner in April, so it was probably a combination of Grace's marriage and Mrs. Gardner's illness that caused them to send Isabella on her fatal errand.

I also noticed in the *Times* report of Isabella's statement in court that it was she who determined that the child was dead and she who put it in the stream. I wonder how she could tell with certainty that the child was dead.

NORTH-EASTERN CIRCUIT

At Leeds, yesterday, before Mr. Justice Wills, Grace Isherwood, 26, married, and Isabella Gardner, 18, single, servant, were charged with the wilful murder of Thomas Gardner at

Slaidburn on the 16 of May last. Mr. Lawrence Gane, Q.C. and Mr. Manisty prosecuted on behalf of the Treasury, both prisoners, being defended by Mr. E. Tindal Atkinson. The deceased was, according to the theory of the prosecution, the illegitimate child of the elder prisoner, and was born on the 15th of December, 1882. The prisoners were sisters, and lived formerly at Dalton-in-Furness. The child had been put out to nurse, and several letters were read showing a deep attachment to it on the part of its mother. From the time of its birth until August, 1884, it had been nursed by various people. On August 3, 1884, it had been received into the Ulverston Workhouse, where it remained until September of the same year. In June, 1884, the elder sister, who was then unmarried and called Grace Gardner, gave birth to another child. In September she became housekeeper to a Mr. Isherwood, farmer at Meanley, having with her the child born the previous June. On the 3d of January, 1885, the elder prisoner was married to Isherwood. Upon the 9th of May, 1885, Isabella Gardner brought the deceased to her sister's house at Meanley, and upon inquiries being made of the prisoners with respect to the child the elder prisoner said that it was the child of a woman called Dockeray. Evidence was given for the prosecution to show that this story was untrue. The child remained in the house until the 16th of May, when the prisoners set out in a trap, taking both the children with them, and saying that they were going to take the eldest child to its mother. They proceeded to the workhouse at Clitheroe, and there saw the matron, and the elder prisoner stated she was a widow with two children, the elder of which she was desirous of leaving at the workhouse as she could not afford to keep it. The matron declined to take it in without an order, and the two prisoners left in the trap with the children and returned to Meanley. Isabella Gardner did not go into the house, but remained outside with something in her arms. She soon afterward started off in the direction of Slaidburn, and was followed by her sister. At about 7 p.m. on the 17th of May the child was found dead in a pool in Easington Beck, a place about two miles from Meanley. The medical evidence tended to show that death had been caused by drowning, but the medical man who gave this opinion stated in cross examination that it was often difficult to say in such cases whether death had been caused by drowning or by suffocation previously to immersion. At the rise of the prosecution the prisoner Isabella Gardner made a statement to the following effect: "Mr. Isherwood was always kind to Grace, but she never dared to tell him about the child. We agreed we would take it to Clitheroe and put it in the workhouse there. When we got to the workhouse we found we could not get it in. We then had to bring it back. We wrapped it in some rugs and laid it at the bottom of the trap on some rushes, and started for Meanley. On arriving there I found the child was dead. We were afraid to take it into the house, and we arranged that I should go up the road with the body of the child, and that Grace should come out as soon as she possibly could. She afterward met me at the Dunnow bridge. We walked from there down Easington-lane to Langcliffe Cross-bridge, and we agreed to put the dead body in the river so that some one might find it. I got over the wall and Grace handed the child's body over, and I put it in the river." The learned Judge, in summing up, made special reference to the medical testimony as to the cause of death and as to undigested food found in the child's stomach. The jury retired to consider their verdict, and on returning into court after an absence of three-quarters of an hour found both prisoners *Not guilty*. A disposition to applaud the verdict was promptly suppressed.

— *Times*, August 5, 1885

In addition to the obvious reasons for not wanting to be the victim in a murder case, most especially the disconcerting fact that you are now dead, there is the problem that sometimes those involved in the proceedings thoughtlessly malign you.

Thomas Gardner was a little boy. He wore petticoats because little boys wore such clothes in 1885. Yet despite having a name and having a gender, when he wasn't referred to simply as "the child," the reporter for the *Times* called Thomas "it."

Not only did the reporter call him it, but his erstwhile loving aunt referred to Tom in her statement variously as "the child," "it," and "the dead body."

Thomas wasn't allowed to be very real to anyone in that courtroom. His clothing played a brief role, as did his caregivers. But as the legal process played out we learned the matron at Clitheroe workhouse had "declined to take it in without an order," and his last breath was reduced to a debate between suffocation and drowning.

Not a person, just an "it."

RESPECTABLE EMPLOYMENT FOR THE GARDNER GIRLS

Jane Gardner still mourned her son, thinking of him secretly as little Sykes. He would be almost ten now, and she was convinced that he would have been a charming handsome boy like his father, although not as feckless. She had just heard of the death of Grace's baby Joseph, and she felt guilty that she had somehow, by starting their brood of illegitimate boys, led them all into a cycle of misery and loss.

Here at Kents Bank, Jane had found a congenial position, not far from her home in Dalton-in-Furness and with daily opportunity to care for children. She loved this kind of work, and the gradual stiffening in her fingers had made fine dressmaking just too difficult to continue.

At last she was out of her parents' home and on her own. She had not thought she would end up a spinster, working as a nurse with the children of others, but it was far better than the workhouse, or the doss-house to which her father had often told her she was destined.

When occasion permitted, she tried to go visit Isabella at the seaside. Thanks to the efforts of her aunt Sarah, Isabella now had a position as the servant for an elderly brother and sister. It was fairly light work, just looking after two people, but Isabella was increasingly frail and she sometimes had to make a valiant effort to keep her employers from seeing how weak she really was. Fortunately, their cousin was a serving girl for a family nearby and she would come over to help out when Isabella felt too ill. Thank goodness for family.

Sitting on the pier in the fresh air, Isabella and Jane were often quiet in each other's company. No longer was Isabella the chatterbox she once had been. When they did converse, much of their talk was rueful reflection on the past. This was not the future that either of them had hoped for.

Jane felt the sadness of being childless and a spinster ever more acutely, while Isabella mourned her own lost dream of finding romance with someone like Mr. Atkinson's young assistant. While she knew in her heart that he would never have settled for the likes of her, she did like to pretend that the sole impediment had been how they met, not who they were.

Both Jane and Isabella talked fondly of Grace and John. Somehow, Grace had escaped the consequences of their birth, her easy ways, even the death of Thomas, and she and John were building a new life for themselves in Haslingden. While they found her stepdaughter Maggie a bit of a minx, the boys seemed agreeable and helpful enough. Despite the loss of little Joseph, she had young William to mother, and it looked as if she might finally be shaking off the shadow cast on her health by the gaol. Isabella so wished she could do that as well.

Isabella continued to speak optimistically about finally losing her cough, but Jane had seen the blood in her handkerchief, and in private conversations the rest of the family had concluded that Isabella was steadily weakening with consumption. Illness had given her an ethereal pallor that made her dark looks more beautiful than she had ever been. Ironically, though neither would ever know, at this stage in her life Isabella looked the epitome of the pale romantic heroine that was the *femme idéale* of Charles Morley, the young man who now worked as a full partner in Atkinson's chambers.

A JURY OF A DIFFERENT SORT

Rita Hirst, our Haslingden connection, also found herself drawn into our attempts to solve the child-murder mystery. It was hard to resist, at least for some of us, and we all enjoyed finding new audiences with whom to share the story.

So Rita mentioned in an email:

> Next month at our October meeting, several of us have been asked to give a 10/15 minute talk. I have decided that this story should be suitable.

David Higham sent Rita a map and photos of the various sites so that she could better visualize events. As she shared her thoughts with us on what she had figured out, they reflected the same kind of twists and queries as we were having:

> I thought the bridge would be lower down nearer to Meanley Farm. They didn't intend the child to be found, if they had, they wouldn't have hidden him at all. They were bound to be found out. They

were strangers to the area. The farmer from Field Head didn't recognize them but it didn't take the police long to arrive at Meanley Farm. They would make a shrewd guess that it was John Isherwood's 2nd wife and her sister who was visiting with a child. I wonder how old James Edward was? He could only have been a baby himself and here she was, expecting another child, she can't have been married long. In those days, you had to marry again to get cheap child care....

At the next meeting of the Family History Society in Haslingden, Rita presented our mystery to a rapt audience. I wish I could have been there. At the end of her presentation, but before revealing the verdict of the jury, Rita asked for a show of hands on the question of the guilt or innocence of the sisters.

That second jury, sitting one hundred and twenty years later in the town to which the Isherwoods had retreated, took a vote. On the facts that were presented to them, the attendees at the Family History Society meeting unanimously found Grace Isherwood and Isabella Gardner guilty of child murder.

JUST ONE OF THE MILL GIRLS

The days had come to seem endless and boring. No longer a part-time worker, Maggie now left the house before seven in the morning to walk to the mill, and didn't get home until almost seven at night.

On the factory floor the women all tended to look alike. It wasn't because they had to wear a uniform, everyone knew that if you didn't wrap your hair up tight and smooth down your apron over your clothes, the machines could easily catch on anything loose about your person. One of the girls had been scalped when her hair got caught in the machine, and after that there was renewed vigour in their braiding and use of hairpins.

At first, Maggie thought she would be deafened by the noise of the machines, the frames banging, and the shuttles knocking all day. But she began to learn the sign language that the other women used to communicate, and she found her good eyesight enabled her to read lips quite accurately.

Her da had always kept a tidy yard and he expected all of his children to be neat and clean, so the discipline and order that was needed to succeed in the mill sat comfortably with her.

They were paid by the piece, and she quickly observed that the fastest weavers inhaled the warp yarn through the shuttle to thread it in a quick sucking motion, though you had to be quick or the thread would go down your throat. With cotton fibres at your feet and floating in the air, it seemed the air one breathed was half cotton as it was.

There were a lot of rules, and she tried to obey them since failure to observe a rule could mean a fine or even a firing. Still, some things were hard to do, like waiting to use the necessaries. You wanted to wait as long as you could, because the closet was so dirty and the smell was so awful, but if you waited too long and you couldn't attract the foreman to get permission, you could end up in a very bad way.

She liked to walk out with her muslin-wrapped dinner, even on bad days, to get away from the noise and the heat and the wet. Her clogs made a clattering sound as she hurried over to sit on the grass and eat her sandwich of thick butter and slices of onion. Thank goodness Grace had a knack for making a nice light loaf of bread.

The foreman was always at them to keep the machines clean, but he wouldn't shut them off so you had to be quick to avoid accident. One afternoon Maggie's friend Lucy got her hand caught fast in a wiper, and it pulled her fingers into the wheels before the machine could be stopped. Her screams of agony were louder than any of the noises from the machinery, and the vision of her mutilated hand came back to Maggie in dreams for years.

Maggie saw friends lost to seduction and lust as well. The mill's overlooker was in a fine position to insinuate that cooperative girls would benefit with better working conditions, and some of her friends fooled themselves into thinking that they were actually loved. The adolescent Maggie understood enough of what had happened to her stepmother and her Gardner aunt Jane to look with disgust at anyone who tried.

Over time she decided she was looking for an older, steadier man, someone hard-working and sober, like her da. She also realized she wanted a different life. Everyone knew that by thirty a mill worker had lost her looks, and the long days standing on the wet floor at the mill convinced her it would eventually take her life as well. She was proud of her pert little figure, and she hoped she might use it to attract a man who wanted something more out of life than the exhausting and tedious life on offer in a mill town.

Sometimes on a Sunday, she and Matthew and brother Jack would talk about their life "before" — when they had all lived at Meanley Farm. While she couldn't remember her ma any more, especially now she had no prompts to aid her memory, she did remember chasing ducks along the stream at the foot of the yard. She could remember rolling over and over on her side down the hills and playing with all her cousins. It all seemed so green and happy compared to their life now.

IT'S A HARD-KNOCK LIFE

I have pored over photographs of women in Lancashire mills lined up in front of their looms. They look clean and tidy, and a little nervous at having their photograph taken. They are dwarfed by the machines, with their huge size and number, and the web of electrical connections in the air around the power looms reminds one of the risk of an electrical spark in the fibre-filled air. These photos are probably a reflection of conditions at their best, since the mill proprietors agreed to let them be taken.

Mill floors were kept damp to avoid sparks that could cause fires, so mill workers wore wooden clogs to try to keep their feet dry. Practical and economical, but the clogs also probably added further to the noise levels.

During a tour of the Helmshore Textile Museum, just outside Haslingden, the staff started up just one loom so that we mill visitors could experience the noise and speed, and we all were shocked at how loud it was. After that, I was really surprised that my grandmother showed no signs of hearing loss.

One can find testimonials on the Internet of children who worked in the mills and were lucky enough to grow old.

Long hours, poor food, noise, air filled with fibres, wet floors, poor sanitation, lecherous bosses, and, even if you weren't dying, the industry was.

Life expectancy for a mill worker was forty-eight years, a shocking figure by today's standards. Work was six days a week and much of Sunday was often spent sleeping.

But there were some positive features of mill work. The salaries were good, especially compared to what girls could earn elsewhere, and the community of mill workers offered friendship and some fun. Music halls and pubs, fish and chips and ginger beer were their kind of recreation.

Married women who stayed at home and tended the hearth and the children had no money of their own. They had to depend on what their husbands and their working children passed on to them. A factory girl had a chance to make money and to acquire a taste for independence.

I remember my grandmother as a sprightly and independent woman, who held strong opinions. She must have been determined and daring to decide to emigrate to Canada. And perhaps she had no deep emotional connections in Lancashire, no life preferable to the unknown.

Before we left the textile museum, I bought some tea towels that had been woven there. I thought of them fancifully as altar linens for my ancestral shrine. I could put them on the shelf where I keep the coffee mug decorated with the Slaidburn Angel.

A MEMBER IN GOOD STANDING OF THE MOTHERS' UNION

I had thought that the newsworthy phase of Grace Isherwood's life ended when she left Meanley. Consequently, I was surprised to learn that the *Haslingden Guardian* had provided its readers with detailed coverage of the deaths of both of the women named Grace Isherwood who were buried in the Haslingden cemetery.

First, in the *Guardian* of Friday, July 22, 1927, was a brief story entitled "Funeral of Miss Grace Isherwood":

> The funeral took place, on Monday last, of Miss Grace Isherwood, who lived in South Shore st. She was in her 23rd year, and was one of those who went to Blackpool a week or two ago with the trip given by Mr. Fred Tattersall, on the coming of age of his sons. She is described as being of a quiet and genial disposition and was connected with the Girl Guides attached to the Parish Church. The mourners were as follows: Mr. and Mrs. J. Isherwood, Mr. and Mrs. W. Barnes, Mr. M. Isherwood, Mr. Dick

Isherwood, Mrs. J.E. Isherwood, Mr. and Mrs. T. Isherwood and family, Mr. and Mrs. W. Isherwood and family, Mr. and Mrs. J. Barnes and family, Mr. and Mrs. Ben Camm, Mr. T. Gardner and daughter, Mr. and Mrs. E. Gardner. Miss Sutcliffe, Mrs. Haworth and Mrs. Unwin. There were a large number of wreaths and flowers, including one from the employees of Messrs. J. H. Birtwistle. The Rev. R. W. Pedder conducted the funeral service. The arrangements were carried out by Messrs. J. J. Hamer and Sons, Blackburn road.

That sad little report explained to me why a young woman called Grace Isherwood was buried in grave C 999. Grace and John Isherwood were a fertile couple, producing Gracie when Grace was forty-four and John was fifty-seven. Little Gracie was the baby of the family by some years, and her "quiet and genial disposition" likely made her a comfort to her parents in their old age.

The death notice implies that her death was sudden, and her death certificate confirms that she died of pneumonia in the presence of her father.

Grace, Maggie's half-sister, was born after Maggie had left for Canada and I don't know if they ever even saw each other. On her death certificate, Grace was described as a cotton weaver, so she did follow in her older sister's footsteps, at least as far as the mill.

The details of the passing of her mother, the former Grace Gardner, came as a further surprise to me. Just under a year after young Grace had died, A. Bremmer, M.D., the same medic who had attended at the death of young Grace, returned to 17 South Shore to certify the death of Grace Isherwood at sixty-eight years of age. The cause of death was a cerebral haemorrhage. Her husband, John, was present at the death.

It must have been terribly difficult for both John and Grace to absorb all of the blows that life had dealt them, and perhaps for Grace the death of her youngest daughter was one blow too many. On the other hand, Grace might have been going along quietly, dealing with life as it arrived on her doorstep, and one day she just had a stroke and died.

According to the *Haslingden Guardian* of June 8, 1928:

FUNERAL OF MRS. G. ISHERWOOD

The funeral took place on Tuesday at Haslingden Cemetery of Mrs. Grace Isherwood, wife of Mr. John G. Isherwood, of 17, South Shore, Haslingden, who is a retired builder. The deceased lady was a prominent worker at the Parish Church, and usually had charge of the tea arrangements at social functions. She was a member of the Mother's Union, which organization was represented at the funeral. The Rev. R. P. Chadwick conducted a service at the house and the Rev. R. W. Pedder read the first part of the burial service at the Parish Church, where a considerable congregation assembled. The hymn "Abide with me" was sung. Mr. Pedder also performed the last rites at the graveside. The mourners were: Mr. J. G. Isherwood, Mr. and Mrs. Walter Barnes, Mr. John Barnes, Wife and family, Mr. Matthews and Mr. Richard B. Isherwood, Mr. and Mrs. Tom Isherwood and family, Mrs Willhena Isherwood, Mr. and Mrs. Ben Camm, Mrs. William Isherwood and family, Mr. Thos. and Miss Gardner, Mr. and Mrs. Edward Gardner, Mrs. A. Townley and Mrs. Irwin, Representatives of Mothers' Union: Mrs. Worsley and Mrs. Higson. The wreathes were inscribed: A token of fond love to Mother, from husband Lizzie and Walter; In loving remembrance of dear Mother, Isabella Walter and John; In affectionate remembrance of a dear Mother, Tom, Maude and children; Lena and Elsie; Mrs. W. Isherwood, John and Alice; Doris; Edna; Brother Edward and Ellen Gardner (Accrington); Little Eric, Jennie and Ellis; Mr. and Mrs. Curran; Mrs Haworth and family; Ladies of Tea Tent, H.C.C.; Parish Church Sunday School; Mr. and Mrs. J. O. Parker; Miss Florence E. Sutcliffe; Brother Wm and family; Dorothy; Mothers' Union, Parish Church. The funeral arrangements were carried out by J. J. Hammer and Sons.

There was "a considerable congregation assembled." Grace and John had found themselves warmth and acceptance in Haslingden. They had clearly succeeded in escaping the taint of the past, and had become part of a new community where they were welcomed and appreciated.

While John was recorded as present at the death of his wife, I wonder at the state of his own health. The newspaper reports that the funeral began with a service in the home, which makes me wonder if John, who was by then eighty-one years old, was too feeble to make his way to the church.

Husband John was joined in floral tribute with daughter Elizabeth and her spouse, while daughter Isabella mentioned her husband and likely a son. Both of Grace's surviving daughters had married a Barnes.

All five of Grace's other children, James Edward, William, Joseph, Grace, and, of course, Thomas Gardner, had predeceased her. Six if you count the little one who was in her womb when Thomas died, but disappeared while she was in gaol. And possibly others, poor little lost souls.

Stepsons Matthew, Richard, and Tom all attended the funeral, while stepson John is not mentioned in the report. Her only stepdaughter, Margaret, had moved to Kaslo, British Columbia, almost thirty years before. It would have taken quite some time for a letter with news of Grace's death to reach her.

Brothers William, Thomas, and Edward Gardner are noted to have attended, but there is no sign of sister Isabella or sister Jane. Where were they, I wonder?

Camm seems an unusual name, so it is interesting to note that a Mrs. Camm was walking with farmer Bargh and his wife near Slaidburn on that night in May 1885, and a Mrs. Camm attended the funeral of both Graces almost forty-five years later.

It is difficult to know what to say about the wreath from the Mothers' Union.

ISABELLA'S FATE

One day my melancholy searching was rewarded: I discovered what became of Isabella.

I had been trying various searches on "freebmd," a remarkable online source of the United Kingdom's births, marriages, and deaths since 1837, when I finally hit upon the right combination of age and district and year and last name, and there she was — Isabella Gardner, dead in Ulverston in 1892 at twenty-five years of age.

The stark appearance of the information on the screen shocked and upset me. Guilty or not, she didn't get to have much of a life.

With the rough date and place of death, Cathryn speedily got Isabella's death certificate, and the information therein was even sadder than I had imagined:

> *Subject: Re: A Hot Lead*
> *Dear Sheelagh*
> *The death certificate has arrived.*
>
> *As you know I sent it to Ulverston, however*
> *Ulverston is the registration district and not the*

town. In fact the certificate was produced by the ever helpful Mr. Henshaw. The registrar at Ulverston had checked their records, realised that it wasn't Ulverston (the town) and sent my letter to Mr. Henshaw....

The details are

Date and place of death — Died 11 August, 1892, 39 Lord Street, Dalton

Name and age — Isabella Gardner, age 25 years

Occupation — Domestic Servant

Cause of death — Contused head, cerebral abscess

Certified by Arthur J. Cross M.D

Signature, description and residence of informant — Grace Isherwood, sister, present at death, 39 Lord Street, Dalton

When registered — 11 August, 1892

Registrar — James Dickinson

I rang Mr. Henshaw to thank him and asked him to confirm that the cause of death reads "contused." It does. (I wanted to make certain that it wasn't "confused.") He said that the cause of death was common, was one that he had seen often at the period, but was not sure exactly what it referred to.

I therefore rang my sister who is an intensive care unit nurse.

Contused means bruised and swollen, so I asked her if this showed that Isabella had fallen.

She replied (without prompting from me) that … "If someone of that age has died from 'contused head, cerebral abscess,' it would indicate some form of systemic disease rather than trauma. You would see cerebral abscess in the final stage of Tuberculosis and the head becomes bruised and swollen (contused) as your brain turns to mush."

I don't think that "mush" is a medical term but
I think that it is very descriptive!

Since dying of TB takes time this is presumably
why Grace had a chance/choice to be there.

I will post the certificate to you.
All the best Cathryn and David

Poor, poor Isabella. What a dreadful fate. Dead from tuberculosis at twenty-five, attended by her sister Grace, with whom she had shared so much during her short life. Whether she smothered the baby or not, she paid the price.

Subject: Wow! What a great amount of information
Dear Cathryn
First of all, we sure owe Mr. Henshaw a debt of gratitude. Does he have an email address where I could write to thank him? Second of all, it is interesting that even though her mother was still alive at that date, Isabella's sister Grace came to nurse her.

As you may recall, Grace's daughter born in 1892 was named Elizabeth Isabel, and her daughter born in 1894 was named Isabella.

Do you think that Isabella might have contracted TB in the gaol? Can you by any chance see where Isabella was living in 1891, was it the same Lord Street address.

What a sad short life.

I have come to think, like David, that Isabella "did it," probably with her feet on the rug on the floor of the trap. My personal theory is that women do not like to get up close in physical violence.

Then I think that Grace lost her baby while they were in gaol, and she was indisposed when the

*trial came around. Isabella read the statement at
the trial and they got off, so I think Grace owed her
a great debt of gratitude.*

*Thank your sister for me for the advice about
"contused." ...*
Sheelagh

The fact that Isabella died in 1892 meant that there was
still another bit of information out there to be found about her
— her whereabouts in 1891 at the time of the census. Back I
went to the census with renewed determination.

The sophistication of the census data and indexing was
improving by the day, and this time I found her quite readily.
In 1891 Isabella Gardner was living in a part of Blackpool
called Layton with Warbrick, at 7 South Parade Promenade.
South Parade Promenade was clearly a good address, and
Isabella was working as a domestic servant for an elderly
retired man named Henry Howorth and his sister, Hannah.
The explanation for her particular employment seems to be
down to family connections. Isabella's mother, whose maiden
name was Cartmell, was from Blackpool and the Cartmell
household at 6 Waterloo Road, just down the way from South
Parade Promenade, included an Isabella Cartmell, nineteen,
a general servant also born in Blackpool. It seems a fair guess
that Mrs. Gardner's relations had helped to find a position
for Isabella with the elderly brother and sister. A household
without children was a good choice.

How quickly poor Isabella had declined from employment
to death, working as a domestic in Blackpool in 1891 and dead
by 1892.

Elizabeth Isabel Isherwood, John and Grace's first daughter,
was born in Dalton-in-Furness in 1892. The picture I am left
with is that of a somewhat enfeebled Grace, either just having
delivered her daughter, or soon to give birth, sitting at her dying

sister's bedside. She must have felt so sad and sorry for the life that Isabella never got to live.

While their mother hovered nearby, it was likely Grace who felt the loss of Isabella and her debt to her most keenly. Only Isabella and Grace knew the truth about what had happened on that Saturday in May 1885. And then only Grace.

GRACE'S VIGIL

Until the baby on her lap started to whimper for attention, Grace sat simply staring at the wall, holding Isabella's chill and stiffening hand.

It had been some time since Isabella had even been able to recognize anyone, but that didn't lessen Grace's present feeling of desolation. She and Isabella had shared so much misery together, enough for several lifetimes, but Isabella had not had much joy.

Grace nursed the child as she reflected on Isabella's life. She had been such a clever girl, but her intelligence seemed to deny her more pleasure than it had provided.

Grace thought back to the dreadful summer after she and John had first been married. It was hard to remember the details: all she remembered was pain and anguish. She owed her life to Isabella, of that Grace was certain, but it was the ridiculous story that Isabella made up and then told to the police that had put them at risk in the first place.

Only James was left to her from the sorry trap load that went to the Clitheroe workhouse that day, and he was just now eight years old.

Even if pressed, she couldn't separate what had really happened from what she wished had happened. Fear, time, and telling had caused her to lose her hold on the events of that day. And there was no one pressing her to get it right anymore; not now.

She looked over at the final peacefulness of Isabella's pale face. Instead of a dead young woman, she saw the lean, dark-eyed girl with her crown of braids, who had stood straight and tall before the court and told them all that she and her sister did not murder that child. Grace smiled slightly at the recollection of the expression on the face of the young lawyer as Isabella had so resolutely spoken her piece. His eyes, behind his wire-rimmed glasses, were quite tender and his look was proud.

Initially, Grace had been reluctant to remind Isabella of that time, so she refrained from mentioning to her what she had observed that day. Later, when she had come to understand how important knowledge of the advocate's admiration, however fleeting, was to Isabella, Grace was willing to describe the scene as often as it was requested.

Grace cried silently, not only for Isabella but for all the grief and loss through which they'd had to wade.

Drying her eyes, she gave the baby a quick pat on the back and went out to find someone to help her with the laying out. She felt eager to get back home to Haslingden and take charge of the household again. With John and Maggie in charge, there was no telling what kind of unsettling new order was now in place.

MARGARET LEAVES THE MILL
BEHIND

Margaret was impatient to get to the church. William's sister Jane had arranged to walk over with her, to stand up for her and sign as her witness, but it was getting late and she was not yet in sight.

She had first thought to ask William's sister Margaret Ann to be her witness. She had met Margaret Ann working beside her in the mill, and it was this friendship that had led her to Jane and then to an acquaintance with their brothers John and William.

Margaret Ann had been surprised that Maggie didn't fancy her brother John, he seemed a livelier match, but it had been William who showed himself extraordinarily determined to win her. Maggie had put him to the test: give up drinking and smoking and come back to see me in a year. To everyone's amazement, he did, and then solemnly insisted on their marriage as his prize. A man that resolute was just what Maggie had been looking for.

Margaret Ann had just been married herself, ceasing to be a Margaret Whittaker just as Maggie was about to become one. It seemed only fair for Jane to get preference as witness, being the only remaining one in the trio who had to go back to the fearsome racket in the mill on Monday and go on trying to keep warm and dry.

It was a chilly mid-December day, but she was pleased that they had chosen to get married in the old century. The prospect of a new life as a married woman in the twentieth century sounded like something out of a book by Jules Verne, and Maggie could hardly wait.

Her thoughts turned to her da, already waiting for her at the church. Unlike the fathers of many of her friends, he had always been kind to her and concerned about her health and happiness. But it was Fanny and Isabella demanding his knee and his stories nowadays, and it was time for her to have a man of her own.

Shivering under her cloak, Margaret could feel the fit of her lacy dress, tight over her shoulders and through to her waist, but she worried that the snow would wet her new shoes. She had saved for months for her finery, and she didn't want it spoiled before William had a chance to see it and, she shivered at the prospect, to remove it later.

At last, there was Jane Whittaker coming down the road. Margaret almost slipped on the icy road running to meet her. She'd have plenty of opportunity to face the consequences of marriage later.

The thin winter sun was setting as Margaret Isherwood, weaver, married William Whittaker, bleacher, at Saint James' Parish Church in Haslingden. The church was filled with Isherwood and Whittaker relations, all celebrating the newlyweds. The fact that William was eight years older than Margaret was generally thought a good thing; he had a little money put aside, and his widowed mother could be left in the charge of his brother.

Margaret Isherwood had departed from the crowded family home at 26 Lincoln Street. William had lived over with his mother on Blackburn Road. But now, as husband and wife, they had a place of their own and the prospect of privacy, a space for just the two of them, even if it was only one room.

Her father looked on thoughtfully at the ceremony. He felt as if he was cutting one of his last ties to Jane, and he was surprised to find he was having a little conversation with her in his head, something he had given up doing long ago. *Well, Jane, there goes our girl, off on her own now,* he thought. *She has your spirit and your smile. I dearly hope she finds the kind of happiness with her William that I found with you, and that she gets to enjoy it for a lot longer.*

John felt a little freshening in the air around his head, as if someone had disturbed it by passing, and he nodded his head. He hoped that Jane and Maggie both knew that he had done the best he could.

The wedding tea in the parish hall, prepared by Grace for their friends and relatives, was ample and well laid out, but of course that was one of Grace's arts — she did have the knack for laying out a gracious tea.

As Margaret had feared, the boys began to get rowdy, but William whispered to her to relax, this was her day and she did not have to worry about those boys anymore.

Her half-sisters, Fanny and Isabella, looked solemn and pretty with their hair in curls, dressed in their Sunday best. Fanny had wanted to know when she might get married, but stepmother had just laughed and told her she should stay a little girl for a while yet. Hearing that, Margaret had wished that she, too, had been allowed to stay a little girl for longer. She still missed Meanley Farm and the Quaker school in Newton.

But today Margaret's mind wasn't on the rowdy boys or her two pale little girl shadows, her mind was focused on the prospect of life in Canada. William's brother had gone ahead and sent them word of the beauty of the mountains with their rich mines of silver, but she knew in her heart he had no mind for assessing the practicality of things. Jack wouldn't have worried about how you might set up a home and raise children in that wild place. His thoughts would be on the adventure of it all.

A VERY LONG JOURNEY

Waiting in the summer's heat at the station for the train to Liverpool, the wedding already seemed long past. It had taken almost seven months for the business matters to be completed and she had watched nervously as William finally set off one morning to meet with Mr. Watson, the secretary of the company in which they had been convinced to invest. William had taken with him with all their savings and he had returned home hours later with two boat tickets and a document attesting to their ownership of 12,000 common shares and a hundred preferred shares in the Arrow Lake Mining Company, corporate address: 6 Spring Vale, Haslingden.

As the train pulled in, William and his brother prepared to load their trunk into the carriage. Frightened, excited, and feeling a bit nauseated by the smoke and the crush of people, she looked about for her father. *When will I see him again?* she worried. But the press of goodbyes from her friends and family quickly distracted her, and when she looked up briefly, instead of the sky she encountered a wall of sooty brick.

Goodbye to all this, she thought. *Goodbye to the soot and the noise and*

Margaret Whittaker — Kaslo pioneer.

the dark house bursting at the seams with children. I am never going to set foot in a mill again.

At last catching her father's eye, she waved and blew him a kiss. Hurrying toward her, he gathered her to his heart, almost forgetting the strength of his stonemason's arms. "Go well," he whispered hoarsely in her ear.

Almost three weeks later, William and Margaret boarded the paddlewheel that took them on the last leg of the journey to their new home in Kaslo, British Columbia. The mine was supposed to be across the lake between Golden and Radium, but they were not going there yet. They were going to see the booming frontier town in which they planned to settle.

Margaret knew she was expecting her first child, and she was eager to have a home in which to welcome the baby. She had heard that winter was harsh in the Rocky Mountains and she wanted the family to be set up safe and warm long before the first snowfall.

By the time Ellen Hazel Whittaker, Jane and John Isherwood's first grandchild, was born on February 13, 1901, Margaret had learned some difficult lessons. The first was that a person who has never experienced a winter in the Rockies cannot possibly even imagine the snow and the cold and the whiteouts, and the sheer sense of isolation and hopelessness it can engender. Another, perhaps even greater, lesson was that mineral mines are fickle and they can suddenly run out of ore.

It wasn't exactly a swindle, more of a gamble you might say. William went across the Kootenay Lake and into the hinterland to help work the mine, and came back on foot across the mountain valleys, half-frozen and lucky to be alive. He had been lost and had walked for days in winter conditions to find his way home.

Margaret was so grateful to have William home safely, and a healthy baby of her own to raise, that she had no will to regret or recriminate. She had already begun to love the blue skies and the big lake outside her door.

"We can make a good life here," she assured William.

MARKED WITH A CROSS

Although I was blessed with the name Margaret, Penny is by birth order and predisposition the curator of our family's historical bits and pieces. She has a generous spirit and has had some big houses with space for pieces of our heritage. Her care for such treasures reveals a deep vein of sensitivity for the arts and crafts of the past.

I don't know where Penny got some of the photos she has saved of our grandparents on both sides, but she kindly spent a lot of money on reproductions of the photos so that lighter travellers like myself could have some historical documents of our own.

I had a vague recollection of looking at some of the photos before, and marvelling at my Grandmother Sadlier-Brown's beauty and my Grandma Whittaker's little waist. There was a famous one with Grandma Whittaker and her four children, dressed in their Sunday best, beside the family cow. Penny has come to believe that photo was taken to send to grandpa overseas during the First World War.

Photos of Grandpa Whittaker, who had died before I was born, reveal a handsome, serious man, whom I had come to think of as a man of few words based, I suppose, on the fact that

I never heard a sound emanate from any of his photos.

As I became more and more immersed in the travails of John and Grace and Isabella, a vague recollection of one of the photos started nagging at me. During a family reunion, my brother, John, his wife, Nancy, and I had been looking at old photographs and we had come upon one taken back in England that featured a smiling young Maggie, another woman, and two solemn girls. I remember asking John if he knew who the other people were, and he said that he thought the other woman was grandma's half-sister Isabella.

At the time there was no reason to doubt him, but as I researched the family history I realized that he had to be wrong. The photograph had been taken about 1898, and Maggie's half-sister Isabella was by then only four years old. Her other sister, Elizabeth, would have been six. So who was the woman in the photo with grown-up Margaret, taken before she left Haslingden for her new life?

Next I wondered if John's name for the person was perhaps correct but the relationship wrong. Could it be a photo of Aunt Isabella, Grace's sister? But then I learned that she had died in 1892.

I decided to look very closely at that photograph when next I had the chance.

As it turned out, I didn't have to wait long. I was in Toronto for the birth of my daughter Meghan's first baby. An actual blizzard was raging outside, but inside Meg's charming cottage in Cabbagetown, the baby and I were tucked up safe and warm. Two-day-old Turner Whittaker Scott and I were blissed out, him sleeping, me casting a protective spell around us.

Turner's exhausted mother happened by while we were sitting there for a quiet hour or three, and she dropped a little envelope on the coffee table nearby.

"Oh, I almost forgot," she mentioned casually, "Penny gave me this to give to you."

When I finally surrendered Turner for feeding, I turned my attention to Penny's envelope. Inside were a large number of

Isherwood family photo.

wonderful photos, beautifully and expensively reproduced. But there was one in particular that made me gasp.

There it was. A photograph of my grandmother, Margaret Isherwood, in her early twenties, an older woman, and two young girls. In Penny's writing on the back was the note: *Fanny, Margaret, ~~~~~, and Isabell 1898 Accrington, Lancs.*

I was briefly confused by the name Fanny on the back of the picture, until someone more knowledgeable than I about the derivatives of nicknames told me that Fanny was a common short form for Elizabeth. John was partially right. Grandma's stepsisters, Elizabeth (Fanny) and Isabella, were in the photograph with her — they were the two young girls.

I held my breath. The older woman in the photograph was obviously Margaret's stepmother, Grace, then in her late thirties. The woman who had become almost more myth than reality was pictured there, surrounded by the other Isherwood females.

I have looked closely at this photo many times now. The young Isabella, with her abundant dark hair, is a pretty girl who seems to share her mother's features, while Fanny seems more Isherwood. If the youthful Grace had the glossy-haired prettiness of the little Isabella clinging to her arm, one can understand her appeal. Or maybe the little girl favoured her namesake, Aunt Isabella.

The woman who inadvertently had decided so many of our destinies was described with a blank on the back of her photograph. But there was more to it than that. What I had initially thought to be damage on the photo caused by the ravages of time, on closer examination looks deliberately inflicted. The older woman in the photo, posed with her two young daughters and her stepdaughter, has a scratch through her figure shaped like an X, as if someone had impotently tried to take out their anger at her on the photograph.

I could imagine that such a feeling might increase, not lessen, as the years went by, and as the alienation from Lancashire in British Columbia took its toll.

Grace. Such a mild looking little woman, such a lot of grief.

LESS A MURDER INVESTIGATION
AND MORE A SENTIMENTAL
JOURNEY

I coaxed Penny into coming to England to help me think about the murder and its impact on our life.

She and I had been sharing insights and feelings, and she was the one who had located the photo of Grace. When I called her to marvel, partly because no one in the house with the newly born Turner Whittaker Scott seemed interested in my ravings about the photo, she said, "I thought it was Grace, but I wanted you to decide for yourself."

Now I needed her to come with me and look at the terrain of Slaidburn and Easington with fresh eyes, and tell me what she thought.

I also needed a dose of "sister." Penny has been both mother and sister to me, but the passage of time and shared hurts and triumphs has made us mainly sisters. I love to listen to the details of her life, and to tell her some of mine, although William privately counsels me to be sensitive about seeming competitive rather than informative. Sigh. My good intentions are so often misconstrued.

We set off on from London on Easter Sunday; Nick (our

youngest child and Margaret's last great-grandchild), William, Penny, and I, plus chocolate eggs, with plans to investigate the scenes of the crime.

William constructed a wonderful Murder Route for us to follow, and the Easter holiday resulted in some interesting sleeping arrangements for the four of us.

The first night we slept in the Coach and Horses Inn in Bolton-by-Bowland, just down from the site of the Magistrate's Hearing. The family seat of the presiding magistrate back in 1885, Lord Ribblesdale, is nearby.

Bolton-by-Bowland is a village, known for its thirteenth-century market cross and a post for putting people in the stocks that stand on the green near the Coach and Horses. The beauty of the place stands in sharp contrast to the horrors that Grace had experienced there: first, the birth of her second illegitimate child, then the magisterial proceedings.

The former courthouse is an attractive stone building, but I feel confident that no one in our family noticed its eighteenth-century features when they attended the Magistrate's Court there in the summer of 1885. On our walk around the village, Penny and I tried to peer through the windows of the courthouse, which is now someone's private home, to get a sense of the building (discreetly, of course, as always).

It was a beautiful spring day, almost exactly a hundred and nineteen years after the hearing, but the village seemed much as it likely had been. We didn't sense any of the angst our forebears must have felt, but it must still have been there, infinitesimal traces in the ether.

We next went over to Slaidburn to show Penny our ancestral village and the scenes of the crime. When I walk in the lanes of Slaidburn I feel the histories of my forebears, and when I sit near the fire in Hark to Bounty I reflect on how many jugs of ale folks with DNA like mine have downed before that fire. I have added a fair few pints of Guinness to the total myself.

Easter is a busy time of year in Slaidburn, with lots of fitness buffs there to walk and cycle on the fells. Our little group had been warned that all that would be available was the "family" accommodation in the Hark to Bounty Inn. On the face of it that sounded all right. We were a family: parents, a child, and his aunt. But our climb up two flights of stairs, the second flight reached through a low door and up increasingly steep stairs, revealed that the family accommodation was one large attic room furnished with four single beds, one over by the bathroom, one against the wall, and two side by side against the wall facing the bathroom door.

A skylight and a small window provide light for the family room. Immediately below is the remarkable, big room that has been used for hundreds of years in Slaidburn as a courtroom, although not on the occasion of the preliminaries of "our murder," where they used the Black Bull tavern across the street.

Penny was cheerful about the arrangements, especially since she was lucky enough to draw the bed near the bathroom door. As she blithely noted, it was not the first time our family has slept in such a fashion over the thousand years or so we seemed to have dwelt in and around Slaidburn.

Once settled, and well-fed by Hark to Bounty's excellent kitchen, we were off to visit the scenes of the crime. We went up the Easington road toward Meanley Farm, which has been gentrified but still proudly reveals its origin as an ancient farmhouse, past Chapel Croft, with its old stone farmhouse and equally old outbuildings.

Then we drove down the lane to the bridge and the stream at Easington Beck. We all piled out of the car to crane our necks over the stone wall, and look down at the paving where the child was found. Having visited the sites previously with Cathryn and David, William and I were able to serve as knowledgeable tour guides.

We tromped around the graveyard at Saint Andrews and sat on the bench beside the River Hodder. Some months earlier, I had sent Penny a postcard of a woman sitting by the Hodder, and if we hadn't known that she had never been there before, William, Penny, and I would all have sworn it was a photograph of her.

We waved, somewhat ineffectually, in the direction of Ash Knott Farm, where the Bleazards had lived. It is very hard to get to, even today.

Of course, Penny and Cathryn Higham hit it off right away, with David putting in a brief, typically modest appearance.

We talked a lot about the crime and the community, and the emotions of our great-grandfather John. We also talked about Grace and Isabella. Two young women half-mad with fear, running about through the fields and lanes with a dead weight, if not a dead child, in their arms in the middle of a summer's night.

Walking through the rough fields was very difficult for us. Grace and Isabella would have done so every day, and they would have known where to put their feet, but they were little women and a two-year-old is heavy.

As we tromped around the countryside, it was clear that Penny was finding the "accident" theory of the crime increasingly hard even to consider, while I had to admit I had never given it much credence. Even today, as Mr. Atkinson argued in 1885, the drive from Clitheroe presents many opportunities to dispose of a body without attracting attention, if murder is your objective. But Mr. Gane's argument, that a healthy two-year-old can't suffocate at your feet without being noticed as you drive along, is much more compelling, at least to me.

The next stop on our family murder mystery tour was Haslingden, the town to which Grace, John, and the six children had decamped to start a new life. By then we had eaten all the chocolate Easter eggs we had brought with us, so the mood in the car was more sombre.

Haslingden is not terribly far from Slaidburn, but even today it is like a completely different world. Compared to the pleasant, verdant fields, the ancient stone buildings and walls, the trees and the daffodils around Meanley, Haslingden seems densely populated, sad, and bleak.

Slaidburn is a charming agricultural village that is in the Doomsday Book. Haslingden is a mill town that flourished in the mid to late 1800s, a bit later than the heyday of Blake's "dark Satanic mills," though the phrase still seems apt.

Using an old map, we drove around Haslingden, locating the homes that the census and marriage records listed as Isherwood residences over the years. And we visited the textile museum to give Penny a sense of the noise and the hardship of life in the mills.

Penny also had a chance to meet Rita Hirst at the local library. And we stayed in quite luxurious accommodations: three separate rooms, each with its own bathroom, at an old vicarage in Bacup now converted into a charming B&B.

Despite the fine hospitality, having carefully surveyed Haslingden, Penny and I agreed that if we had been working in a mill there in the 1890s, we too would have taken our chances in Canada. Maybe it's in the genes.

QUESTIONS JUST KEEP TURNING UP

In the years since Penny first directed me to the Slaidburn site, I have read over the legal proceedings reported in the various newspapers several times. Each time that I do so, I notice something new.

Most recently, I noticed a seemingly small discrepancy. After the inquest, the *Preston Guardian* reported that:

> Jane Hayhurst, of Chapel Street, Slaidburn,
> deposed to washing the deceased and laying it
> out. She found a black mark on his forehead
> and a few scratches on his cheek. There were no
> other wounds. The child was healthy looking.

Some days later, the Guardian reported on the magisterial proceedings:

> Jane Hayhurst, of Slaidburn, who laid out the
> child, and found no marks of violence on the
> body, repeated her evidence.

The newspaper reports of the actual trial make no mention of any testimony by Jane Hayhurst.

The change in testimony, although small, seems worth noting. In all likelihood, the minor nature of the black mark and the scratches made it natural for all involved to discount them. I doubt that would be the case today.

Modern forensic theory and practice would suggest that scratches on the cheek could be caused by placing something over the mouth and nose to cause suffocation. A black mark or bruise on the forehead could have occurred during a little struggle or the moving of the head from side to side to try to get free to breathe. Or the marks might have been the normal bumps and scrapes of childhood.

The evidence that the child was healthy looking is also significant. For all his being handed from one person to another, Thomas sounds as if he was a resilient little boy, which makes his death all the more mysterious.

MY EMERGING THEORY OF THE ACQUITTAL

Originally I thought the sisters were found "not guilty" for two main reasons: Grace's obviously pathetic condition, combined with Isabella's articulate explanation; and Judge Wills's disinclination to sentence another trapped and hopeless young woman to death for using a desperate measure to get rid of an unwanted child.

Now I think that while those reasons may have played a role in the acquittal, there were other forces at play.

I took the opportunity at one of our delightful lunches to ask my friend Elaine, one of the smartest lawyers I am not related to, what she thought about the death of the child and the trial. She is from a legal family based in Manchester and I wanted to know if she heard or understood something in the story that was different from the way that I understood it, especially the statement at the trial given by the teenaged Isabella. I also wondered if she could cast some light on the fact that Grace seems to have sat mute throughout the trial.

Elaine's chief insight was that the sisters were certain to have benefited from the rather rudimentary forensic work that was conducted in 1885. She felt strongly that today there would be no doubt about whether the child had suffocated or drowned, and the evidence on the contents of the stomach would have been quite exact. But in those days the young women would have received the benefit of the doubt.

Rereading the reports of the trial, I notice that while Doctor Bridgman testified that the post-mortem evidence seemed to indicate drowning, on cross-examination Mr. Atkinson got him to concede, as reported in the *Times*, "that it is often difficult to say in such cases whether death had been caused by drowning or by suffocation previously to immersion."

The *Preston Guardian* included the information that Mr. Scattergood, a lecturer in forensic medicine from Yorkshire College, also testified that "while the evidence was consistent with suffocation by covering the mouth, the probabilities were in favour of death by drowning."

That is where the prosecution went wrong. Mr. Gane, Q.C., and Mr. Manisty focused the prosecution on proving that Isabella's story about Elizabeth Dockray and John Stables was untrue and that the women had drowned the child in the beck.

As the "Summary" in the *Yorkshire Post*, August 4, 1885, read:

> At the Leeds Assizes yesterday the most important case was a charge of child murder against 2 sisters — Grace Isherwood and Isabella Gardner. The child was the illegitimate son of the young woman, Isherwood, a farmer's wife, and it was alleged that she had, with the connivance of her sister, drowned the boy in Easington Beck, near Slaidburn. The case was not concluded when the Court rose.

The prosecution either did not know or did not pay sufficient attention to Isabella's testimony that on their return to Meanley from Clitheroe, she had discovered that the child had suffocated during the journey, and subsequently she and Grace had disposed of the body at Langcliffe Cross Bridge. The women were admitting that the child had died on the return trip from the Clitheroe Union Workhouse to Meanley, but claiming that his suffocation had been accidental.

The prosecution likely was caught off-guard by the fact that no witnesses were called for the defence. As a result, Mr. Gane had to deliver his closing arguments immediately after Isabella's statement. In closing argument, as reported by the *Yorkshire Post*, he called the attention of the jury "to the improbability of the suggestion the child was suffocated in the rugs. Considering the size of the child, its healthy condition, and the nature of the journey from Clitheroe, could it be believed that the child could meet its death in this way without the attention of the women being called to it?" However, neither Mr. Gane nor Mr. Manisty seems to have offered any evidence on the type of rug the child was alleged to have suffocated in, how the crowded floor space in the trap was allocated between the child and the day's purchases, or how Isabella was able to determine so quickly when she lifted him down that the child was dead.

With an all-male jury, it seems reasonable to assume that they would be less likely to know from intimate knowledge how robust a two-year-old can be, and how insistent, even though it is probable that Thomas was an undemanding little boy.

And what about the child's clothes? Where does the removal of the child's coat, hat, and shoes fit into the defence? As the *Yorkshire Post* reported, in closing, Mr. Tindal Atkinson argued "that the defence was, and had been throughout, that the child was dead when it was put into the water, and did not meet its death by drowning."

A clever argument, narrowly framed. No wonder that within a year, Edward Tindal Atkinson "took silk," which in the English legal world means becoming a Queen's Counsel (Q.C.). My great-grandfather certainly got his money's worth.

The outcome was fortunate, not only for Grace and Isabella but for Margaret and John and the rest of their descendents. If Grace had been convicted, she likely would have been sentenced to death, with the sentence subsequently commuted to life in prison.

John, emotionally and financially spent, would still have had to give up Meanley Farm, although he might have tried to move to somewhere close to where Grace and Isabella were imprisoned so that he could visit. Even a deep love would have been further tested by those circumstances.

Margaret would have had to become the woman of the family, staying home to look after her brothers and her father. With the stain of murder on the family's reputation, it is hard to guess who might have sought to marry her, and she might have ended her days as a spinster, keeping house for her father and her unmarried brothers. The Canadian branch of the family would never have sprouted.

THE PASSING OF A DECENT MAN

John Isherwood had been unwell and weary for some time, and finally his heart just gave out. Fanny sat at his bedside at the end and held his hand, as he had done for her mother. She and her husband, Walter, had been living in the South Shore house for some time, caring for father, who had been sinking steadily ever since Grace had died some eighteen months before.

In recent months, John had been lost for much of each day in thoughts of the past. Some days he simply spent remembering things like how he had courted Jane and how they had dreamed of being tenants at Meanley. He would smile to himself when he thought about Meanley, such a fine place for animals to graze.

He still missed Maggie, even after all those years. She had spunk, that girl, and she was his first girl baby. She often wrote to tell him how she and William and their children were faring, but it was hard for him to imagine her life way over there in Canada in the shade of the Rocky Mountains. Hazel, Ross, Dean, and Ivy — funny names for children — but then, Maggie always did try to be different.

Grace had never really liked Maggie, and he guessed he understood why. Grace was afraid he favoured his daughter, and in some ways he did. But surely Grace realized that in standing by her through all their travails he had more than proved his devotion. Even with his fourscore years and three, a biblical age if ever there was one, he still found the minds of women mysterious.

Travails. A good word for the fear and suffering they went through that summer. He had never satisfied himself that he knew what had really happened to that little boy. Long ago, on that late walk home from Slaidburn after the boy had been "delivered," he had told himself that there would be no profit in inquiring after all the details, and he remained convinced that he had been right.

He felt terribly tired now, just bone weary. In his mind, the faces of the people he remembered shifted and shaped themselves into a tender look with a loving smile, somehow more an enfolding embrace than just a picture.

Hello, my darling, he sighed, *I've been watching out for you.*

KASLO PIONEER VISITS ENGLAND

In August 1951, seventy-five-year-old Margaret Isherwood Whittaker took a lengthy journey by airplane from British Columbia to Britain. She landed in Scotland and then made her way by train to her brother's house in Haslingden. I think the brother must have been Tom.

She wrote of her travels for the newspaper back home, the *Kootenaian* (named for the Kootenay Mountains in which she lived), and her first letter, which ran to a full column, is filled with lists of things she had to eat. I suspect she had heard stories of rationing and post-war shortages, but as she commented in her letter: "Doesn't look like starvation in England."

While in Haslingden, she visited three brothers' widows and their families. James Edward and William, her stepbrothers, had both married and predeceased her, and a passing reference to "my brother Dick's wife who has a television-radio-gramophone," suggests that Richard, too, was now dead.

Her letter closed with the news that she would be leaving on Saturday to go to Slaidburn, her home village, and she signed off as "Margaret Whittaker, the Wanderer."

Margaret lived in Haslingden from 1885 until 1900, almost fifteen years, while she left Slaidburn before she turned ten. But when she was in her seventies she still described Slaidburn as her home village.

It was October before the *Kootenaian* published "Another Letter from England" and Margaret had written this time from Clitheroe. She had been up to the Lake District, through Barrow-in-Furness and Dalton-in-Furness, which suggests that she was visiting Gardner connections up there.

Her letter is full of comparisons of the cost of food and the availability of appliances, and she seems impressed by the standard of living of those she had visited. When we leave a place for a long time, we do tend to imagine that it has stood still, unable to progress without our presence, and when we return we are surprised and perhaps even a little miffed at what they have been able to accomplish in our absence.

Margaret seems to have been treated a bit like visiting royalty, as her report about Slaidburn includes the information: "A few people own their houses, but King Wilkinsons own most of the houses in Slaidburn, also all surrounding fields and farm houses. They are what are called landed gentry. I was there for tea. Mr. King Wilkinson has an aunt in Creston and once lived on Creston Flats. He is a photographer."

In closing her letter, grandma wrote: "I wish all people could see my old home. They'd wonder why I left it. But I guess I wanted to see the world, like the little duckling in the story. Hope I get safe home like him and be content to stay. Ever a Canadian MARGARET WHITTAKER."

No mention is made in her letters of the court case that was the real cause of the family's departure from Slaidburn, or her work in the mills of Haslingden. Ever the tough little optimist, grandma was quite happy to forget all of that.

VARIOUS VERDICTS

The defence that little Thomas suffocated accidentally in the trap on the road home from Clitheroe seems just too serendipitous. An otherwise healthy toddler conveniently smothers as his mother is on the way to confess his existence to her new husband, possibly at the expense of his love and protection? I think not.

Cathryn, like me, is unable to swallow the "tragic coincidence" argument.

David, as we know, became convinced that Isabella "did it," and I think that I have joined him in that opinion. I have hypothesized that females prefer to approach the harming of others from a bit of distance, and that Isabella may have found a way to tighten the rug over Thomas's face with her feet. It makes me feel ill even to write that, but the fact is that the baby was dead when they got to the farm, and Isabella knew, without making any effort to wake him or hit his back to fill his lungs with air, that Thomas was dead when they arrived at the farm. Not to mention that black mark and the scratches.

Penny, the lawyer, believes that the women behaved hysterically once they had returned to Slaidburn, running about the countryside with the child's dead body, but that the source of their hysteria was their fear of being found out, not their fear that they would be blamed for Thomas's accidental death.

Discussing the case after Rita Hirst's presentation, one woman commented that, sadly, things are still much the same. Girls still get pregnant with the boy next door and children are raised with more than one father. As Rita wrote to me:

> When we go to Slaidburn we often cross Langcliffe Cross Bridge. I always remember poor little Thomas, so unloved and unwanted, passed from woman to woman to be cared for. I think nowadays the verdict would have been manslaughter.

My husband, William, who is almost as deeply steeped in the evidence as I am, is convinced that the death of little Thomas was an accident. On the one hand, I wonder how he could think that in the face of all the evidence. On the other hand, I wonder if I am biased against stepmothers, even though I am one. But William is most representative of the jury of peers that found Grace and Isabella not guilty, so he is not the first hard-working, thoughtful man to believe the accident story.

To get on with his life, John Isherwood had to embrace the notion of the innocence of the sisters. Or did he? Maybe he just had to believe that Grace was innocent, and that Isabella, as young people sometimes do, just went too far.

BEING ISABELLA

Isabella sits sadly in the back of my mind.

My feelings for her are contradictory, and certainly not guided by a simple moral principle. I think she probably was a murderess, but I also have a great sympathy, verging on empathy, for her.

For me, Isabella is somehow more real than Grace, more present in my mind, even though I now realize that I did hear stories about Grace — stepmother stories — when I was a child. Isabella's voice is the voice of the crime and the cover-up, and the ultimate plea to the jury for acquittal. Hers is the voice that speaks through the carefully inscribed notes of the police officer who was first on the scene, clumsily peopling their alibi with the names of her neighbours in Dalton-on-Furness.

Hers was the life that never got a real chance to tell a different story.

When I think about my life and my formative influences, I always come back to Penny. Penny showed me what a mother should be like. Penny defined my experience in so many ways. She taught me the importance of lullabies, no matter how tunelessly rendered.

When I have tried to imagine the relationship between Grace and Isabella — Penny gets to play the role of Grace, Pillar of the Mother's Union and tea-maker extraordinaire, while I get to be Isabella.

Isabella was the adoring younger sister, who thought Grace could manage to look after everybody; John, baby James, John's five children, Thomas Gardner, and perhaps even Isabella herself. When she realized, too late, that it was all too much for Grace, perhaps she just panicked and tried to help her older sister out of the mess she was in. In her confusion, Isabella probably thought that without young Thomas her sister could go on to have a good life with John Isherwood. And, in fact, Grace did.

I am an adoring younger sister, and I would go a long way to help Penny out of a tough spot. I don't think that I would murder anyone, but these are different times. It would be almost unendurable for me to see Penny deeply unhappy, especially if I could do anything to save her from it. In my own protective way, I worry about her relations with her children and her husband, and whether or not she has enough money to do all the things I think that her remarkable generosity and sacrifice have earned her a right to do.

Isabella was in service at fourteen and dead at twenty-five, with a few months spent in gaol, indicted for murder, in between. Weakened by consumption, she would have known for months, if not years, that she was dying.

Isabella was very brave to stand up at the trial and read her statement, and she must have been quite compelling. Or maybe the combination of her little speech and her sister's wan presence made the difference.

But her sister went on to have at least five more children and live to be a respectable member of the community, while Isabella just wasted away.

I'm touched that Grace was there at Isabella's deathbed, leaving behind her large family to look after her dying sister. No question there was a deep bond there.

And what if Isabella didn't do it? Here she is, in the brief immortality of a story, condemned as a murderess even though she was acquitted. The saying goes that you cannot libel the dead, but that implies that they are past caring. Prospectively, I doubt that I would ever be past caring about my reputation, even when I am dead.

While I write, I have been thinking of this book as a kind of a memorial for Thomas Gardner, the little boy whose death, accidental or not, was scarcely mourned. But I have felt Isabella reaching out to me, trying to get me to understand how she got caught up in a circumstance where she had little or nothing to gain and where everything was lost.

So, even though they make a strange pairing, this is a requiem for the toddler Thomas Gardner and for his youthful Aunt Isabella too.

A MEDITATION ON THOMAS GARDNER (DECEMBER 15, 1882, TO MAY 16, 1885)

Twenty-nine months of life. Not enough to really get started being.

A child approaching two-and-a-half years old is a child on the brink of speaking, of complaining about being hungry or cold in ways that can be readily understood. Little Thomas could have been getting ready to become a little person, with a personality and, maybe, a sense of humour or a capability to accurately observe the world around him.

We adopted our son Daniel when he was twenty-two months old. He had not been abused, or knowingly neglected. In fact, he had been loved. His problem, or perhaps misfortune, was that he had been cared for by someone with a mental illness who often wasn't capable of understanding his needs.

Nevertheless, or maybe as a result, Daniel was unnaturally quiet and acquiescent. He behaved as if he was unaccustomed to being fed when he was hungry. Instead, he waited patiently until someone was ready to feed him. And he didn't seem to expect to be comforted if he fussed or cried. He was quiet and seemingly thoughtful, but he didn't begin to speak until he was almost three.

Little Thomas might have been like that. He had been passed from his mother to a wet nurse, to another, to a workhouse, to his grandparents, and back to his mother, all in a span of twenty-nine months. He probably had no idea who, if anyone, to love or trust. Each time he was cared for, or even settled, he had been cast off or moved. Near the end, he had suffered a long journey with a woman he couldn't know was his aunt, arriving at a house full of children and noise.

Little Thomas would not have understood that Grace and Isabella wanted to leave him at the workhouse in Clitheroe, only that he had been on another long journey, this time in a trap, where he had to sit on the floor on a bed of scratchy rushes.

He would also not have understood that he was not merely inconvenient, but that his mother believed that his very existence threatened her own well-being and that of his little brother, and of the baby she was carrying. And his Aunt Isabella was tired of hauling him about the countryside.

I am sure that Thomas was a passive child, life had not encouraged him to be anything else, but he was "well nourished" and not likely to have given up life without a struggle.

I hope he didn't struggle for long.

PARADISE LOST

In June 1963, as Maggie approached ninety years of age, she wrote a letter to her son Dean. In it she reminisced:

We were on a large farm in Yorkshire when I was a little girl. I had a Horse called Bonny and did a lot of riding around the Farm looking to the fences. Herding up the Ducks. They would stay all night a quarter of a mile in the Pond and the Foxes would eat them up. So I drove them home and shut them up safe. I also liked looking and watching where our hens stole their nest in the Hedges to lay their eggs. My Brothers did all the hard work. Milking cleaning stables etc. For Father would keep the Stables Barns and Farm yard so very clean they had scuts shoes or clogs to wear while doing the Work.

School clothes and shoes changed for School. I was the only girl in the family until I was 17 years old. Then I had a step sister arrive. She is still alive in England. I saw her the last time I was in England.

I guess you saw her Dean or did you while you were in the Army. She looks like stepmother.

I get around using a stick for walking. I am well and hope I will be able to come to Edmonton to see Tessie. How is she.

I hope you come and bring the girls.

Love Gram

Glad John did so well. Gram

A KIND OF IMMORTALITY

One chance at immortality is to live on in the thoughts of others. Even if one is neither wealthy nor accomplished, your life can have meaning to someone who comes later.

You can find the village of Slaidburn in the Doomsday Book, and Saint Andrew's Church can be traced back to the eleventh century at least. There is a cheeky pagan sculpture looking down at worshippers from the church wall that speaks of even earlier times.

Nothing much has changed in Slaidburn in the last century or two. When I walk in the cemetery, between the gravestones, I somehow expect it to communicate with me, to tell me something through the engravings on the stones or through the grass under my feet.

Many of my Isherwood forebears were stonemasons, so I expect to be related at least in this way to more of the tombstones than I can identify. One of the few I can claim with certainty is the flat stone on the ground over behind the grave of Henry Bond. When you push the grass back you can read: "Thomas, son of J and M Isherwood, inter Nov 26, 1806 also Christiane their daughter inter May 19, 1808, infant."

More dead children. My great-great-great-uncle Thomas and aunt Christiane.

The parents J and M Isherwood described on that stone are John and Mary, the grandparents of John Green Isherwood, who was in turn my great-grandfather. Married in 1803, this John was a stonemason and farmer and they lived at Chapel Croft Farm. But I can find no stone in St. Andrews Cemetery that commemorates either John or Mary.

Penny and I have a plan to memorialize someone at the church who was not related to us, but who changed the direction of our lives. We have plans for a memorial plaque to be fastened to the wall of Saint Andrews, acknowledging the presence in that cemetery of the tiny remains of Thomas Gardner, aged two-and-a-half years, died May 16, 1885.

To us it seems only right that on the plaque there be an engraving of the Slaidburn Angel, a little figure in petticoats found lost by the riverside, accompanied by the inscription:

After all, tears have been shed for you

APPENDIX 1

Excerpt from the *Yorkshire Post*, Tuesday August 4, 1885:

Leeds Summer Assizes

Crown Court — Monday
(Before Mr. Justice Wills)
His lordship resumed the business of the court shortly after eleven o'clock.
ALLEGED CHILD MURDER BY TWO SISTERS
Grace Isherwood (25), married, and Isabella Gardner (18), single, servant, were indicted for the murder of a child named Thomas Gardner, alleged to be the illegitimate son of the older prisoner, at Slaidburn, on 16 May. Mr. Lawrence Gane, Q.C. and Mr. Manisty prosecuted, and the prisoners were defended by Mr. E. Tindal Atkinson.

Mr. Gane remarked in opening his case

that the evidence was mainly circumstantial. It was not a case in which the prosecution could lay before the jury the positive testimony of eye witnesses to the acts of the prisoners, who were sisters, coming from Dalton-in-Furness. In September last year the elder, then unmarried, went as housekeeper for a respectable farmer named Isherwood, at Slaidburn, taking with her an illegitimate baby. For some time she stayed with Mr. Isherwood in the capacity of housekeeper, exchanging that position for that of wife in January. On May 9 Gardner visited her sister, being accompanied by a boy, some two years and two months years old, stated by her to belong to a woman named Elizabeth Dockray, who had entrusted it to her for nurse. That child was on May 16 found dead in Easington Brook, near Slaidburn, by a farmer named John Barge. The body was lying in a pool about eighteen inches deep in the middle. Perceiving that the child was dead, Barge went to Slaidburn for a policeman. He afterward returned with a constable, and the body was then in the same position as it was before. Near the spot there went over the brook a Bridge, to protect which a sort of pavement extending about thirty yards along the edge of the brook had been laid down. The child lay with half its head under the kerbstone of the pavement. Now the prisoners were charged with having by drowning caused the death of this child, which was alleged by the prosecution to be the offspring of Grace Isherwood. Before he married the elder prisoner Mr. Isherwood was a widower, having one daughter nine years of age. The daughter would state that on the day in question the prisoners left her father's house with the two children with the intention of going to Clitheroe. They borrowed a neighbour's trap and arrived between twelve and one o'clock at Clitheroe, where they made some purchases and afterward visited the workhouse. There they saw the matron, Mrs Lofthouse, to whom Isherwood stated that she was a widow with two children, one of whom she wished to leave at the workhouse, not being able to support them. The matron refused to accept the child without an order, and the prisoners then returned to Slaidburn. Mr. Isherwood's daughter would say that on their return at about six o'clock, Isabella remained outside the house, having apparently the older of the children wrapped in a shawl. She did not see the face of the child nor hear it speak. Gardner went away with the child in the direction of Slaidburn as was shortly afterward followed by Grace Isherwood. Barge, who found the body, would prove that at a quarter past seven o'clock the same evening he saw two women proceed to the bridge referred to but these two persons could not be positively identified. Later, Mr. Isherwood was seen accompanied by two women going in the direction of his house. A Mrs. Tomlinson, would prove that at about seven o'clock that evening she saw Isabella on the road leading to the bridge but could not say whether she had a child with her. The next day (Sunday) Isabella told her she had been taking the child to its mother. A constable who went to Isherwood's house after the child was found was told by the younger prisoner that the child they had had with them belonged to Elizabeth Dockray. Enquiries resulted in it being proved that although there were living in the neighbourhood two women named Dockray neither was the mother of the child referred to.

John Barge, farmer, Fieldhead, Slaidburn, gave evidence with regard to the finding of the body as described in the opening statement, and added that one of the women he saw on the Saturday evening was carrying what appeared to be a child in her arms, wrapped in a shawl. The body was found in a pool three or four yards square, and could not be seen from the bridge. In cross examination the *witness* stated that he could not tell whether what one of the women carried was a child or not. Anyone standing by the pool could have been seen.

Margaret Isherwood, nine years of age, daughter of John Isherwood, of Meanley Farm, Slaidburn, said the child upon whose body the inquest was held was Thomas Dockray, who had been brought to her father's house by Isabella Gardner. There was another child, a baby named James, her half brother, then in the house. She remembered Thomas, the baby, and the two prisoners going away to Clitheroe and described what clothes Thomas was wearing that morning. She identified a suit of child's clothes, including underthings, produced as what she had seen Isabella dress the baby in. Her evidence further bore out the statement of counsel as to the return of the party from Clitheroe.

Edward Hansen, an earthenware dealer, Clitheroe, stated that at about twelve o'clock on Saturday 16th of May, the prisoners visited his house having with them two children. He saw them at his house again at three o'clock in the afternoon. The elder of the children was then riding in the bottom of the trap in front. In cross examination by Mr. Atkinson witness described at some length the road that the prisoners would traverse on their return to Slaidburn.

Walter Embley, assistant at the Clitheroe Cooperative Stores, gave evidence as to the prisoners purchasing some groceries there on Saturday May 16th. There were then two children with them — one about two years and a half old, and the other about six months. They drove away in a trap at half past three o'clock, the older child then being seated in the bottom of the cart.

Mrs. Lofthouse, matron of the Clitheroe Workhouse, gave evidence in accordance with the opening statement as to the visit of the prisoners to that institution.

Mrs. Camm, wife of a farmer at Slaidburn, spoke to having met two women, whom she could not identify, on the night of Saturday May 16th, near the Easington Brook bridge. One of them was carrying what appeared to be a child, wrapped in a shawl.

Mrs. Franklin, of Harrop Hall, gave similar evidence.

A witness named *Walmsley* stated that between half past ten and eleven o'clock on the night of Saturday, 16th May, he met

John Isherwood and two women going in the direction of Meanley Farm. One of the women carried a loose shawl.

Police Constable Sutcliffe, of Slaidburn, proved that some of the clothes identified by Margaret Isherwood were upon the body when found. When he visited Isherwood's house on the Sunday night he asked the elder prisoner if she had a little boy, and her reply was that she had not. The younger prisoner then said, "I had a boy named Thomas Dockray at my father's house, No. 3 Victoria Terrace, Dalton-in-Furnace." She went on to say that in consequence of a letter she received she took the child to Clitheroe, to give it up to the mother, Elizabeth Dockray on the previous day. She saw the mother at the Railway Station, but did not give up the child, the reason for keeping him being that the mother asked her to be at the Black Bull Inn, Slaidburn, with him at ten o'clock that night. She added that she did so meet Dockray at Slaidburn, and handed over the child to her; and further gave a description which she said referred to the woman Dockray and a man accompanying her at Clitheroe whose name was Stables. On leaving Isherwood's house the elder prisoner said she wished they had taken the child to the workhouse and Isabella remarked; "Happen it is as well as it is." Cross-examined by ATKINSON, *witness* admitted that he had not stated this last conversation before the magistrates.

Anne Tomlinson wife of a farmer at Waddington, stated that on the night of the 16th May she saw Isabella Gardner when she was going to Slaidburn at about seven o'clock. She did not then speak to her, but on Sunday morning she asked Isabella whether she was not on the road as stated, and she replied that she was — the she went in to take the child to its mother at the Black Bull Inn. She further stated that Stables, who was at the public-house with Dockray, went with them toward the Easington Bridge. On the way she asked for money for nursing the boy, and Stables then threatened he would do away with both her and the child if she made another request of the kind. She took away some of the clothes the child was then wearing.

Mrs. Wilson, who had known the prisoners for ten years, said that she had visited Meanley on the Thursday before the discovery, and was then told by Isabella that she was nursing the child for a woman named Dockray. On Sunday evening witness went to church with Isabella who told her that on the previous night that she was at Slaidburn and gave the boy up to his mother at the Black Bull Inn.

Superintendent Inman, of Settle, read a statement made by the younger prisoner, which he took down in writing in an interview with the accused on Monday May 18th. This set forth that Isabella lived with her father at Dalton, and that about two years ago she and Dockray were living in service in the same village near Bootle. Dockray was at that time something of a loose character, and was afterward confined of a child at Dalton. She did not see Dockray again until four months ago at Dalton, when she arranged with her to nurse a child until Whitsuntide at

4s 6d a week. Dockray sent the child to her in the evening. The statement repeated what had been said by other witnesses as to the interview at the Black Bull. The prisoners were charged separately after being apprehended. Grace in reply said nothing and Isabella said, "I have not done it." A certified copy of an entry in the registry of births at Dalton which witness had examined was produced, showing that a male child, born in December 1882, was registered in the name of Thomas as being the son of Grace Gardner, domestic servant.

The case was not concluded at the rising of the court. It was stated that there were yet eighteen witnesses to be called for the prosecution.

APPENDIX 2

Excerpt from the *Yorkshire Post*, Wednesday August 5, 1885:

Leeds Summer Assizes

Crown Court — Monday
(Before Mr. Justice Wills)
His lordship took his seat in the Crown Court at half past ten o'clock.
THE ALLEGED CHILD MURDER BY TWO SISTERS AT SLAIDBURN
The prosecution of Grace Isherwood (25), married, and Isabella Gardner (18), sisters, on an indictment for the murder of a male child, alleged to be the offspring of the elder prisoner, at Slaidburn, on May 16th, was resumed. Mr. Lawrence Gane, Q.C. and Mr. Manisty appearing to prosecute, and the accused being defended by Mr. E. Tindal Atkinson.

Inspector Prosser, of Bolton-by-Bowland, stated that in the township of the district including

Clitheroe he had made exhaustive inquiries with the result that no trace had been discovered of persons answering to the descriptions the accused gave of Dockray and Stables. The jacket, frock, socks, and boots worn by the child he afterward received from John Isherwood, at Meanley Farm.

Dr Alexander Gray, Dalton-in-Furness, deposed that he attended the elder prisoner in her confinement at her father's house on 15th December 1883. She was then delivered of a male child. When attending the prisoners' mother in April of this year he saw a little boy apparently just over two years of age at the house.

Agnes Creary, wife of John Creary, Lower Brook Street, Ulverston, stated that at Whitsuntide, 1883, the elder prisoner, then Grace Gardner, visited her at Ulverston with a baby a few months old. She said the child's name was James Thomas Gardner, and that its father was a man named Dockray, living at Dalton. As she (Grace) was going to a situation, she wished to place the child out to nurse, and witness undertook the care of it for 4s 6d a week. She kept the child for 27 weeks during which time she received several letters. As she was unable to read or write, these were read and answered by a neighbour's daughter named Dempsey. Some of the letters contained money. In consequence of not receiving her money regularly, she returned the child to Grace's father's house.

A girl named *Dempsey* stated that certain letters produced were those she read to Mrs Creary, purporting to come from Grace Gardner. She had written to Grace Gardner at the request of Mrs Creary.

Mrs Coward, Dalton-in-Furness, gave evidence as to nursing a child called Thomas from the Gardner's house in November 1883. She kept it till June, 1884.

Mrs Jane Gordon stated that she in the course of last summer nursed the child known as Thomas Gardner. He was the same child whose body she saw at the Black Bull, Slaidburn, at the Inquest. Some of the clothes which had been produced were worn by the child when with her.

Further evidence was given respecting the letters received by Mrs. Creary, which were afterward read by his lordship. The writer, who was then in service at Crosshills, chiefly concerned herself with the welfare of the child, and the struggle she had to pay the money necessary for his maintenance. There were also several letters to Mrs Gordon from Meanley, one or two of them after Grace Gardner was married, and these also referred to the child and the payment for its nursing.

John Stables, labourer, Prince Albert Cottages, Upper Frederick Street, Liverpool, stated that he formerly lived in Dalton, which place he left in October last. He had never been to Clitheroe or Slaidburn. Knew a girl about 15 years of age in Dalton. There were many Dockrays there, but he had never had any conversation with the prisoners respecting a child belonging to any of them.

Elizabeth Dockray, aged 15, living at Dalton, said she saw Isabella on one occasion this year, and she then told her she was going to see her sister, and would take her sister's child, Thomas. Did not know any other Elizabeth Dockray in Dalton.

Dorothy Dockray, an inmate of the Ulverston Workhouse, said she had a child — the only one she had had — which was in the workhouse with her. She knew John Stables, but was never at Clitheroe or Slaidburn with him. Grace Gardner did on one occasion ask her to nurse the child, Thomas Gardner, but she declined. Grace had told her that the father of the child was William Dockray, a miner.

Mr. H.A. Bridgman, surgeon, Slaidburn, who made the post-mortem examination, attributed death to asphyxia by drowning.

Isabella Gardner here read a written statement to the jury in which she said that John Isherwood had been very kind to her sister. He suggested the child was hers, but she denied it to him, and said it was Elizabeth Dockray's. She being afraid that he would find it out they arranged to get it into a workhouse in Clitheroe and failing that they agreed to take it home her sister saying that she would tell John all about it. They accordingly wrapped it in the rugs, and it was quiet all the way home. She (Isabella) lifted it out of the cart and placed it on its foot, but it fell to the ground as though it were dead. They dared not take it into the house, being afraid that her husband would think they had done something to it. They agreed that she (Isabella) would take the child in the direction of Slaidburn. Grace following as soon as she could. She went and turned back again and then met with her sister and then went with her along the Easington Road to Langcliffe Cross Bridge. There they decided to put the child into the water, Grace remarking that they should take the coat off. They did so and Grace then passed her the little dead boy. She decided to put the body where it would be seen, and carried it to the river. Neither of them did anything to it.

Mr. GANE, there being no witnesses for the defence, then addressed the jury, whose attention he called to the improbability of the suggestion the child was suffocated in the rugs. Considering the size of the child, its healthy condition, and the nature of the journey from Clitheroe, could it be believed that the child could meet its death in this way without the attention of the women being called to it?

Mr. TINDAL ATKINSON said that the defence was, and had been throughout, that the child was dead when it was put into the water, and did not meet its death by drowning. He further eloquently pictured the painful position in which the mother of the child was placed as the wife of a respectable man who was unacquainted with the fact that she had more than one illegitimate child, and who with the knowledge that there was another child would probably become estranged from her; and then went on to argue against the improbabilities which in his mind were mentionable in the case for the prosecution. He pointed out that on the way from Clitheroe to Slaidburn there was every opportunity of disposing of the child had the women entertained this murderous design, and it was simply inconceivable that having this idea the child should have been brought all the way to the farm and then taken where any and all theirs was open to the view of anyone passing the bridge. He showed how the medical evidence came to no definitive conclusion on the question of death by drowning, and urged the fact of undigested food which had been partaken of at Clitheroe being found in the stomach as conclusive evidence that death must have taken place before the body was placed in Easington brook.

His LORDSHIP having exhaustively reviewed the facts of the case, the jury retired to consider their verdict.

After an absence of three-quarters of an hour, they returned into court at 6:40, finding both prisoners not guilty, a decision which was applauded by a crowded attendance.

FAMILY TREES

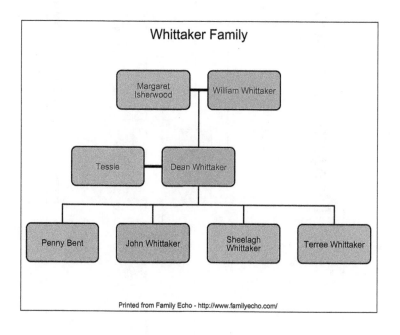

Margaret Isherwood's Family

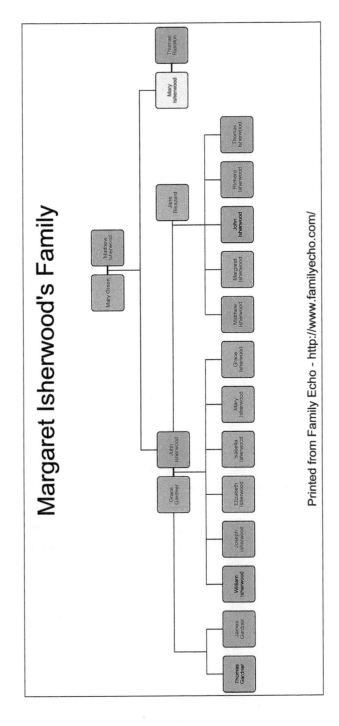

Printed from Family Echo - http://www.familyecho.com/

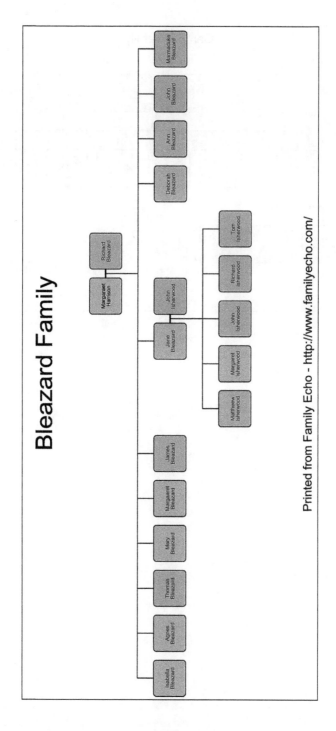

Bleazard Family

Printed from Family Echo - http://www.familyecho.com/

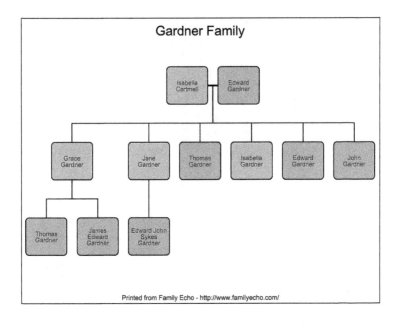

ACKNOWLEDGEMENTS

Of course, it was Penny and William who made me write it. Then, much later, William demonstrated his genius, and his generosity, by editing the result.

In between, Cathryn and David Higham, tireless researchers who became good friends, were instrumental in investigating the original events and placing them in the context of Victorian-era Slaidburn. Rita Hirst's insights helped, while Grace Ibbetson's enthusiasm was infectious.

Our children each contributed in their own ways. Daniel read two early versions and issued helpful comment. Meghan and Abigail were genuinely enthusiastic readers. Nicholas remained steadfastly proud and encouraging throughout, while Matthew and Emily showed their implicit faith by just letting me get on with it.

In London, the ladies of "The Texas," all of them true friends and excellent duplicate bridge players, were an important source of support. Nancy Gough, Ellen Davidson, Kay Lloyd, Emma Forbes, and Wanda Cristali read and discussed the manuscript with me. Barbara Harrison even returned the copy I had given her to make sure I wouldn't miss typos she had found.

Harvey Schachter surprised himself by reading the whole thing and gravely pronouncing it "publishable." Then, as if to prove Harvey right, Linda Cameron found me a publisher … and what a publisher!

Beth Bruder and Kirk Howard gave me what turned out to be my first "author's lunch," Kirk staying on despite terrible back pain to make sure that both I and *The Slaidburn Angel* felt properly welcomed to Dundurn Press. With Kirk and Beth having set the standard, Cheryl Hawley and Marta Warner contributed to making my experience with Dundurn consistently responsive and helpful.

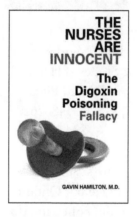